What ~~People Are Saying~~ About
Chicken Soup for ~~the Soul~~ ...
Stories for a Better World

"What a splendid anthology of stories that tell so eloquently how each of us can make a difference as a peacemaker; sometimes spectacularly on the international level, but more often no less spectacularly, on an intimate personal level."

Archbishop Desmond M. Tutu
Nobel Peace Prize laureate

"I am proud to have my story included among dozens of other vibrant and inspiring perspectives on the never-ending struggle for peace. This is a volume that will open your eyes and gladden your heart."

Oscar Arias
Nobel Peace Prize laureate, former president of Costa Rica

"Every story in *Chicken Soup for a Better World* is a vision of peace for our future. Here is my challenge to you as you read this book: open your minds, listen with your heart. You can make a difference!"

Muhammad Ali

"Learning how to create a peaceful soul is the most important calling of our time . . . for ourselves, and for the future of our world. This book is a loving and instructive guide."

Marianne Williamson
Author, *The Gift of Change*

"*Chicken Soup for the Soul . . . Stories for a Better World* is unique in its wisdom, full of inspiration and insight. I hope it will be widely read."

Howard Zinn
Historian, author, *Voices of a People's History of the United States*

"Years ago, when I wrote the lyric, 'Weave, weave, weave me the sunshine, out of the falling rain. Weave me the hope of a new tomorrow, and fill my cup again,' I never thought I'd read a book that would powerfully bring this hope and dream to life. To create joy and healing from sorrow and suffering is the stuff of the moving stories told in these healing pages. They hint that everyone can find his or her version of this great gift—one to be shared in different, perhaps, but always extremely significant ways."

Peter Yarrow
of Peter, Paul, and Mary

"This collection of stories of real people making a better world by practicing nonviolence demonstrates that it is always possible to actively cultivate understanding, love, compassion and forgiveness, even in the face of misperception and conflict. These stories also confirm that practicing nonviolence is far from passive and requires courage."

Thich Nhat Hanh
Zen master, Nobel Peace Prize nominee

"This book of dynamite stories is a 'must-read'! These true stories will inspire you and encourage you to get up, get out and act with new energy. By reading this treasure trove, you will be powerfully convinced that each person's words and actions truly do have the power to lift and heal the world."

Midge Costanza
first woman to serve as assistant to the president,
appointed by President Carter

"This book is a lovingly compiled and painstakingly profound work detailing the possibilities of the human spirit. It shows us in story after story how we CAN make this world a better place—and not merely wish it so."

Laurie Beth Jones
author, *Jesus, CEO*

"This collection is a treasure chest! Inside readers will find beautiful gems of celebration, appreciation, creativity, strength and joy."

Virginia E. Law, J.D.

president, PeacePaths, LLC

"These stories of our humane beingness comfort us to the core. In simple acts of essential humanity, we find where we all belong."

RAFFI Cavoukian, C.M.
singer/composer

"In this age of information overload, one of the rare things people really remember are metaphors, parables, short stories, pictures and photos, because they speak to the heart more than to the intellect. This is the immense value of the *Chicken Soup* series, which explains its unending success over the years. Many of the enclosed stories brought tears to my eyes: they cut across all barriers, because they speak to that common strain of humanity in all of us, to the original innocence and spontaneous compassion which lies—albeit sometimes dormant—in the heart of every human being."

Pierre Pradervand
author, *The Gentle Art of Blessing*

"At a time when we are inundated with what is wrong, failing and to be feared in our world, I can think of no more courageous act in advancing a global culture of peace and compassion than to acknowledge, together, all the good that is erupting around us. This remarkable book goes a long way in advancing that dialogue, and the practical hope it brings. Be part of the emerging global consciousness. Read it with your family and friends. Read it to your children!"

Steve Olweean
founding director, Common Bond Institute

Life on earth is sacred, and we've got to learn to live in peace with each other. We can fix everything in the world if we decide to do it! This book's powerful stories will surely inspire readers to do just that—to right the wrongs in our world! The stories also provide so many moving examples of HOW it is truly possible to live in peace with each other, on all levels.

Helen Caldicott, M.D.,
Nobel Peace Prize Nominee, Author,
If you Love this Planet: A Plan to Heal the Earth

These stories show so powerfully that, when we listen with

empathy, and speak and act with compassion, we truly can transform even the most volatile and challenging conflict into a situation where mutual understanding and respect triumph in the end! Our world will, without a doubt, be a better place when the multitude of readers of this book begin to put into practice the joy and wisdom of connecting with others in the ways they find in these wonderful stories.

Marshall Rosenberg, Ph.D.
author, *Nonviolent Communication,*
and founder, Center for Nonviolent Communication

Peace Lovers, rejoice! Here is a book that will open your heart to inspiration and action. These stories will re-awaken the living spirit of peace within you. They will thrill you, entice you, and invite you to remember that you too can make a difference, that you too are a builder of peace. Please do yourself—and the world—a favor by reading this book and passing it on to a friend or loved one. Then go out and make your own peace dreams come true!

Louise Diamond, Ph.D.
Author, *The Peace Book: 108 Simple Ways to
Make a More Peaceful World*

Making peace has never been easy, and I cannot remember a time when it was more difficult—or more needed. It calls for courage, self sacrifice and hard, hard work, the best that we can muster. Many are indeed rising to answer this call, and they need lots of inspiration and support. This wonderful collection will help them.

Michael N. Nagler
author, *The Search for a Nonviolent Future*

This excellent collection gets down to the real essentials where everyday peacemaking really happens. Peace is about everything that makes us human our laughter, joy, tears, celebration, our desperation to ease anotherís pain and our delight at the beauty all around us. This book reminds us of something we all know in our innermost hearts: peace cannot be delegated, but rather starts with you and me and the choices we make today.

Mansukh Patel and **Savitri MacCuish**

CHICKEN SOUP FOR THE SOUL... STORIES FOR A BETTER WORLD

Chicken Soup for the Soul Stories for a Better World
Jack Canfield, Mark Victor Hansen, Candice C. Carter, Susanna Palomares,
Linda K. Williams, Bradley L. Winch

Published by Backlist, LLC,
a unit of Chicken Soup for the Soul Publishing, LLC. www.chickensoup.com

Front cover design by Larissa Hise Henoch
Originally published in 2005 by Health Communications, Inc.

Back cover and spine redesign by Pneuma Books, LLC

Distributed to the booktrade by Simon & Schuster. SAN: 200-2442

Publisher's Cataloging-in-Publication Data
(Prepared by The Donohue Group)

Chicken soup for the soul : stories for a better world / [compiled by] Jack
  Canfield ... [et al.].

  p. : ill. ; cm.

  Originally published: Deerfield Beach, FL : Health Communications, c2005.
  ISBN: 978-1-62361-030-2

  1. Spiritual life--Anecdotes. 2. Anecdotes. I. Canfield, Jack, 1944- II. Title:
Stories for a better world

BL624 .C457 2012
158.1/28   2012913033

PRINTED IN THE UNITED STATES OF AMERICA
on acid free paper

21 20 19 18 17 16 15 14 13 12   01 02 03 04 05 06 07 08 09 10

CHICKEN SOUP FOR THE SOUL... STORIES FOR A BETTER WORLD

Jack Canfield • Mark Victor Hansen
Candice C. Carter • Susanna Palomares
Linda K. Williams • Bradley L. Winch

Backlist, LLC, a unit of
Chicken Soup for the Soul Publishing, LLC
Cos Cob, CT
www.chickensoup.com

A Prayer Written for
Chicken Soup for the Soul . . . Stories for a Better World

Goodness is stronger than evil;
Love is stronger than hate;
Light is stronger than darkness;
Life is stronger than death;
Victory is ours through God who loves us!

Archbishop Desmond Tutu

We honor and
celebrate all who envision,
live for and move us
toward a better world.

Contents

2. LOVE AND KINDNESS

3. DEFINING MOMENTS

4. A MATTER OF PERSPECTIVE

5. ANSWERING THE CALL

6. INSIGHTS AND LESSONS

7. ON WISDOM

8. GIVING BACK

Introduction

You are holding in your hands a very special book—the 101st book from *Chicken Soup for the Soul*. For us, 101 has always been a magical number. It is the number of stories in the first *Chicken Soup* book, and it is the number we have striven for in every single book since. We love the number 101 because it gives you a sense that you are not reaching an ending, that the "extra" story carries you forward into a world of stories beyond those that have been captured within the pages of a particular book.

That is what we hope you will take with you from this our 101st book—a sense that you can carry the *Chicken Soup* message forward beyond the experience of reading. That you can use the inspiration, understanding and love within these pages to make your world a little bit better every day. That by improving your life you can change the lives of those around you. And maybe, just maybe, together we will truly make a difference.

That has been our goal all along with *Chicken Soup for the Soul.* We never set out to sell books. We set out to touch the heart of one person in the hope that that person would in turn touch another person, and that person another person, and so on down the line. We admit it: Twelve years ago we were naïve enough to think that stories could make the world a better place. And we were right. More than 80 million people have been inspired by *Chicken Soup* stories around the world!

For us, *Chicken Soup for the Soul* isn't just a book series; it's a feeling and a life philosophy. It's strength in the face of adversity. Friendship in a moment of loneliness. Hope to brighten the depths of heartache. Love as a response to pain. *Chicken Soup for the Soul* is the belief that we are all good people and that, by truly listening to each other, we can begin to heal the hurt within ourselves, within our communities and throughout the world.

We all have a story to tell. An elderly relative of Linda K. Williams, one of the coauthors of this volume, was murdered by a drug addict for her Social Security check. Instead of letting that terrible act beat her down, Linda turned her pain into a movement to put an end to senseless violence. That is a *Chicken Soup for the Soul* moment, for there is nothing more central to our philosophy than the belief that when you reach out, instead of in, you broaden the circle of life and the circle of love.

Every story isn't as dramatic as Linda's story. Sometimes hope arrives in a moment as timeless as a small child giving water to her puppy. Their innocent love is a window into a better world. Sometimes that window is as simple as a smile.

Every story has a message; every story is from someone like you; every story can change your mind, your heart and your life. This is as true in this 101st *Chicken Soup for the Soul* book as it was in the first book—and every book in between. We hope you'll take a moment now to think back on the stories that inspired you—whether you read them in our books, in other books or lived them in your own life—and rekindle the sense of wonder you felt when you experienced those wonderful goosebumps of emotion for the first time.

At *Chicken Soup for the Soul,* we know that stories make a difference. We know because of the letters we receive telling us how much these stories mean to you. But we also know it because these stories have changed our own lives. They have inspired us, and when you're inspired, no matter who you are, you will change the world.

Jack Canfield and Mark Victor Hansen

1

MAKING A DIFFERENCE

What is making a difference?

*It is the opportunity to take the time each day
to acknowledge the beauty around us, to
appreciate the amazing people who touch us,
and to leave the world a better place each day
through our thoughts, words and actions.*

I am making a difference each day by
sharing myself and my gifts with grace and
ease with all those who come into my life.

Going Home on the D Train

Once we discover how to appreciate the timeless values in our daily experiences, we can enjoy the best things in life.

Harry Pepner

I've lived in New York City for all of my seventeen years and can't imagine living anywhere else. It's an amazing city full of sights and smells and sounds unlike anywhere else on Earth. Its being a city with a population of more than 8 million adds to its excitement, as well as to the mistaken belief that it's filled with cold, aloof and uncaring people. Taken as a total number, it's hard to imagine connecting with all its citizens, but when you deal with one person at a time something different happens.

It was a cold November day, and New York City was still reeling from the devastation of September 11. All the members of my soccer team were glad to have an excuse to get out of school. It was the first game of the year, and we had suffered a horrible defeat; still, we were just excited to be starting the new season. We were twenty high-school girls walking and laughing through the streets of the Bronx, ignoring the occasional whistles from the men we passed. We got to the subway station just as our train was coming in. Piling onto the D train, we glanced around the car, finding it full of blank stares and vacuous expressions. As the train started moving, twenty boisterous voices erupted at once, discussing everything from the attitudes of the girls on the opposing team to our plans for later that night.

All of us lived in Manhattan. Even though Manhattan and the Bronx are both boroughs of New York City, they're pretty far apart, so we had at least an hour-long train ride ahead of us. To amuse ourselves and pass the time, we began to sing. Various genres of music filled the train's car, from Bob Dylan to Christina Aguilera. Even though only one of us could really sing, we all sang along as loudly as possible; what we lacked in musical talent we made up for in volume and enthusiasm. I wish I could freeze that moment: being with my friends, feeling happy and not thinking about anything else. It was an amazing feeling that got even better as the train moved on.

Our fellow riders had different feelings. A few smiled in our direction, but most shot us disgruntled looks (was it our obvious lack of musical talent?), and some were downright hostile.

All our voices stopped almost simultaneously as an old man entered the car from the subway platform. His clothes were tattered, and his face was covered with a stubbly beard. In his hand he held a Styrofoam coffee cup emblazoned with "I Love NY." Despite his shabby appearance, he carried himself with dignity. He spoke softly, but his voice projected through the car: "Hello, ladies and gentlemen. I hope everyone is staying warm and healthy this winter. I am going to sing a couple of my favorite old songs for you during your trip. Please listen, and I hope you enjoy."

No one on the train looked up. Most people slid down behind their newspapers or feigned sleep, but we girls watched him carefully. As his lips parted and he began to sing "Joy to the World," we were so carried away by his eloquent voice and presence that we found ourselves chiming right in. After we had finished, we heard clapping and looked around to see that the people who had been in their own worlds a few moments before had now crossed over to ours to listen and marvel at this rare moment. His exquisite voice leading ours made it all sound so beautiful. The singing continued for a few more songs, then the old man sang a song he introduced as his own. When he was finished, he was lauded just as before when we had sung along with him.

For his final song, he chose something that was sure to move everyone: "God Bless America." With this song, not only did the twenty of us join him, but so did everyone else in the car. The stirring strains of "God Bless America" rang through the subway train and out into the station where we stopped. Many people left their own cars to come and see what was happening in ours—and to join us. This impromptu chorus on the D train, this medley of voices and unity of spirit, was real and marvelous. Its significance became clearest to me when I noticed a woman holding a baby in her arms, singing through the tears that were streaming down her cheeks.

The power of this moment will be with me forever. A moment when a group of strangers, all New Yorkers, tough and jaded, connected with a group of high-school girls and a ragtag homeless person, and allowed their voices—and their hearts—to be as one.

Simone McLaughlin

A Gift of Peace for the Homeless Heart

It was three in the morning, and I had a feeling that I should go to the ocean and play my guitar. I packed up my guitar and drove to Ocean Beach, California. It was overcast in the beach area, and a slight rainy drizzle was in the air. The usually crowded boardwalk was deserted except for two people. On one side of the beach was a woman who appeared to be troubled and was wielding a broom; on the other was a lone figure sitting on the retaining wall and staring out to sea. I chose a spot equidistant between them and began to play.

As I played, the troubled woman with the broom swept her way right next to me. She stopped sweeping and leaned on her broom, smiling at me. She appeared to be homeless and was covered with dirt. Her clothes were tattered and mismatched.

"How are you doing?" I asked to break the awkward silence.

"Just fine," she said. "I'm cleaning this place up. Somebody has to do it." She pointed to the beach. "Just look at all that sand . . . gets tracked everywhere."

She went on, "You sure play beautiful music. I never heard a guitar sound like that before. I think my friend would like your music. I want to hire you to play for her." She pointed to the lone figure staring out at the ocean down the boardwalk, then produced a few coins from her pockets. "I ain't got much, and I know you're worth a lot, but if I give this to you, will you play a song for her? She's had it pretty rough. I know the music will make her feel better."

I told her I'd be happy to play a song for her friend for free.

As we walked over to her friend, the Broom Lady told me that her friend never talked and not to be offended if she didn't seem to hear me . . . that she'd appreciate the music just the same. We approached, and the Broom Lady introduced me. "Annie, I got you a present to cheer you up. It's a guitar man who's going to play a song special for you."

Annie did not move. She was wearing dark sunglasses and had a tattered coat pulled up to cover most of her face. She looked to be in her mid-forties, but it was hard to tell because the streets age a person fast.

The Broom Lady informed me that she had a lot of boardwalk left to sweep and urged me to get on with it. She swept her way back down toward the pier again.

I sat next to Annie and played. As I played I put every thought into having good things happen for this woman. I played for quite a while.

Suddenly, Annie turned toward me and asked, "How do you do that?"

"Do what?" I asked, astounded that she'd spoken.

"You play, and you make it so beautiful. I can feel it inside my heart."

She took off her sunglasses. She had tears in her eyes and a smile on her face. She held out her hand to me. In her palm were a few coins, mostly pennies. She said, "I can't pay you much 'cause I'm having a run of bad luck, but I want you to have this."

"Oh, no!" I told her. "This is a gift from your friend."

"She's nuts, you know," she said, "but she is a friend. I guess it's not bad luck."

I told her, "When I play, good things happen."

"Go ahead and play then," she said in a sad voice, "'cause I like to believe that."

I sat on the retaining wall and played for Annie. I lost myself in the music. I couldn't tell you how long I played or even what I played. I can only tell you that I was totally connected to the instrument, and an overwhelming peace ran through my entire body and seemed to radiate out of me.

When I stopped and looked up, I was startled to see a small crowd around us. A smiling man stepped forward and said, "I've been standing here listening for a while. It was amazing. I have to give you some money."

"I can't take your money, but if you give it to help out this woman beside me, I would be grateful."

The man reached into his pocket and pulled out a wad of bills. As he gave it to Annie, he grinned and said, "This is from that guitar man. It's your lucky day!"

As I packed up my guitar, the Broom Lady was sweeping toward us again. I was headed back to my car when I heard Annie say, in a quiet voice, "I believe you now."

The Broom Lady stopped sweeping. As I walked by her she was muttering out loud. "She talked. She never talks—I can't believe it! She talks!"

KEV

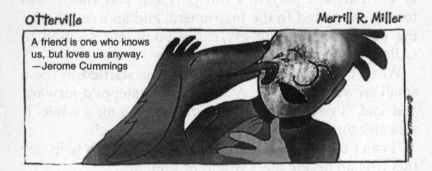

Otterville   **Merrill R. Miller**

A friend is one who knows us, but loves us anyway.
—Jerome Cummings

"The Impossible Dream . . . ?"

Poverty is the worst form of violence.
                                        Mahatma Gandhi

It was happening again! Only a little milk swirled in the bottom of the pitcher, and several tiny, hollow-eyed children were still waiting patiently, cups eagerly outstretched to be filled. If only he didn't have to promise the Red Cross—for which he worked—that he would drink a quart of milk each day for his own health! What was wrong with this picture? Swallowing hard, Dan had to accept the fact that at least one more of those children would starve to death this day.

He slept fitfully that night, as he did most nights since coming to Spain during the Civil War of 1937-38. He kept thinking of the children lying in bed hungry. And the next day wasn't any better. *Too little milk, too many empty cups.* The cows had been killed by rebels to eat or simply as an act of violence. There were no jobs, little food, inadequate clothing, empty schools—and always fear. Even many of the houses had been destroyed. It was the suffering of mothers, children and old people that made his heart ache. What caused people to do these terrible things to each other? Dan knew who most needed his help—the "little people": the poor, the hungry, the cold, the powerless, the uneducated, the young, the old. It warmed his heart and inspired him to know that his father, Landon West, had helped slaves to escape the terror and abuse of their bondage during the Civil War in the United States. Would those people in such desperate need have been able to change their life situation without help from Landon and the Underground Railroad?

Dan's mother had done her part, too, by baking extra loaves of bread, which she left in the shed for the escapees. Now Dan himself was giving handouts. But the milk was gone too soon. Spanish families would never know peace if the food was always running out. They needed milk today, and tomorrow, and the next day—and the day after that, and on and on. . . . Wouldn't it be better to give the Spanish people cows, rather than cups of milk? Not a cup, but a cow! Folks able to help themselves in a sustainable way seemed to be peace-loving. Could giving cows help bring peace, maybe even help end war?

Dan West had grown up in Ohio farm country, where fat cows munched in the meadows and fresh cool milk was served at every meal. These were common elements in the daily life of every child there. As he sat under an almond tree after another day of observing the frustration of so many desperate people, he became aware of the bubbling stream and the soft grass under his hands. These people had been farmers. If they had cows, they would be able to supply milk for their children. Could cows possibly be sent here, to Spain, from Ohio?

Returning to the States, Dan was greeted by his children, Janet and Joel, one and three years old, rosy-cheeked and healthy, as farm children usually are. As his little ones drank their milk, in his mind's eye were images of the skinny, sad-eyed children in Spain. Surely something could be done to share the rich bounty of American farm country. But what could one man do?

He talked about it to anyone who would listen. And Dan was easy to listen to, dynamic, eager, passionate. Even the kids playing around the buildings where the grown-ups were talking listened to Dan. His vision was exciting: green pastures with healthy cows delivering calves and giving wholesome milk to healthy children; parents proud to be able to clothe their children and send them to school. The way Dan described the terrible conditions in Spain, the questions he asked, the way he listened with appreciation to the creative new ideas people offered—all this helped make people feel that it was their own vision. Would his family and friends, and his neighbors and fellow church members, help?

His wife Lucy said, "Dan, maybe this is an impossible dream." But she was willing to help him anyway, because she loved him, and she knew he was trying to help people who couldn't help themselves. The news got around that Dan needed help with his vision, and a plan began to emerge. One day, Virgil Mock, a farmer from Indiana, said, "I'll donate a cow." Then his neighbors, O. W. Stine and his son Claire, said, "We'll feed and care for it until it can be sent to Spain." Another farmer said he could spare a cow; then another and another. . . . And some said they would be willing to care for animals until they were ready for shipment. But how to get them to Spain?

Soon, there were questions flying everywhere. Where would they get a ship to take the animals? How long would the journey take? Wouldn't the cows have to be milked? What to do with all that milk out in the middle of the ocean? And what about the manure?! (The children listening at the door that day held their noses and gave a huge "Yuck!") It could be thrown overboard, but who would shovel it? There would be a great deal of work and expense involved. Was this really an impossible dream?

There were three main problems with shipping the cows: They needed money to pay for the costs, people to care for the animals and a plan for how to save all that milk. Isn't that what this whole thing was about: milk?

John drawled, "Well, there wouldn't be any milk if we send heifers."

Duh! To experienced farmers, this was a no-brainer. A heifer is a pregnant young cow that has never before produced a calf, and therefore, cannot give milk yet. And when the calf was born, there would be another animal! In fact, someone suggested, each person receiving a pregnant heifer could promise to give the calf to another family. People receiving would become givers. They would be *passing on the gift!* Could that be a motto?

"Well, if farmers donate the animals, maybe city folks would donate money for the other expenses," someone ventured. Excitedly, people began to think of uncles, brothers and friends in the city, and the churches could take up collections, too! Now, how about the caretakers on the long sea voyage?

"I'll go!" came eager shouts from the doorway. "I'm good with cows!"

"I'll be a cowboy! I'll go! I'll go!"

Seeing the excited children, the adults realized that some of the older teenagers, indeed, might be able to do that job. Some of the men volunteered, and so did some women. Willing workers seemed plentiful enough. What could stop them now?

It took six years to make the dream happen, but by that time the war in Europe prevented sending cows to Spain. An urgent plea in June 1944, however, resulted in the first three donated cows—Faith, Hope and Charity—along with thirteen of their "girlfriends" and one calf being sent to Puerto Rico. After the end of World War II, shipments were sent to Europe, Asia and South America, and a project was also started in Arkansas.

In the sixty years since, more than 7 million families have been helped in 125 countries around the world. From alligators and alpacas to camels and cows, from donkeys and ducks to geese and goats, from llamas and yaks to even bees and trees, the list now includes twenty-nine living things that are donated by Heifer International. Great care is taken to send the species best suited to the environment and needs of a particular people. Camels are not sent to swampy areas, nor are fish sent to the desert.

Dan West's dream might have seemed an impossibility at one time, but now, cows are exchanged for guns in Kosovo and Albania. And warring tribes in Africa and Armenia—and former rival gang members in the United States—have learned that cooperation in farming ventures can help both sides; they've learned to work side by side, building lasting relationships, mutual respect and trust.

When the hungry can feed themselves, peace happens.

Florence Crago, Ph.D.

A Child Survivor and Her Hero

To map out a course of action and follow it to an end requires some of the same courage that a soldier needs. Peace has its victories, but it takes brave men and women to win them.

Ralph Waldo Emerson

My friend Vera is alive today because of a *real* superhero. He was brave and just and awesome. His name is Raoul Wallenberg; Vera calls him her "miracle-maker." Raoul Wallenberg saved Vera's life when she was a twelve-year-old girl living in Hungary during World War II. She lived through the nightmare of the Holocaust when 6 million innocent Jews were killed—1.5 million of them children. Vera was one of the lucky Jewish children. She was rescued by Mr. Wallenberg, a Swedish Christian who, amazingly, saved the lives of a hundred thousand people of a faith different from his own.

Raoul Wallenberg was officially the secretary of the Swedish delegation in Hungary, and he had the authority to issue passports. It was this authority he capitalized upon to save thousands of Jews from deportation to Nazi death camps. When Jews were in danger, Wallenberg would issue Schutz passes and often showed up in person to offer help. He walked along death marches to give out food, water, medicine and fake passes that he printed to fool the Nazis. Without a weapon—but armed with the important-looking and life-saving passes—he jumped on top of trains to save families headed for the concentration camps. He gently sang to frightened children and once even scared a Nazi general—stopping him from killing thousands of people. This genuine hero risked his own life over and over again because he believed in the human rights of everyone. Vera calls him an angel.

Today, my friend Dr. Vera Goodkin is a professor at a college in New Jersey. When she visits schools, churches and synagogues to talk about her superhero, the children listen very quietly—sometimes with tears misting their bright eyes. Vera tells them that Raoul Wallenberg not only saved her life, but he restored her self-confidence and self-respect. She goes on to explain this to the children by sharing one of her vivid recollections from the frightening time she spent in a holding prison:

"After years of suffering so many cruelties at the hands of the Nazis, you begin to think that you really are not worth saving, that the freedom you remember might have been just a dream." Vera pauses, then continues, "When Raoul Wallenberg put his life on the line to save Jews— with a special place in his heart for the children—he helped them to believe in themselves, and in their past, once again. Because he believed the Jews were 'worthy of saving,' this righteous Christian gave them back their dignity." Vera concludes her story with a smile—her voice as hushed and reverent as in prayer.

By now, Vera has become a grandmother. She appreciates that her precious new grandson never could have been born if Raoul Wallenberg had not saved her life all those years ago. She is thankful, too, as she watches children of all faiths find hope in her true story of Mr. Wallenberg. Maybe they could grow up to be amazing like he was, a real superhero: strong and compassionate, bravely saving strangers from endless darkness.

What about Raoul Wallenberg? When the Russian Army liberated Budapest, the Russians took him prisoner. No one knows exactly why they did that—or what became of the heroic Swedish diplomat. In 1981, the United States recognized Wallenberg's courage and heroism and made him an honorary citizen. He was the second person that America so honored; Sir Winston Churchill was the first. Wallenberg's name is also found in the *Guinness Book of World Records* for having saved the lives of more people than any other human being—and he saved them all without violence.

Ilene Munetz Pachman

The Writing on the Wall

Hate is easy; love takes courage.

Several years ago, I spent one day per week working in a small, new "alternative" high school designed for high-risk, adjudicated youth. In other words, this educational setting was for kids who had been expelled from regular public schools and arrested for serious crimes. To avoid incarceration, students had to attend classes regularly, make satisfactory academic progress, participate in a skills-training program and keep their noses squeaky clean.

The school administrators, faculty and other staff had numerous meetings to prepare for the first class entering in the fall. Kathy, the new art teacher, and I occasionally participated in order to learn how the school would operate, but we mostly wanted to know more about the troubled teens who so desperately needed the help, understanding and encouragement of a dedicated staff. Initially, we were horrified that the kids would be searched daily, that there would be armed guards on site and that there was an incredibly strict zero-tolerance policy. Veteran teachers cautioned us about being too naive and "touchy-feely." We soon learned that these students all belonged to warring gangs. To eliminate flaunting of this rivalry through gang-related clothing, accessories and visible tattoos, male and female students were required to wear the exact same boring uniform. Kathy and I agreed that this environment wasn't as harsh as some of the "boot camp" schools we had heard about, but it still seemed sad to us that these teens had forfeited the chance to express their individuality and needed to be monitored every minute like criminals, not kids.

My assignment every Monday was to teach social-skills classes and girls' physical education, provide individual counseling, conduct psychological testing and assess students for previously undiagnosed learning disabilities. Kathy had four art classes and lunch duty. Far from prepared for the year ahead, we faced our first day with mixed feelings. Part of us was scared, part was excited, and part was hopeful that we could somehow make a difference in the lives of these kids. For some, it might be their "last chance" to avoid entering the adult judicial system. With the support of a more experienced staff, Kathy and I felt a little reassured that we could get all the help and advice that we needed.

In my social-skills classes, I asked everyone to complete questionnaires that measured self-esteem and self-efficacy (the perception that they had control over their lives). As tough as these teens tried to appear, few truly felt good about themselves. Most felt hopelessly trapped in their circumstances, with no expectations that anything would ever get better. Meeting with these students one-on-one, I easily understood why they joined a gang for support and protection. They believed that their life scripts were set in stone. How could I possibly convince them that they could make choices, write new chapters for their future?

During the first two P.E. classes, an armed guard stood in the gym. The girls obviously felt inhibited around him. I wanted to earn their respect and trust, so I obtained permission for the guard to sit outside the gym door, readily available if problems arose that I couldn't handle. Still young enough to sit cross-legged on the floor without getting stuck in that position, I donned matching gym clothes and joined everyone in a big circle on the floor. Girls from rival gangs glared at one another.

"So," I said, breaking the awkward silence, "y'all don't seem crazy about playing basketball or doing calisthenics, but we do have to get some exercise. Any suggestions?" I eagerly scanned a couple dozen faces, finally making eye contact with an angry girl known as "Big Bertha." She oozed hatred toward me.

Don't let her intimidate you, I reminded myself, feeling my heart beating furiously. I maintained the gaze and asked calmly, "Your thoughts?"

"I think you should watch your back, lady," she hissed.

"Tag! Good idea!" I responded with a thumbs-up.

Everyone, even Bertha, laughed. "O-o-o-r-r-r . . . ," I said mysteriously, "we could dance our butts off! Heaven knows, I've put on a little extra down there!" The girls laughed again, but then vehemently protested when they realized I was serious. I sadly learned that none of them had ever been to a school dance; none of them even danced around the house! Dancing was associated with frivolity, and life was far too serious to dance. The next week, I brought in a radio to ensure that we had popular music. Even when I pumped up the volume and suggested just moving to the beat, the girls all stood there, motionless. Only when I demonstrated some simple steps, instructing them to copy me, did they finally let go and start having fun. Oh, how I wanted soothing rhythms to heal their pain, uplifting movements to lighten their souls! By the time the semester ended, we had choreographed some dances. My favorite was their chorus line, in which everyone kicked in unison, arms wrapped around the shoulders of the girls on either side, oblivious of which gang they belonged to.

Meanwhile, Kathy was trying to connect with her students through artwork. Like me, she was getting some success. Many of the students had small jobs around the school in order to develop responsibility and acquire marketable skills. John's assignment was to wipe off the cafeteria tables after lunch. One day, Kathy stopped to chat with him. He suddenly held up the liquid cleanser as if he were going to spray it at her. Kathy smiled and said, "You wouldn't do that to me—you're too sweet!"

No one knows whether John took that comment as a challenge or was posturing for someone nearby, but he instantly pressed the trigger, spraying burning chemicals into the face of the teacher who had befriended him. Flooding Kathy's eyes with water was not enough. She had to be rushed to a hospital for medical care. John was tackled, handcuffed and taken to jail by the guard.

Fortunately, Kathy's vision wasn't permanently damaged. She returned to school the following week, still shaken from her ordeal. It was a difficult lesson to learn. We never heard what happened to John, but his actions had a profound impact on others. Even his friends agreed that what he did wasn't cool. I was amazed at how quickly Kathy bounced back, warmly interacting with her kids again as if none of them ever had the potential for violence. She wasn't just an art teacher; she was an art therapist in the truest sense of the word.

I don't know how she generated the idea, but one day I arrived late and discovered rival gang members working side by side, collaborating as they began to paint a mural on the wall, the entire length of the hallway. One of the kids had written in the lower left corner, "By the graduating seniors." My eyes met Kathy's, and our tears flowed instantly. I walked over to hug her. We didn't have to say a word; the wall said everything.

Karen Waldman, Ph.D.

The Five-Year Nightmare in Denmark

Nothing can be politically right that is morally wrong; and no necessity can ever sanctify a law that is contrary to equity.

Benjamin Rush, 1786

An unexpected and amazing stream of experiences began in our family when my eighteen-year-old son Dan agreed to a blind date with seventeen-year-old Lise, a Danish exchange student. Eight years—and a fortune in long-distance telephone and travel costs—later, Dan and Lise were married in two separate ceremonies, one in Copenhagen and another in San Diego.

Currently, Dan, Lise and their small children Emil and Lucia live in Denmark, which has prompted me to visit often. During these trips, I have been intrigued by amazing facts about the Danes and the history of Denmark that I've learned from Lise's family and friends. I have also formed friendships with two Americans, Hennie and Svend, a married couple who emigrated from Denmark in the 1950s. They, too, have enriched my life and shared remarkable childhood memories of their homeland. From among these stories, I have found the most inspiring those that focus on the Nazi occupation of Denmark during World War II, especially the ones about how the Danes heroically helped save their Jewish citizens from the horror of the Nazi concentration camps.

Typically, Danes are proud without being arrogant, accepting of others, and stalwart in their loyalty to country, family and friends. Because of the breadth of their international contacts, Danes are tolerant, open-minded and rarely categorize one another. Jewish citizens were Danes; it was as simple as that. It was a shock to the Danish people to learn that the Nazis had a different view of their fellow countrymen. This rumor became reality in 1940 when their beloved Denmark was invaded. A terrifying five-year nightmare had begun.

In Denmark, two legends prevail around the Nazi invasion and occupation. In the first, when King Christian X was informed that the Nazis demanded that all Jews wear armbands with the Star of David emblazoned on them for easy identification, he contacted the Gestapo and told them he himself would wear such an armband the following day, and every day thereafter as he took his daily horseback ride through the city. At that, the demand was withdrawn. In the second, Christian X also informed the Nazi leaders of his intention to have a soldier take down the Nazi flag with its swastika and put back the Danish flag on Amalienborg Castle. When he was told that the soldier replacing the flag would be shot, the king responded, "I will be that soldier!" Again, King Christian X won the day.

Whether fact or myth, these stories sent a strong infusion of pride and courage to the Danish people, who were routinely harassed and deprived of necessities by the Germans. Of course, for Jewish Danes it was far worse. Soon, the day came when an order went out to round them up in surprise raids for transport to concentration camps in Germany. Legendary numbers of Danes did what they could to save their Jewish countrymen.

Svend, my Danish American friend, tells about a horrifying event he personally witnessed when the Gestapo invaded the apartment of friends of his family. "Our apartments were in different buildings, but next to each other and on the same floor. They were so close, we could see practically everything that went on in one another's lives. They were a poor Jewish family of nine in that little two-room apartment. The father was a tailor making suits for rich men by hand at the window during the day and under one little lightbulb at night. All of them ate and slept in the other room. Unbelievably, they were always clean and neat as pins.

"When our friends heard the Gestapo on the stairs, the boys ran as fast as they could up to the roof. They jumped to the roof of the next building and ran down that staircase. From there, nobody knew for sure where they went until years later when they returned. Moving more slowly, their father trailed behind them. I watched the Gestapo brutally herd the mother, her baby and her three small daughters out of the apartment to a waiting truck.

"I kept watching out the window. The boys didn't go to the street, but I saw their father come out of the next building and run down an alley, only to run straight into a large wagon and collapse into unconsciousness. Somebody managed to get him to the hospital. Over the years that followed, no matter how much the Gestapo tried to pry that poor Jewish tailor out of the hospital, the doctors would not release him. They insisted that he was still in no condition to travel!"

There were many incidents of individual efforts to shelter the Jews during the Nazi occupation. Most astounding, however, was how the Danes responded as a nation to save their Jewish countrymen. It was an autumn day in 1943 when the order came from Berlin to round up all Danish Jews and deport them to Theresienstadt and other concentration camps. But the well-organized and highly effective Danish resistance had been tipped off, and they in turn informed the Jewish community. In one night of heroic and concerted effort, nearly eight thousand Jewish men, women and children were smuggled out of Denmark to safety in neutral Sweden. This daring and well-organized effort coordinated hundreds of fishermen to transport the Jews to safety in small fishing boats across icy waters. Bribes were also paid to guarantee that the German patrol boats would be in for repairs the night of the rescue.

On that bitter-cold October night, anxious Jews, old and young, alone and in family groups, waited along the Danish shore for the signal to wade out into frigid water, from which they could be hauled into the fishing boats, stowed like fish in the cargo area and covered with smelly canvas to avoid detection. The arduous journey to Sweden was nerve-racking for the Jews and fishermen alike. But in that one night of courage and compassion, nearly every Jew in Denmark was pulled from the horrors of Nazi anti-Semitism and carried to safety.

Today, a beautiful statue of a girl joyfully blowing a long, curved horn stands in the seafaring town of Gilleleje, where the Jews were smuggled into the boats. The statue is a visual reminder of that fateful night and the power of people who possess an inherent sense of justice and are willing to risk their own safety to protect their fellow men.

Gerry Dunne, Ph.D.

Shared Tears of Grief and Hope

*What diminishes one of us diminishes us all.
But when a person is raised up, to that degree,
the whole world is lifted.*

Mahatma Gandhi

The men and women clad in colorful, hand-woven garments lining the dirt road looked like a rainbow. These were the rural Maya of the Guatemalan highlands, survivors of nearly three decades of raging civil war that had killed an estimated four hundred thousand of their people.

In the summer of 1995, I joined thirty volunteers to hold a health clinic for them. Each day of the four-day clinic, more than five hundred people would arrive for help, and we would be able to treat only about a hundred of them. As I walked along the "rainbow" with a nurse and translator, seeking out the most life-threatening cases, I was shocked at what I saw.

One woman had a horribly swollen leg that had been broken a month earlier and never set; the bellies of a half dozen toddlers bulged from malnutrition and parasites; Pedro, age eleven, sobbed in pain, his blood-red eyes having been burned with solvent nearly a year earlier. Then there was little Jesús, age five, whose head was soft on top due to parasitic worms. It had taken three of us to assist the doctor in removing the peanut-sized bot fly larvae incubating in his head. Afterward, we found a secluded back room where we held each other and cried bitterly from the horror. No child should have to go through that!

On the third day, we were running low on antiparasitic medicine and planned a trip to stock up in San Juan Ostencalco, about an hour away. Gretchen and Ehlers (novice and veteran humanitarian workers, respectively) volunteered to accompany me. They hopped into the back of a well-used pickup. I climbed into the cab to drive—something that always made the locals smile. In Guatemala, it was still uncommon in 1995 to see a woman behind the wheel of a car, let alone a truck. Finding medicine was easy; we didn't need a prescription, and it was quite inexpensive. Jubilant at our success, we headed back down the bumpy, dusty road to the clinic.

I was the first to see them. They stood like misplaced statues in the middle of the road ahead—three men wearing black ski masks. They were holding machine guns, which they raised and pointed directly at the truck. I paused for a moment before turning and saying calmly through the open cab window, "I think we may have some trouble."

Ehlers and Gretchen were still facing backward. Gretchen turned around first, gasping and covering her mouth as she caught a glimpse of the ominous figures. Ehlers saw them and stayed very cool, answering simply, "Okay."

As we drew near, they motioned us to pull over. One man approached the car. I felt my face flush and my heart speed up. Perhaps this would be the last moment of our lives. Had I failed at keeping my team safe? I took a deep breath and focused on making the moment full of peace and acceptance.

In Spanish, I asked if there was a problem.

"You'll have to come with us."

As if in a dream, I replied, thinking of the others waiting for us at the clinic: "We're really busy right now. Is there any way we could do this another day?" (The things people say in life-and-death situations!)

I will never forget the man at the window repeating what I had said to the other two, then the three looking at each other and laughing.

"Drive down this road," the man at the window said to me sternly, motioning toward a dirt path, "and don't try to turn back or we may have to shoot you."

I remember thinking, *Okay. Got it.* I felt relatively calm and focused.

We soon reached the town square at Concepción. The village had only one road in and one out, and it was the perfect place to stage a mandatory public meeting. The Commander, a light-skinned man with green eyes and a beret, spoke to the crowd of about three hundred:

"Corrupt politicians have taken away our land and our children's future. We want to work, but there is no work; we want to learn, but there are few schools or teachers in our rural villages. We need medical care, but there are few clinics and less medicine. All we have left is the hope that we can take back what is rightfully ours."

The crowd clapped softly, apparently fearful of taking sides.

The three of us, fair and tall by local standards, stood out painfully in a crowd of dark-haired people who were generally much shorter. Almost immediately, the Commander's eyes found mine. He began to make his way toward us and was joined by a half-dozen associates clad in tattered uniforms.

I greeted the Commander with a firm handshake and looked him directly in the eye. Ehlers followed suit. Gretchen hung back, thoroughly and justifiably frightened.

"Pleased to meet you," I said. "We are humanitarian-aid workers."

He replied, "As a humanitarian worker, I know you understand suffering. I have people in these mountains who are fighting for the rights of the poor and who need medicine. Will you help us?"

This was a terrible moment. If I said yes, our entire team could be in great jeopardy; at this time in history, the Guatemalan government did not take kindly to groups helping what they called the "guerrillas" [revolutionary fighters]. If I said no, perhaps the three of us would be killed on the spot.

In a moment of trust, I decided to speak my heart: "Sir, you are the commander of a group of people whom it is your duty to protect. In the same way, I have to protect my people. If we give you medicine, the government may believe that we are affiliated with your movement, making it impossible for us to return to help your poor."

I paused for a moment to think. He studied my face, clearly undecided about whether to treat us like friends or enemies—or perhaps dispose of us without further ado. My heart ached for these ragged young soldiers at his side, many of whom wore blood-soaked bandages.

"We never ask who comes to our clinics," I offered. "Our clinics are open to *everyone*."

The Commander's gaze was intense, as if he was searching my eyes and the nuances of my expression for the truth of my heart. I had spoken in earnest and offered the best compromise I could muster. This situation was now out of my hands.

The Commander motioned for his colleagues to follow him, and they convened to speak just out of earshot.

Ehlers, Gretchen and I stood by, unable to do anything but wait.

When the Commander returned, I noticed immediately that his eyes had softened, and I was dumbstruck to see tears welling up!

"God bless you for the work you do helping our poor," he said kindly. "You are free to go."

In stunned silence we drove back to the clinic. Somewhere along that dusty road, we began to weep. In the oddest of ironies we would speak of later, our tears made each of us feel a kinship with our kidnapper. We realized we were crying over the same injustices and suffering that had moved the Commander to tears. What a surprise it was to know we both shared the same grief and hope for the people of Guatemala. Perhaps some day we would be sharing only hope.

Leslie Carol Baer

"Peace" in a Bottle of "Joy"?

There is no duty we so much underrate as the duty to be happy. By being happy we see anonymous benefits upon the world.

Robert Louis Stevenson

I always kept a bottle of Joy liquid dishwashing detergent on my classroom sink. If my students were not having a peaceful day, they were to go wash their hands with the soap to get a little more "joy" in their lives. The students believed that if they didn't have joy in their lives, they wouldn't have any peace. If they lost their peace, then they would lose their joy.

I had been working with an inner-city first-grade class, and their behavior was very challenging. Every time I visited the classroom, we discussed how we could keep our peace and not fight and hit everyone. I left a bottle of Joy in their classroom on one of my visits, hoping it would help remind the students to keep joy in their lives. I visited the classroom one last time before school was out for the summer. When I entered the room, there seemed to be a calmer feeling among the students. The teacher had been spending more time doing activities where the students worked on building relationships with each other. The time spent was paying off. The classroom actually felt peaceful.

I praised the class for their efforts, and as I left, I noticed the bottle of Joy was gone from the sink. I was thinking it must have taken a lot of Joy to make their classroom peaceful. As I was walking down the hall, a little boy ran after me, yelling for me to wait. I turned and saw Jerrome, one of the most challenging children in the class, following me.

"Wait, wait. I want you to take this," he yelled. I looked down, and in his hands was the bottle of Joy wrapped in rough brown paper towels and secured with a copious amount of tape. Scrawled on the top of the package was "President Bush."

"I want you to mail this to the president. Maybe this will help the people fighting find their peace."

Tears were in my eyes as I left the school with the special package in my hand. I sent a note to Jerrome to thank him for his kindness, only to have it returned to me with a note that said: "Jerrome has moved. This will be the seventh time he moved this school year, and we do not have a forwarding address."

I just hope that Jerrome can find the peace in his own life that he was so eager for others to have.

Barbara Pedersen

P.K.'s Mission

It's better to light a candle than to curse the darkness.

Eleanor Roosevelt

P.K. was the center of his mother Talia's universe, and she was very happy to spend what little free time she had with her beautiful boy. P.K. was the youngest of three children and the last one to live at home. P.K. didn't know his father. When the other children in his neighborhood asked him about his father, he explained that his father was not around, but his mother was happy having him all to herself.

P.K.'s neighborhood was crowded and dangerous, plagued by unemployment, poverty and violence. From a very young age, P.K. was taught to avoid trouble, and he was good at it—most of the time. P.K.'s uncle, who until recently had lived two blocks away, often took P.K. along on his bread-delivery route during the summer. P.K. absorbed the words of wisdom his uncle judiciously dispensed between deliveries—much of it focused on how to stay out of trouble and how to pick friends. To P.K., his uncle was much larger than his 150-pound frame. P.K.

looked forward to being a few years older so that he could go on all-night catfishing adventures with his uncle on the river that bordered the city.

A good student, P.K. paid attention in school. His mother checked his homework every night. P.K. heeded his uncle's words about choosing friends and avoiding fights. Also, P.K. was a good friend; all the other third-graders knew that they could count on P.K.

One warm October afternoon, P.K.'s mother walked six blocks to pick him up after school. A new job and a bigger paycheck prompted a sense of hope in P.K.'s mother. Her steps were light and brisk. She anticipated P.K.'s surprise and pride at her coming to pick him up after school. On the way home, the two would buy the school supplies that most students brought with them on the first day of school, but which Talia could not afford until now because of her new job. A slice of pizza and an ice-cream cone would celebrate the paycheck and guarantee a memorable day together.

Heading for the store, P.K. and his mother rounded the corner to head up Mill Street. P.K. felt his mother's hand grab his shoulder tightly as his slight torso was drawn to hers. Their feet stopped so abruptly that they leaned forward, off balance. At the end of the block, two groups of young men were screaming threats at one another. Shots were fired, the sound of them bouncing sharply off the hard, graffiti-covered factories and storefronts. Tires squealed and cars dashed through stoplights to get away from the area. The noise stopped as abruptly as it had begun. The young men disappeared into the crevices of the city. Sirens interrupted the interminable, numbing silence.

P.K.'s mother lay bleeding at his feet, her eyes staring blankly upward. The ambulance came, but it was too late: Talia was dead.

When the funeral was over, P.K. was shuttled among relatives and friends—a month with his aunt and uncle, a couple of weeks with his mother's best friend, a month with his older sister and her family—the length of his stay determined by the available room and resources. P.K. shared beds and slept on couches; often, he slept on the floor.

P.K. was quiet in school. He stared blankly as his teacher's explanations and assignments went unheard. His grades dropped, and P.K. found himself drifting further and further from his friends. Gradually, his friends tired of encouraging and consoling P.K., whose once-familiar laugh became a distant memory. And as the weeks and months dragged by, the reassuring words of relatives and his minister became hollow. Anger and despair competed for P.K.'s attention.

One day, a woman visited P.K.'s school and spoke to his class about starting a peer-mediation program. P.K. came to life, bouncing in his seat and waving his arms to ask questions. He waited until she finished her presentation about peer mediation, then bolted to the front of the room to sign up for training.

"Are you sure, P.K.? You have seen so much conflict and violence. I am afraid that mediation will make you think about your mother," his teacher cautioned.

"Yes, I'm sure about the training," he answered. "And yes, I'm thinking about my mother. This is exactly who she would want me to be."

Roberta Anna Heydenberk, Ed.D., and
Warren Robert Heydenberk, Ed.D.

The Family Circus, Bil Keane, ©2000, reprinted by permission of Bil Keane.

An Extraordinary Woman

*All around the world people are waging peace .
. . and it is working.*

Robert Muller, LL.D.

Zainab Salbi was an undergraduate student at George Mason University when the idea came to her to form the relief organization now known as Women for Women International. She was watching the evening news, listening to reports of the genocide in the Balkans, the repeated and systematic rape of an estimated twenty thousand Bosnian women by Serbian soldiers. As the stories unfolded before her eyes, her thoughts turned to her childhood in Baghdad, to growing up during the Iran-Iraq conflict. She was on intimate terms with the vulnerability war engenders, with the fear of annihilation and the pervading sense of disconnection and loss that are the con - sequence of war. She knew what lay in store for these Bosnian women, particularly the strain of trying to shape a life in the aftermath of war. As these familiar images played themselves out before her on television, she vowed to use her life experience to help these Bosnian women. It was, she believed, her moral and spiritual responsibility to do so.

In the days that followed, Zainab telephoned various relief organizations to volunteer her services. Agency representatives were sympathetic, but no one was, at this early stage of the conflict, prepared to provide aid. With no experience in disaster-relief organization, no professional contacts and no funds of her own to draw on, twenty-three-year-old Zainab Salbi did the only thing she could think of: she backtracked through the list of organizations she had telephoned and asked total strangers to help her form a nonprofit organization to support the women of Bosnia. One group agreed to act as the administrative arm for the fledgling project for a year. It was just enough time to get Women for Women in Bosnia up and running.

Today, Women for Women International serves indigent women in Bosnia, Kosovo, Herzegovina, Croatia, Colombia, Rwanda, Nigeria, Bangladesh, Pakistan, Iraq, the Democratic Republic of Congo and Afghanistan. It provides emotional support and financial aid through a one-to-one sponsorship program. It offers job training, including leadership development and human-rights awareness that teaches women how to grow a postwar economy. And it funds a micro-credit lending program that provides capital to create women-owned entrepreneurial ventures. In 1995, two years after it was founded, Women for Women International was honored at the White House for its achievements. To date, it has raised over $18 million in direct aid and helped thirty-three thousand indigent women become self-sufficient.

"There came a point when I needed to move beyond my idea to only help rape victims. While we were in Croatia, someone asked me how I planned to identify the women I wanted to help. Would I put up a sign that said, 'Rape victims line up here for aid'? Singling them out would be another slap in the face; it would stigmatize them even more. I couldn't do that.

"Then I met a woman who told me about escaping from the Serbian soldiers who destroyed her village. She was shaking as she described how she and her sons ran into the mountains, how she turned back to see her house in flames. She wasn't raped. She wasn't held in a concentration camp. But the image of her house burning terrified her. Who was I to say she did not deserve aid?

"I decided then that I would not ask a woman what had happened to her. I would not ask if she was married or single or what she believed politically or spiritually or what her ethnicity was. What is relevant is that she is a human being who is poor and needs help. There isn't one definition of a victim. There isn't one definition of the most horrible thing that can happen to a person. You can't compare atrocities. You can't compare human misery.

"A Rwandan woman I worked with lost six children in a brutal massacre. She was in church praying with her family when the soldiers came. The bullets began to fly, and her children were killed. They all fell on top of her as they died. The soldiers walked through the church to execute the survivors and assumed she was dead because she lay still underneath her children's bodies. She was pregnant at the time this happened. She left her home, moved to another town and had her baby. By the time I met her, she had adopted five children who had lost their parents in incidents similar to her own. Taking those children helped her give meaning to her own loss.

"I've come to respect these women as unique individuals who know their own hearts. My responsibility is to support each woman in her process, to give her exposure to different options, but ultimately, to let her choose what she feels will restore her dignity. Step by step, they find ways—small ways, at first—to regain their power. For one woman, it was a simple gold bracelet she received from her sponsor. It was all she had, and it became her connection to life itself. It was not the material value of the bracelet that was important to her, but the friendship it symbolized. Someone out there cared about her; someone was there for her if she needed help."

Margaret Wolff

From Angry Kid to Peace-Prize Winner

Anger is a great force. If you control it, it can be transmuted into a power which can move the whole world.

William Shenstone

A hush fell over the banquet room. It was time, and my heart was beating wildly. I couldn't believe I was here, and that, in a moment, all eyes would be on me. I stood as I heard my name called, and with sweaty palms I began my walk to the podium amidst thunderous applause. As I stood there, acknowledging the outburst of approval from my peers, I couldn't help thinking how my old friends from my tumultuous high-school days would roll over laughing in disbelief if they could see me now!

I was the angry kid who had joined them in petty thefts, joy-riding in stolen cars and various acts of vandalism, and I was about to accept a California Peace Prize from the California Wellness Foundation! My second thought was, I really can't get into any public conflicts anymore! How embarrassing would it be to read in the newspaper that "Wayne Sakamoto, Safe Schools Lead Coordinator—who is responsible for violence prevention, conflict resolution and gang prevention in San Diego County—has been in a fight!" I chuckled to myself as I smiled and accepted the prestigious award. "Thank you. I am honored to be here."

It had been a long journey to this evening's recognition. I remembered the anger I had felt as a little boy confronted by racism. My parents had tried to prepare me for the discrimination, but I was still surprised and deeply hurt by it. The first time it happened, I was about seven years old. There was this playground equipment in the park that I wanted to climb. It was like a rocket ship with a capsule at the top. It was difficult, but I made it to the top, only to be confronted by some older kids who were up there.

"You don't belong up here!" they yelled at me. "You're a Jap!"

"What do you mean? I'm an American!"

"No, you're not! You're a Jap!"

I was outraged and so confused. There weren't any adults around to help me. I went home. I didn't tell my parents. I had learned from them that there are some things—and feelings—you don't talk about. I knew that they had been interned during World War II as teenagers. Only rarely did they talk about it, giving me the briefest glimpses into what it must have been like. My mother spoke of the cold draft that was always blowing through the shack they were forced to live in. They both spoke of the shortage of food, of going hungry. The property their families had owned before was taken away from them, as well as scholarships to college (their only way to attend), the senior prom and all the social activities so important to teenagers—so many things that could never be replaced. In spite of their losses and humiliation, they were fiercely patriotic Americans. But the injustice of it all smoldered inside me.

I started experiencing more and more of these discriminating messages. *No, you don't belong! No, you're not one of us!* I became more and more angry. I began hating myself. I didn't fit in. I was filled with rage. The name-calling continued, and I started getting into fights. I never told anyone that it was because of the racial name-calling.

By the time I was in the fourth grade, we had moved from Orange County to Riverside County. We were the only Asian family in the *barrio*. Recess time from the first day on was a time to fight—until I could prove I was pretty tough. I was always proving myself.

My only escape was at night when I told myself stories to get to sleep. I was always the hero in my stories, living in a big house, being the best athlete and having wonderful parties. When I got older, instead of stories, I went over in my mind what had happened during the day—how I could have changed the outcome, what I could have done differently. I think a lot of our youth today don't have an opportunity to do that.

When I work with an angry kid now, I ask, "Where do you think your anger is coming from?" I encourage them to reflect on their lives. Looking straight into their eyes, I tell them, "Until you can accept who you are and what you cannot change, you will not be able to move on."

I certainly did not change all at once. It was very gradual—baby steps. The first person to really help me was my sixth-grade teacher, Mrs. Madeline West. She entered my life on the playground when I was still in the fourth grade. She saw me shoving another kid, and she grabbed my arm and told me how unacceptable my behavior was. I saw her watching me after that and hoped that she would never be my teacher. I was really worried when the sixth grade came around and she *was* my teacher! I knew she knew who I was, but she never said anything about the past. Instead, she saw potential in me. She believed that I could do better in school. She helped me believe in myself. When she talked to me, it was genuine. I wasn't over being a knucklehead, but meeting her was a turning point in my life. Kids do need adults in their lives to care about them. It's a slow process, but they do make a difference in a kid's life.

In my work, I don't try to change kids. I just give them information. I tell them about my own experiences, how my own anger felt when I was a kid. I talk about the joy I felt being connected with other guys as angry as I was, inflicting hurt on those who had hurt us—and those who hadn't—and the addiction of the adrenaline rush. Kids recognize authenticity. I tell them that anger is a natural emotion; it's how you channel it—or don't—that makes it a problem. So channeling your anger is what's important. Kids tend to think that conflict, no matter how minor, always turns into a violent confrontation. They don't understand that there are other ways to resolve conflict. We must give them tools to communicate their anger other than a physical fight—or a tragic school shooting.

My dream is that all adults will realize that they are involved in developing young people, no matter what their role is with them. It *does* take a village to raise a child! We need to share our values, teach them manners, tell them what we think makes an ideal man or woman, and give them hope that they can make a difference.

The sound of applause penetrated my reverie. Looking out into the sea of faces, I began, "Ladies and gentlemen, I want to tell you a story about an angry young man. The important part of the story is how teachers and adults like you made a difference in his life. I want you to be inspired to be that person in another child's life. . . ."

Wayne Sakamoto
As told to Barbara Smythe

And a Little Child Will Lead Them

I will act as if what I do makes a difference.

William James

It was the summer of '67, and America was being turned inside out by unrest at home and war abroad. Activists were making disturbing accusations about the motives of their government's involvement in Vietnam. Women were birthing a new feminist movement that men were resisting. And blacks were loosing themselves from the chains of segregation that had chafed their bodies and bled their hearts for over two hundred years. Every prevailing opinion was brought into question, every imaginable assumption brought into doubt.

It's hard to say what ignited it all in downtown Detroit that summer, but it was mid-July when the trouble began. Within a matter of days, the city was engulfed in what was to the white community a riot and the black community a rebellion. For both groups, long simmering over years of resentment and suspicion, the kettle finally boiled over. Arson, vandalism, gunfire, fistfights—Detroit was dancing precipitously close to the brink of destruction, and there was little in the way of either wisdom or will to pull her back.

"Our city was dying," recalls Carl Andreas, a United Auto Workers employee who, with his wife and two sons, lived in the Lafayette Park neighborhood, close to downtown. "Everywhere you looked you could see fires or the vestiges of fires, smoldering rubble, burned-out hulks of buildings, charred timber where somebody's business or home once stood. It was so very painful.

"We didn't know what to do, but as a family we knew we had to do *something*. We are Mennonites, not only committed to peace, but to the things that make for peace. But like everyone else, we were at loose ends."

The Andreases tied up at least one of those loose ends when one single, simple idea arose during dinner conversation one night. They made a sign. It read: "This House Is Unarmed." They hung it in their living-room window, visible from the street.

"If nothing else, the sign at least gave us the opportunity to proclaim *our* nonviolence," Andreas observed. "It was our own little witness. And if others wished to join us, well, they were welcome to do so." And so, a message was born.

Others did join them. Despite protests from some neighbors who feared it might attract trouble, a few more signs started appearing, sporadically, in living-room windows dotting the neighborhood. And the message spread.

"We then had a few printed up," Andreas remembers. "Maybe a dozen or so. They had the image of a dove and a home, and the words, of course. And we gave them out to our friends." And so the message spread a little more.

"Some of us made our own," recalled Rev. Nancy Doughty, new to the city at the time. And the message spread a little more.

"Eventually, one of the progressive churches in town took up the idea," says Andreas, "and actually printed quite a few. It may have been hundreds. Maybe a thousand. I don't recall exactly how many, but I know it was more than we could've made." And the message spread a little more.

An inspired idea became something of a movement, and for the duration of the unrest, all reports indicate that none of the houses that bore the signs were touched by so much as a scintilla of the violence.

We so often believe that great ideas can only come from great leaders, that effective protest can only be driven by saintly figures. How inspiring to realize that any one of us has the ability to imagine a workable solution and can then turn that idea into powerful action.

Most amazing of all, it was the Andreases' eleven-year-old son, a child, not the power and might of experience, who thought of a sign proclaiming "This House Is Unarmed." This child's simple idea became the spark that gave protection and helped restore peace to a violence-torn city.

Erik Kolbell

Harriet Tubman:
A Battle of a Different Kind

Since justice is indivisible, injustice anywhere is an affront to justice everywhere.

Martin Luther King Jr.

"If a fire is lit properly, it will burn," her mother said.

"I know, Mama. And if it rains, there will be puddles somewhere."

"I'm telling you, Harriet, some things don't change, and they're never going to change. Just like fires burning and water puddling. And being a slave!"

"Mama, you told me the story of my great-grandma being kidnapped and brought here to be a slave. She was free before she came here. I can't change fires burning or rain falling, but I will change what I can change. I won't always be a slave. I'll be free some day."

Harriet Tubman was no more than five years old when she was sent to work in the Big House. The house where the plantation owners—*her* owners—lived was very different from the shabby cabin in which she slept. Her jobs in the Big House began when the sun rose and ended when the sun set.

"Harriet! Why is that baby crying? You're not rocking the cradle gently enough! Go help the cook prepare lunch."

Harriet rubbed her own growling stomach as she went off. She hadn't eaten since the night before.

Harriet was a slave because her family all were slaves. Her great-grandmother had come from Africa, but it hadn't been by choice. She had been captured, put on a crowded ship, taken to a country on the other side of the globe and sold. She didn't want to stay, but she no longer had her freedom, so she had to stay. By the time Harriet was born, ship captains had been bringing Africans to America for two hundred years, and more than 4 million black slaves worked on farms and plantations.

Harriet washed, scrubbed, rocked—and thought. And if she thought too much and her master didn't think she'd worked hard enough, she was whipped. As she grew older, she always feared that if she didn't please her master, she might be sold as her sisters had been. As a slave, she could be sold just like a horse or a piece of furniture. She knew she had to leave before that happened because if she were sold, it would be farther south and much harder to reach the North.

Harriet longed for freedom. She didn't want to work in the fields without being paid; she didn't want to be an unpaid servant. She wanted to be free. But escaping was not as easy as opening a door and leaving, because leaving was illegal. Harriet was a slave in the state of Maryland. There were other states that were slave states, and there were nearby states that were considered "free" states. In order to escape, Harriet would have to leave Maryland and go north to a state that did not allow slavery.

* * *

Except for the early-morning light peeking through the openings between the logs, Harriet's cabin was dark. Harriet was sitting on her rag-covered bed of straw. Her mother looked over at her.

"What were you and your father talking about last night?" her mother asked.

"Well, Mama, we were talking about fires burning and rain puddling. You know, all those things that don't change."

"You were out there for a long time, Harriet. You were talking about other things besides fire and rain."

"We were talking about something else, Mama, about something else that doesn't change. We were talking about how the North Star shines. We were talking about how some things might change."

"Harriet, you are looking for trouble if you are talking about the North Star. If you have been listening to all those folks talking about going north to freedom, you are just listening to them wishing they could. If you try following that star to the North, they'll come hunting for you with dogs. They'll put out a money reward. I'm frightened for you."

"Mama, I'm afraid, too, but I have to leave. If I can escape and reach the North, I can find work, and I can help our people become free."

Harriet made her escape in the middle of the night. Following the North Star as her guide, she traveled only under the cover of darkness until she reached safety in Philadelphia.

In the North, there were many people who wanted to help slaves leave the South. Harriet joined those people and became an important part of an escape route called the Underground Railroad. There were no trains on this railroad, but there were stations. The stations were hiding places along the way. Very little of it was underground, but it was a secret, and calling it "underground" reminded those who were helping that the secret had to be kept.

All too often, the words bravery and courage remind us of battles and battlefields. Harriet's battles were of a different kind. They didn't take place on a battlefield, but they did require bravery. They took place in darkness and in secret places. Her courage was special because, even after she was free, she continued to risk her life and her freedom. She couldn't enjoy being free when she remembered the ones who weren't free. The battle she fought was for something she believed in: freedom for all.

* * *

"Come quickly," Harriet said as she noiselessly entered the slave cabin. "We have a long way to go, and runaway slaves don't have much time."

Harriet's troop of escaping slaves entered the forest, huddling together and waiting for her directions. Each time, she used different paths, different safe houses, different boats, different wagons.

"We will cross the river here. Take off your shoes and hold them above your head. The water moves quickly, but it is not too deep. You'll dry off on the rest of the journey."

"You sound like a general giving orders," one of the escaping slaves said.

"I've been called General Tubman before," she answered, laughing quietly as they reached the dark woods on the other side of the river.

* * *

As she guided escaping slaves to safety in the free states, Harriet's bravery was tested many times. Slave hunters were offered thousands of dollars to capture her, but she continued taking small groups through forests, hiding on boats, in attics and in underground tunnels.

With special handshakes and passwords, her friends on the Underground Railroad helped her.

Her own escape took great courage, but it was her return to the South and the danger of recapture for which she is remembered. Fifteen times, she returned. She helped more than three hundred slaves find their way to the North. Always at night, always in secret, always in danger.

The success of the Underground Railroad as a way to freedom in the North was the result of Harriet Tubman's courage and her belief that she could change things. None of her "passengers" was ever recaptured, and Harriet was even able to rescue her own parents. Her journeys in darkness to help others to freedom are reason enough to remember her name—Harriet Tubman—a heroine in a battle of a different kind.

Susan Finney

Consider Me Your Bird

The future belongs to those who believe in the beauty of their dreams.

Eleanor Roosevelt

It was a naive and childish idea, but I was only fourteen years old and filled with hope, in spite of the terrible circumstances surrounding me during the 1950s. My home was the Mekong Delta region of Vietnam. It is a place of great beauty and agricultural richness—as well as of war and natural disasters. The families living there, who tried to make their living from the land, suffered great losses from the warring factions, both revolutionaries and foreign forces. Many were killed and maimed, their small farms destroyed.

I felt desperate for the children and their families, but I refused to be helpless. I decided: *Where I am, I can do something. I cannot stop the war, but I CAN help the children.* I began going from house to house, knocking on every door and saying to each person who answered my knock, "I know that you are kind and give the birds that come to your yard a little rice. Please consider me your bird. Give me only a handful of rice each week when I come to your door. I will take it to the temple where it can be given to the hungry children."

No one seemed to mind giving me a small handful of rice, even when they had little themselves. On Sunday, I would go to the temple and give my handfuls of rice to the monks to give to the children. My teenage friends saw what I was doing, and they also wanted to help. Soon, there were many "hungry birds" like myself, going door-to-door for our handfuls of rice.

One day, I came to a house that had much to give. I told my story and asked if I could be their bird. The woman called her daughters, and each one gave me fifty cents, as well as the handful of rice! I began to ask for change and rice from the other "bird feeders," and they gave it to me. Everyone was happy to be helping those who were suffering, even in only this small way. The temple was soon able to help everyone who came to them for food and clothing.

"Consider me your bird." My naive and childish idea had not stopped the war, but in a small way, it was creating peace.

Sister Chân Không
As told to Barbara Smythe

2

LOVE AND KINDNESS

What is love and kindness?

Love is the power to forgive, to heal, to create joy, to build communities and families. Kindness is a contribution that we can each make to those around us through the power of our compassion, our courage, and our honoring each other's differences and similarities. These two powerful qualities can assist us in transforming our families, communities, countries and the world.

I am sharing the love and kindness that is in my heart with those who are near and far.

Sleep in Heavenly Peace

The world is moved along, not only by the mighty shoves of its heroes, but also by the aggregate of the tiny pushes of each honest worker.

Helen Keller

Somehow, I knew my spirit would change that day. Perhaps it was a premonition; perhaps it was simply being in the presence of such an amazing place, born of a phenomenal woman who forever changed this city—if not the world. Whatever it was, I felt the butterflies of anticipation as I descended the steps to Prem Dan, one of the homes of the Missionaries of Charity founded by Mother Teresa in Calcutta, India.

I stepped into the main room where the Sisters housed and fed the women in their care. The large cement room was dimly lit, with beds laid out side by side and in long rows like a military bunkhouse. The Sisters moved quietly about, tending to the various needs of the poor souls who ended up here. I was completely overwhelmed by the sight. After almost a month in this country, including travel by third-class trains, cockroach-infested beds, bodies cremating before my eyes and starving lepers in the streets, I thought I had seen it all, but once again, India was proving me wrong. I was all too weak in the shadow of her power. Women in all stages of life and forms of sickness lay about, moaning and talking, crying and sleeping. Skeletal silhouettes shuffled in circles with nowhere to go; others were literally disfigured from lying too long in the fetal position. Dark eyes emptied of hope long ago gazed up at me from hollow sockets; only a few seemed to really see me.

I suddenly wondered if I could do this, if I could make myself stay and work with these poor, forgotten people, wasting away and waiting for death. I began to question why I came here. Was it merely to tell other people that I went to Mother Teresa's in Calcutta? Was it a sense of obligation to India and her people for allowing me a glimpse into the mysteries of life here? Or, perhaps, was it out of respect for one of my idols, a simple woman who so impacted the world through her unfailing belief in God? For a fleeting moment, I thought that I could leave. I would just be another volunteer come and gone. But deep inside I knew I couldn't. Wouldn't that be defeating the whole purpose of the trip? Hadn't I come to India to fight my fears, to find some answers that lay deep within my soul, and to share peace with people from the other side of the globe? *Besides,* I thought as I looked around at the dismal scene, *these people can't escape. And, therefore, neither will I.*

I felt drawn to a small form lying on a bed in the corner of the room. She couldn't have weighed more than seventy pounds, and her dark skin seemed to merely lie on top of her skeleton. Her eyes were closed, and her three remaining teeth protruded from black, rotted gums. I couldn't determine how old she was, but her head was nearly bald, and she reeked of the stale odor of age and disease. But what frightened me most was her breathing.

Every breath was drawn in sharply, her lungs gasping for air with great effort. I could tell from the way she occasionally grimaced that she was in pain, suffering with each raspy breath.

I looked around, surprised that she was alone. The Sisters were kneeling throughout the room, quietly tending others. I gingerly sat down on the bed next to her head and gently took one of her leathery hands in mine. With trepidation, I stroked her head, internally scolding myself for being afraid to touch someone whom I thought of as so dirty, so repulsive, so diseased. I felt helpless. I knew that, regardless of whether she could hear me, my words would mean nothing to her because I couldn't speak them in her language. But then I remembered the words of Mother Teresa, and I imagined this poor woman as God in disguise. I felt a flood of compassion storm over my heart, washing away fears and drowning my hesitations. And I suddenly couldn't bear to leave her alone. Nothing other than some unknown twist of fate determined that I was the one holding her hand, and not the other way around. The least I could do was let her know that she was not suffering alone in a dimly lit corner of an impersonal room.

So I decided to sing, just as a mother sings to comfort her crying baby. Music speaks beyond words, beyond language. For some inexplicable reason, the most soothing song I could think of was "Silent Night," and I began to sing it softly. I stroked her head gently with one hand, holding her skin-and-bones hand tightly with the other, and I sang. I could see her visibly relax, her tired and undernourished body release some tension. She began to breathe a bit easier, and I knew she was listening. She knew I was there.

I was encouraged and I continued on, not caring whether anyone else could hear my unmelodic voice, not caring that I sang the same words over and over. I focused on her, pouring every ounce of energy, love and peace into her body through my hands, my voice and my soul. I wondered if she had a family somewhere in the world. I wondered if, in her life before she fell ill, she had ever held her child in her arms and sang him to sleep. I wondered if she had friends, if she had ever laughed, if she had ever fallen in love. And if she had—if any of my wonderings were true—why was she alone now? Where were they, her friends and loved ones, and why had they forgotten her?

Suddenly, she opened her eyes, looking quickly and directly into the center of my pupils with a clarity that stunned me. For a moment in time, the gap was bridged, and no racial or linguistic boundaries existed between us. We were just two women, bound together in time of need, each staring deeply into the other's spirit. I felt tingles dance along my spine and reach into my soul; I knew she was saying "thank you." She winced in pain again, and the moment slipped away. I resumed singing, falling into rhythm with the rasps of her pained breathing, wondering how anything back home would ever seem important again.

Soon, she relaxed into a deeper stage of sleep; before long, I noticed she was no longer breathing. One of the Sisters saw my desperate glance and walked over to me. She nodded, confirming my fear. I guess I half expected it, and I just nodded. Death is a very real part of life in India, and I shouldn't have been bothered by it. Though I found myself fighting tears, I searched the innermost sanctum of my heart and found not sorrow but peace.

India had been hard on me; I had difficulty adapting to the poverty, the filth, the endless challenges that living in the Third World brings. But if the sole purpose of my entire journey was this—if all my fears, discomfort and homesickness were not in vain but to allow me to be by a lonely and frightened woman's side while she lay in her last hours on Earth—then it was worth every moment. I found comfort in knowing that my song soothed her, that my loving touch made her feel less alone until the moment that she crossed over to a place where she didn't hurt anymore. I knew that, because of her, my life would change. The frivolities of my "problems" back home in America would seem shallow now, and finding my purpose in life would have new meaning. Part of her would remain in my heart forever, and some day, when it is my turn, I may find her on the other side waiting for me. We will smile and sing "Silent Night" in our common language of the heart and dance in the glory of an existence without sadness or pain.

And, I realized as I filed this life-changing lesson away in my heart, that I didn't even know her name.

> "Silent night, holy night,
> All is calm, all is bright. . . .
> Sleep in heavenly peace,
> Sleep in heavenly peace. . . ."

Stacy Smith

Be Careful What You Teach Them

Don't worry that your children don't listen to you. Worry that they are watching everything you do.

Weatherly

Katie was in trouble, and I mean BIG trouble. She was such a sweet and caring kid; I just couldn't imagine what she had done to make her mom so angry. A third-grade teacher always dreams of having a classroom filled with Katies. She worked hard, loved learning, did her homework, had concerned and active parents, was attentive *and* a risk taker. And she was *never, ever* a discipline problem.

So when I received a phone call one evening, I was surprised. Katie's mom was not the type to overreact to situa - tions, and she said she needed my help. It seemed that Katie had been running up sizable charges in the lunchroom. Her mother and father explained that she did not have permission to be buying snacks at school. She brought a great homemade lunch each day, and there was no reason for her to be charging extra items. They assumed a sit-down with Katie would solve the problem.

It always had in the past. But when they got another bill from the school cafeteria the following month, her mom and dad became very concerned. It was so unlike Katie to purposefully misbehave, and it was totally out of character for her to ignore her parents.

It was at this point that her parents asked me if I could help them get to the bottom of this situation. I told them that I would try to find out what was going on and would be in contact with them by the end of the week. When I went to the cafeteria to inquire about Katie's charges, the lady told me that Katie charged a lunch every day and took the tray to her table and ate it. This made no sense at all. I had seen the lunches Katie brought and had thought to myself that I wouldn't mind if her mom packed me a lunch once in a while. There was no way that Katie would prefer to eat the school lunch. Hey, nothing against school lunches, but really!

I asked Katie to stay in for recess the next day, hoping to solve the mystery. I had a few theories of what might be happening, but I planned on letting her tell me the story in her own time.

She was a rock.

She wouldn't crack.

I couldn't believe it!

There was no way Katie could ignore the stern manner I took with her . . . but she did. I have a pretty good "disappointed teacher" look, but it had no effect on her.

"Why are you charging lunches, Katie?" I asked.

"Because I need to eat lunch," she responded.

"What happens to the lunch your mother makes for you every morning?" I countered, sure that I had her with this one.

"I lose it," she responded, matter-of-factly.

"You lose it?" I asked incredulously.

"Yup, I lose it."

"Every day?" I asked.

"Every day."

I leaned back in my chair, fixed her with my sternest gaze and said, "I don't believe you, Katie."

She didn't care. . . .

Well, as upset as it made me to be ignored, there was something about all this, something that just didn't fit.

So, I took a new tack.

In my most understanding and concerned voice I asked, "Is someone stealing your lunch, Katie? Is that what is happening?"

"Nope," she said in a tight-lipped sort of way.

"Katie, if someone is bullying you and stealing your lunch, I can help." I really thought I was on the right track with this theory.

"No one is stealing my lunch, Mr. D. I just lose it."

Well, she had me. There was nothing else I could do.

Schools have a law that a student with no lunch must be provided with a lunch. The family is to be billed for the lunch unless they qualify for a free or reduced lunch. There was no way Katie's family qualified for free lunch, so they would have to pay the charges as long as Katie asked for a lunch.

I called her parents on Friday night. We talked about the whole situation, bouncing different theories off one another, but nothing made sense.

The problem was still unresolved the next week when I noticed a boy who was new to the school sitting alone at a lunch table. Other kids had not warmed up to him very quickly, and he always looked sad. I thought I would go and sit with him for a few minutes. As I walked toward him, I noticed the lunch bag on the table in front of him. The name on the bag said "Katie."

He was munching away on a big, delicious, homemade sandwich.

Now I understood.

I talked to Katie that afternoon.

It seemed the new boy never brought a lunch, and he wouldn't go to the lunch line for a free lunch. He had confided in Katie and asked her not to tell anyone that his parents would never take a "handout" from the school. And if he did charge a lunch, he got in a lot of trouble at home. Katie asked me not to tell her parents.

But I did. I told on her.

In fact, I drove to Katie's house that evening after I was sure that she was in bed. I have never seen parents so proud of their child. Katie didn't care that her parents had grounded her. She didn't care that I was disappointed in her. She didn't care about any of these things as much as she cared about a little boy who was hungry and scared and keeping his embarrassment a secret.

Katie still buys lunch every day at school. And every day, as she heads out the door, her mom hands her a delicious homemade lunch.

David Diamond

Nonno Beppe's Gift

No act of kindness, no matter how small, is ever wasted.

Aesop

There I was, seven years old and back in Italy, the land of my birth. Uprooted from my life in America, I was bundled off to Europe in a rush by my mother so that she could recover and regroup after a traumatic divorce from my father. Being a war bride in America had been trying. She needed the support of her family and their simple way of life. She was sad and lonely in America. Now I was feeling the same way in Italy. I was living with my grandparents in their three-hundred-year-old farmhouse in a tiny village high in the mountains north of Florence. My mother, needing medical care and rest, was staying in the city.

I was used to an American way of life. Now, suddenly, I was in a place that had changed little since the eighteenth century, living with people I didn't know and struggling to understand a language I had never spoken. I was used to television, riding in cars, bright lights at the flip of a switch and indoor plumbing—none of which existed in this village. Here, plows were pulled by oxen, water came in buckets drawn from a spring, and houses were lighted with kerosene lamps. My grandmother cooked in the open fireplace; our bread was baked in the ancient community stone oven. Clothes were washed in the river, and the toilet was a village outhouse.

I missed my father, my bedroom, and all the people and things I was familiar with. I was homesick, lonely and scared. I cried a lot those first few days. My grandparents and everyone else tried their best to ease the transition, but there was no TV to distract me—no toys, games or books. Children played with nature's ornaments—stones, pebbles, sticks and the like. The people of the village were all subsistence farmers. Days were spent growing, harvesting, storing, preparing and eating food. The old farmhouses were furnished with only the barest necessities. Life was simple, uncomplicated, lived at the most basic level—but for me, it was, in a word, miserable.

One chilly fall day, my grandfather, Nonno Beppe, announced that he was going to walk down the mountain (indeed, he had no other way to go) and into the town of Baragazza, which had modern conveniences like electricity, running water and shops. I was made to understand that the purpose of his trip was to bring back a special gift for me. Perhaps I was starting to adjust to my new life just a little because this stirred my interest, and I felt a tinge of excitement. Although I didn't understand why, things suddenly didn't look quite so bleak and lonely. My seven-year-old mind began to hum with anticipation. What could this special gift be?

It was a long trudge down the mountain on a trail that was little more than a goat path. Because of the great distance and time involved, such trips were infrequent, never taken on the spur of the moment, and always had multiple purposes. But on this day, Nonno Beppe's trip was just for me. Nonno Beppe knew exactly which shop to visit. He had carried fresh vegetables down the mountain. These he traded for not one, but two, gifts, which he carefully placed in the inside pockets of his heavy wool coat, one on either side. Then he prepared for the long trek home.

Walking back up the mountain took more time than going down. Although the air was cold by now, Nonno Beppe was sweating and had to rest often, but he knew my gifts were safe in his inside pockets. It was after dark when he finally reached home, and the whole extended family—aunts, uncles and cousins—had gathered around the fireplace in anticipation of his return. When he burst through the door, he was flushed with excitement. I jumped up and down as he opened his coat, reached into his pockets and pulled out . . . two small, gooey sticks.

For a brief moment we looked at each other in surprise. I thought, *What's special about these messy little sticks?*

He must have thought, *They were ice cream when I put them in my pockets.*

My uncles, who were a bit more familiar with twentieth-century delicacies, burst out laughing. They immediately understood that the ice cream had melted in the warmth of Nonno Beppe's pockets. My grandfather had never sampled ice cream in his whole life. His only thought was for me. He was certain that ice cream would make his little granddaughter, used to American luxuries, feel at home. As we started to grasp what had happened, everyone began laughing hysterically—including me.

I didn't get any ice cream, but somehow, it didn't matter. I couldn't explain it then, but at that moment, something wonderful happened. In all the hilarity, I was transformed. My inner turmoil was replaced by a feeling of peace. I understood that these people loved me more than I'd realized—really loved me and were there for me.

The real gift I got from Nonno Beppe that day was the knowledge that what we do for others is not as important as caring enough to try. The ice cream might have been eaten and forgotten, but because it melted in the loving warmth of my grandfather's coat, I've had Nonno Beppe's greater gift every day of my life.

Susanna Palomares

Tammy's Trauma

It is only with the heart that one can see rightly.
What is essential is invisible to the eye.

Antoine de Saint-Exupéry

Tammy* was a cheerful, determined, resourceful and loving kindergartener. She smiled a lot. When her father picked up Tammy at the kindergarten door, she would jump into her father's arms and wrap her legs around the man like a toddler would. Tammy's love for her father bubbled up and spilled over like the foam of root beer running down the side of the glass.

I spent many special moments hugging Tammy, providing snacks (since she rarely brought one from home) and just plain loving her. Then, one horrible day, her father committed suicide. Tammy was out of school for several days.

I remember entering the floral shop and ordering a fruit basket to be sent to Tammy's house. With tears streaming down my face, I said to the young man behind the

*Names have been changed.

counter, "Please make this a children's fruit basket. Four children under the age of eight have lost their father. Make this basket as joyous as you possibly can, so if their mother cannot attend to them, they can just reach up on the counter and grab something good to eat."

I was tormented about what I should do to prepare for Tammy's return to school. I wanted to make the whole thing go away, just like a bad dream. I decided not to mention anything about it to the class. My intuition told me that I would have to respond to whatever Tammy brought with her into our classroom family. I couldn't possibly prepare the class because I had no idea what had actually happened, and I didn't know what Tammy had been told. I prayed for guidance.

When Tammy returned to school, we sat for our opening meeting as we always did. At first, she didn't mention anything about her father. I prayed. After fifteen minutes, she said, "Mrs. DeLucia, my daddy died."

"I know, Tammy. I'm so sorry."

She continued by clutching both her hands around her little neck and choking out these words: "He took a rope and did this until his face turned red."

The class sat speechless.

I managed to utter, "Who told you this?"

She responded, "My grandma."

Then, from behind Tammy, came the tender and caring arm of Sarah. She rested it gently on Tammy's shoulder. She spoke spontaneously, "It's okay, Tammy. Even though you'll never see him again, he'll always live in your heart."

Goosebumps covered my entire body as I heard myself say, "Tell her again, Sarah." She obediently repeated the words, and across Tammy's face came a smile that I can't even describe.

God had truly answered my prayers. Without any fore-warning, Sarah's genuine and sincere compassion had rescued us all in a moment of need. Nothing I could have said would have had the power and magnificence that came through the arm and wise words of one five-year-old and into the heart of another.

Maureen Murphy DeLucia

Compassion in a Preschool

When I worked as a nanny, I also assisted one day each week in a cooperative preschool where the twin girls in my care were enrolled. They had been to school the year before, and were comfortable enough to run off and play without needing my attention. A few children were newcomers and a bit shy, but most were busy. They pounded and rolled clay, or giggled and talked while trying on hats and shoes in the dress-up corner.

One day, I was busy setting up the easel paints when the peaceful, happy sounds of play were interrupted by loud screams coming from the hall. Through the open doorway, I could see a dark-haired two-year-old sitting on the floor. Tears were streaming down her face. "No!" she yelled, with the force of her whole small body, and threw her shoes away. I didn't hear what the teacher said, but in a short while, she returned to the class, shook her head and sighed, "She won't put her shoes on."

Next, a parent went to the child and brought back the shoes. "Everyone has to wear these at school," she said. Again, the little girl threw them down with an emphatic no and began hitting anyone who came near her. Her screams grew so loud that all the children in the room stopped what they were doing and just stared in disbelief.

The mother who had tried to help came back to the room, shrugged her shoulders and frowned. The child, left alone, was still screaming in the hall. I could see that she was frightened, so I asked the teacher if I could help. She readily agreed. The child, she said, was just two and a half, and though she spoke a bit of English, her speech was a hodgepodge of several languages. Maybe she didn't understand the rule about wearing shoes at school. That, added to the fact that I didn't know the little girl, gave me a moment's pause. I had taught preschool some years before and had helped other children adjust, but only after we had gotten acquainted. This child and I were complete strangers. How could she trust me? I didn't know, but I couldn't leave her so upset and all by herself. So I took a small chair out into the hallway and sat next to her.

"It sounds like you're feeling angry right now and sad, too," I said. I wasn't sure she understood because she kept crying and screaming. I stayed there anyway, just listening. My heart went out to her. Then, in a moment or two, she pointed again and again at the door that led to the outside.

"Did Mommy go out?" I asked.

Right away, she screamed, "Mommy! Mommy! Mommy!" Now, she sounded more scared than angry. Her large brown eyes were filled with fear, and alternately, she began to sob and gulp.

"Are you scared because Mommy went out?" I asked. It dawned on me that maybe no one had told her her mother would come back! How terrifying for a two-and-a-half-year-old! Even if someone had said that her mother would return, she might not have understood or might have been too upset to hear.

"Mommy went out that door, yes," I said, "but she is coming back."

The child stopped sobbing and, for the first time, looked straight at me. Then I remembered a song I had made up once to reassure another fearful child, so I smiled at this little one and sang it.

Mommy goes out, but Mommy comes back,
Mommy comes back, oh back, oh.
Mommy goes out, but Mommy comes back,
Mommy comes back, oh back oh.

She was quiet now, listening, her large, dark eyes still teary, but fixed on mine. I sang it several times, and when I stopped, she reached out. I took her small hand, picked up her shoes and said, "Want to go play now?"

She nodded yes, so we played with a train set in a room across the hall for a few minutes. She was smiling now, even laughing with me, while we moved the trains along the track. It was easy to put on the shoes after that. In fact, she put out each foot to help me. Later, her mother arrived, dressed in a colorful sari, and I noticed that the woman's feet were bare. Now it all made sense.

After that, I continued to bring the twins to school once a week. And each time, the dark-haired little girl called out my name, ran to me with a big smile and grabbed my legs to give me a strong hug. I always knelt down and hugged back. She also insisted on saying good-bye to me daily. Although I had spent no more than twenty minutes with her when she was so upset, the empathy I had offered had made a lasting impression. I felt surprised by this, deeply touched and grateful.

It warms my heart still, remembering that child—her rage and tears, as well as her hugs and smiles. And I feel thankful for each of my teachers who taught me about compassion: how to listen without judgment and offer empathic reflection. How grateful I am that I could pass it on.

Patty Zeitlin

December Snow

It was three days before Christmas, and I found myself riding in an old Chevy truck filled with rusting animal traps. We traveled down the two-lane country highway on that gray, frigid day, mostly in silence. I was too lost in my own pain and grief to take much notice of nature's gifts of winter.

My life was in complete turmoil. Just prior to that fateful holiday season, I thought I literally lived a storybook marriage with a husband who truly loved me. I was too blind to understand why, in the past few months, Jack* had become cruel and unreasonable. It was only after he left me in September that I finally had to accept what I didn't want to believe: Jack had returned to a former love, a woman he had never really left.

I turned to my family for love and support, which they provided in abundance. However, the holidays were too much for me to bear. Christmas not only represents a time of love and togetherness, but Christmas Eve was my wedding anniversary. While others were singing carols and making merry, I would go behind closed doors to

Names have been changed.

break down in tears. Although I found myself in that stage between grief and anger, I still could not bring myself to rail against the man I once believed was the love of my life.

My childhood friend Kathy lived in the house next door, and she had introduced me to Billy, a man several years our senior. Most of his education came not from books, but from life experiences. His red hair and beard had long since turned white, and he looked remarkably like Santa Claus. Unlike jolly Santa, Billy was very quiet, although he would watch you intently with piercing blue eyes. Silent Billy, a Vietnam veteran, was still haunted by memories. Before Kathy left to visit family for the holidays, she instructed Billy to "watch over Angie" while she was gone. Totally unaware of this request, I was surprised that winter afternoon to find Billy at the door.

"Darlin', you and me are going for a ride," he said with a strong Texas drawl.

Too startled to reply, I grabbed my coat and jumped into the old truck, wondering what life had planned for me next.

Billy turned off the main highway and onto a long country road that eventually took us to a small, heavily wooded park. In the summer, this little park was filled with visitors. Needless to say, now Billy and I silently sat in the parking lot alone, with only the sound of the cold wind blowing around the faded, old truck.

Finally, Billy turned and looked at me. "Darlin'," he began gruffly, "I have been watching you these past few days, and I recognize that you have been going through a war of your own. Years ago, when I returned from Vietnam, I was in bad shape, just like you are today. I couldn't do anything to help myself because I couldn't talk about the hell I'd just gone through. A very good friend recognized my deep pain, and he helped me through it. I want to pass that gift on to you."

Billy jumped out of the truck, walked around and opened my door. I followed him into the woods, too numb to be curious. Suddenly, Billy stopped, turned around to me and pointed to a large oak tree in front of us. "I'm gonna stand over there, and you are gonna talk to me. But when I go over to that tree, I'm not Billy anymore. I'm Jack, and you have permission to say anything to me that your heart desires. You can do this 'cause I am not gonna say a word back to you. I just want you to tell Jack how you feel. You will be perfectly safe here."

Without another word, Billy walked up to the tree, turned around and faced me.

My eyes welled with tears. I just couldn't do this. But Billy stood there, not making one move, not making one sound. Finally, I turned, closed my eyes and began talking to Jack. My words were soft, pleading for reason and understanding. After about ten minutes, I shook my head. Billy nodded, and I followed him back to the truck. Neither of us mentioned what had just taken place in the cold, lonely woods.

The next afternoon, Billy showed up again at my door. Again, we took the trip back to the oak. And again, I closed my eyes and started my pleas of reason. After a few minutes, the pleas became mixed with occasional words of frustration and anger. When I was spent, Billy took me back home. We did not speak of our secret.

The third day was very difficult, for it was the dreaded wedding anniversary. I was actually relieved to see Billy at my door that afternoon. I found myself walking ahead of Billy to our special spot in the woods.

Billy silently took his place in front of the tree. This time I stood in front of "Jack," looking him right in the eye. "How dare you treat me the way you did, when I loved you so much." I took a deep breath. "I was there for you all those times when you said the world was against you. You knew I would do anything for you, and you threw me away like garbage."

By then I was feeling very angry. My voice, filled with pent-up emotion, became forceful and loud. I suddenly lost that desire to tiptoe around the situation. Every word I screamed carried away some of the incredible pain I had harbored for so long.

After several moments of release, I dropped to the ground. Totally exhausted, I sobbed with a sense of rebirth. Billy walked away from the tree, dropped to his knees and held me. With tears running down his own rugged face, the big Vietnam vet said in his soft drawl, "Darlin', for two days, I stood here and listened to you plead your case, and that told me how lost you had become. I also knew that today would be the day that you would start to reclaim yourself. Now that you and I both know what a good and caring person you are, maybe you can start to see what Jack allowed himself to lose. You deserve to restart your life away from someone who will-fully caused a beautiful young woman such hurt and pain. I knew you could do it."

And with those words, the wind died and large snowflakes began to fall. I could actually feel my spirit being cleansed and renewed.

Billy eventually moved back to his beloved Texas. A few years later, I met and married a man whom I knew would truly love and cherish me for the rest of our lives. Once again, the holidays are a time of peace and happiness. And every Christmas Eve, instead of memories of sad-ness, I smile and remember my friend holding me in the soft December snow.

Angie Rubel

Reaching for Peace

*Can I see another's woe, and not be in sorrow,
too? Can I see another's grief, and not seek for
kind relief?*

William Blake
Songs of Innocence

Paul was dead. My delightful twenty-one-year-old son was murdered in a carjacking attempt, and my world collapsed. The bullet that ripped through his heart shattered mine, destroying my peaceful world forever.

Just as it seemed things would be easier for us, his life was taken senselessly, and now, mine had no meaning. I raised Paul as a single parent, and we were so very protective of each other. He was a senior in college, planning to marry a wonderful young woman, and my life would be moving into another dimension. I would no longer need to send a check each month to help with his college expenses. We chatted the evening before he was murdered about what I would do with all the money I wouldn't be spending after his graduation.

There are no words to describe the rage I felt toward the seventeen-year-old who asked Paul for a ride, then killed him in cold blood. So many times in my life I had wanted to be taller than my five feet, two inches, for it seems that power comes with height. I sat in the Austin courtroom looking at a young man, over six feet tall. If looks could kill, he would have met his doom, for nothing came from me but utter hatred.

Charles White received a forty-year prison sentence, and again I was enraged! Paul was dead, and a worthless, hardened criminal was allowed to live. My taxes would feed him, pay for his guards and furnish him with clothes to wear and food to eat. *Paul is dead.* That was all I could think of. It gave me no peace to know that the murderer would serve thirteen years of "flat time" for Paul's murder. Paul would never be alive again, not in thirteen, twenty-three or thirty-three years!

Every three months I sent a scathing letter to the Board of Pardons and Paroles, pouring out my great anguish and pain from the depths of my soul. How I wanted to know that someone would read those words and know the continuous, overwhelming pain that results from the murder of a loved one. Two times a year, on February 18 (the date Paul was murdered) and again each August, I made a personal trip to Austin to speak with a staff member and get an update on Charles's actions in prison. I was elated when he got in trouble and "lost good time." That proved that he was a really bad guy.

Years passed, thirteen to be exact, and I had no peace. I continued my letters and personal visits of protest and lived to hate the murderer of my precious Paul. One day, as I opened the mail at my office, I received a letter from the parole board informing me that my son's killer was being considered for parole. I became physically ill and had to leave the office. My staff did not know what was wrong, but they knew something drastic had happened. How could they even think of allowing him to go free? Paul was still dead, and I felt so overwhelmed with helplessness. Through the years, I was told, "He won't be released," but after reading the letter I knew that I had to take immediate action: I would go talk with my son's murderer.

The state of Texas has a program that allows victims to meet with perpetrators, and I made the dreaded call and received confirmation that I could participate in the program. Even greater anger consumed me, for it was my responsibility to pay for my trips to Austin to work through the program. Charles, on the other hand, languished in prison, and my taxes paid for the mediator to help prepare him to meet with me.

The meeting was scheduled for June 9, 1998. Again, I paid for a trip to Austin, but was taken to the prison site in a state vehicle. Though I had been in numerous prisons as a speaker for the victim impact programs, it felt different when I went inside that prison. *HE IS HERE! This is HIS prison!* My heart beat frantically, and I did not know if I could go through with the meeting.

In preparation for the time we would spend together, I had meticulously decided what I should have with me for this momentous meeting; I was ready! I sincerely hoped to shatter any shred of peace he felt. When I left, he would know that he had destroyed my world with a single bullet.

To say that the meeting was awkward is putting it lightly. Everyone in the room, including the guards, was deathly quiet, and frequently my soft voice was barely audible. I had not slept at all the night before; I paced the floor in the tiny hotel room, alone with my thoughts and questions. I had been instructed to write out the questions that I wanted to ask Paul's murderer and have them in order so that the meeting could progress in an organized manner. Of the seventy-seven questions I had written down, the one I asked first was simple: *WHY?*

The young man, who did not look much different from when I last saw him thirteen years earlier, had no answer for me other than to shake his head and say, "It was just a stupid thing to do. Stupid, just stupid, stupid, stupid . . ."

I felt no pity for him; he senselessly murdered my son. I wanted him to squirm and feel my pain. Tears streamed down my face as I spoke of Paul, and I said to him, "If you knew how much I loved him, you would not have killed him." He sat across the table from me, showing no emotion.

For this meeting, I had Paul's photos enlarged to fourteen by eighteen inches. I wanted him to know Paul as a real person, not as "him, the dude, the kid," as he referred to Paul in his writings to the mediator. He said he didn't even remember what Paul looked like, and I wanted to scream, "How can you not remember him? You killed him!"

I became pensive and, as if to myself, I began to talk of how Paul would call to see if my car was okay. If I thought it sounded funny, he would tell me that he was coming home over the weekend to take care of it for me. I spoke of how he would ask about our yard, telling me that he'd come home because I was "too little to mow the lawn."

Something touched Charles at that point. I could not believe the tears that streamed down the face of the man across the table from me. What was going on? Charles put his head in his hands and sobbed. Without thinking, I pulled a tissue from the box on the table, handed it to him and said, "Here." Those tears of shame and remorse touched me deeply. The tone of the meeting changed; suddenly, the mother and the murderer began to connect. I listened to how Charles was raised in extreme poverty, one of several children, living mostly in the streets. Paul, by contrast, was an only child and knew only love and all the security I could provide.

For the very first time, I really looked into the eyes of my son's murderer and was amazed that I felt no hate. I encouraged him to stop being violent in prison. I asked that he attend classes and get a GED. He looked at me in disbelief, for he seemed to realize that my rage was gone. The meeting ended with him agreeing to attend classes and stop his violence. I thanked him for meeting with me, folded my hands and closed my eyes. I felt a great need to put my hand across the table and take his, but I dared not do that. He had murdered my son. If I did that, I would be reaching out to the hand that held the pistol that killed Paul. Again, I felt that I should reach out to the killer across from me. No, I just couldn't do it.

Then, almost against my will, my hand reached across the table to grasp the hand of my son's killer. A great cry of anguish was released from the depths of my soul as I felt him take my hand. He covered my hand with both of his, and his tears of remorse washed over them. The same hand that, thirteen years earlier, had held a pistol and pulled the trigger, releasing the shot that shattered my peace, now clung to mine as if I were his lifeline. Though Charles never said, "I am sorry, please forgive me," and I never said the words, "I forgive you," we came to our place of peace. Our communication continues to this day.

Thomas Ann Hines

A Safe Place

There is no trust more sacred than the one the world holds with children. There is no duty more important than ensuring that their rights are respected, that their welfare is protected, that their lives are free from fear and want, and that they grow up in peace.

Kofi Annan

Can you imagine a little boy attending school for the very first time in his life and being so afraid that he could not speak?

Can you imagine the frustration of the kindergarten teacher who knew only that the child came from a violent home, but not whether he was capable of speaking? To make matters worse, the child's mother refused to come in to discuss her little boy.

Many years ago, as a Title I teacher, I had the privilege of working with a class of no more than six children at a time. These were children with social/emotional problems that made it almost impossible to integrate them into the regular classroom. All of them cried out for help in one way or another, but that year, my biggest challenge was a boy who cried out in silence. From the day he entered our class until the third month of the school year, he never uttered a word. To add to the problem, the school had absolutely no information other than that he lived with his mother and had been removed from the home a number of times because of suspected abuse. As I said, this happened years ago when it was much harder to remove a child from a bad home situation—in fact, almost impossible unless there were signs that the child's life was in danger.

The day that James* was brought into my kindergarten class, the school social worker asked if I would work with him and discover whether he could talk. So far, they had not heard him say a word or even make a sound. My heart immediately went out to this seemingly lost little soul, and I promised to see what I could do. Knowing only that his home life was traumatic, my strategy was to create a place of safety, solace, peace and love for James—a place without any demands. And I decided to let him discover at his own pace that this was a safe haven.

All my other children vented their problems and daily frustrations by acting out. I spent much of my time trying to help them find acceptable ways to interact with each other—and me. James was just the opposite. Because of his fears, he spent most of his time hiding under a card table that had three heavy-duty brown-paper walls around it. Occasionally, he would venture out to look at the many things happening in the room . . . always avoiding me. Over the next few months, I patiently continued to greet him warmly each day, letting him choose from moment to moment what he would or wouldn't do. By the end of the third month, I was beginning to question

*Name has been changed.

my strategy of loving and accepting him, of making a safe place for him that was free of demands. Would it eventually pay off? But even with these moments of doubt, I continued to hold in my mind the vision of him coming to me to be held—and, of course, speaking his first words.

Then one day, as I was quietly doing my work, James ventured out from under his safe haven and lay down on a small rug. He curled up and started sucking his thumb. I slowly made my way over to where he lay. Mirroring his posture, I lay down on the rug beside him and slowly stuck my thumb in my mouth. When he looked over and saw what I was doing, he jumped up, socked me full in the face with his tightly clenched little fist and yelled, "Take your G-d d--n thumb out of your mouth!"

As I recovered from the surprise of the blow, I was suddenly overcome with the realization of the emotional prison in which this child was living. He must have lived in terror day after day, the threat of violence ever looming over his head. And when he innocently sought comfort by withdrawing and sucking his thumb, he was cursed and beaten—just as he cursed and struck out at me. I sat up, and he ran back under the table. But I knew I had finally broken through, and tears came to my eyes.

As the weeks went by, James began speaking gibberish from under the table, venturing out from time to time only to scamper back to safety if anyone moved toward him. Still, I never gave up my vision of James coming to me to be held and to reemerge from his world of silence. More weeks passed; then one day, I looked up to see James creeping out from his safe place and slowly moving toward me. I continued what I was doing, but watched him from the corner of my eye, not wanting to look directly at him and scare him away.

James moved closer and closer until he was right beside me. I turned very slowly toward him, and for the first time, his eyes were free of fear. As he continued to look into my face, he pointed to his safe place under the table and said, "I don't have to hide in there anymore."

After that, James came out more and more. At first, only when we were alone as a class, but eventually, he ventured out even when we had a visitor. As the year wore on and James came to trust that the classroom truly was a safe place, he continued to make slow, steady progress.

Still, when the last day of school arrived, James and I were far from my vision of him coming to me to be held. Late in the day, as I sat in my chair pondering this and watching the children, I noticed James beginning to move slowly toward me. My heart beat faster as he finally drew near enough and held his arms out for me to pick him up and settle him into my lap. He snuggled into my arms, looking up at me with eyes full of childhood innocence, and clearly spoke these words: "You know what? You're special. I'm special, too."

Tears streamed from my eyes, and my heart rejoiced with the pure pleasure of finally connecting with James.

On this very last day that I was ever to see James, he had come to me and manifested the miracle I had hoped for.

Lynea Corson-Hadley

Connected in Spirit

Resolve to be tender with the young, compassionate with the aged, sympathetic with the striving, and tolerant with the weak and the wrong. Sometime in your life you will have been all of these.

Dr. Robert H. Goddard

When my mother was dying of cancer, my family and I went for our daily visit to see her at the hospital. As we were walking down the hallway to her room, we heard an excruciating cry coming from one of the other rooms. It turned out to be an older woman who was sitting up in her bed, rocking back and forth, crying out, "Oh, I'm in so much pain. Please, someone help me. I just can't take the pain anymore." We briefly peeked into her room in amazement, only to find that there were no nurses or anyone else responding to this white-haired lady's call for help. My wife and six-year-old son continued walking toward my mother's room, but I just stood there in the doorway, holding my one-year-old baby girl.

The lady couldn't see us because she was paying

attention only to her pain. She shut her eyes tight and continued to rock back and forth, screaming in agony.

Then it happened. I heard a voice inside me say, *Take the child and place her on the bed in front of the lady.* I slowly walked into the room, fearful that I shouldn't even be in there. What if she had some sickness that could have been given to my child or to me? What if she opened her eyes and was so startled that she had a heart attack? All these thoughts raced through my mind as I ventured closer and closer. Still, no hospital staff came into the room.

Without the lady noticing, I set my baby girl down in front of her and said, "There is a beautiful baby girl in front of you."

The screaming lady opened her eyes and seemed to suddenly lose all sense of pain. Her face lit up as if she were a little girl and had just received the Christmas surprise of her life. Her painful expression was replaced with one of joy, and I knew I had witnessed a miracle. She said over and over in an almost trembling voice, "Oh, what a beautiful baby." And the tears and pain just melted away.

Richard Gutherie

The Endless Time-Out

You will find as you look back upon your life that the moments when you have truly lived are the moments when you have done things in the spirit of love.

Henry Drummond

One Saturday morning, my normally bright and happy sixteen-month-old daughter Kate awoke in a foul mood. All morning, nothing suited her—breakfast was all wrong, her toys were all wrong, and her mother was most certainly all wrong. As a result, she sought out every possible way to demonstrate her frustration. She cried; she whined. She did every single thing she knew she was not allowed to do—and she did each one repeatedly. Pulling her away from the television set for the fifth time, I decided to remove her from temptation by taking her upstairs to change the shirt she'd smeared with jelly while rejecting her breakfast. Sitting on the changing table as I struggled to remove her shirt (she certainly wasn't going to cooperate!), she began yanking hard on my dangling earrings. When I scolded her, she hit me.

My patience completely expended, I put her into her crib for a time-out. She sobbed during the forty-five or so seconds that I was out of the room. When I returned, I said to her sternly, "No hitting!" As soon as I picked her up, she hit me again. So I put her in time-out again.

We went through the process several times: I'd return to the room, admonish her sternly not to hit, then pick her up—only to have her hit me again each time. During the final time-out, I realized that there was no possible way to change her behavior until I changed mine. I returned to her room, looked down at her and said in my kindest tone, "Kate, I love you. I am sorry that you are having a hard morning, but I still love you very, very much. You are a wonderful baby."

I didn't know if my words would have any effect, but as I lifted her from the crib, she immediately reached up—and hugged me.

LeDayne McLeese Polaski

3

DEFINING MOMENTS

What is a defining moment?

It is the moment in time when the caterpillar becomes a butterfly or a baby is born. We experience defining moments daily. Some may seem catastrophic, while others are elating. Each moment is one that defines us.

I am seeking the gold in each defining moment and learning the lessons that will aid me in creating a better life and better world for myself and others.

Rice for Peace

We don't have to engage in grand, heroic actions to participate in the process of change. Small acts, when multiplied by millions of people, can transform the world.

Howard Zinn

In the mid-1950s, the pacifist Fellowship of Reconciliation, learning of famine in the Chinese mainland, launched a "Feed Thine Enemy" campaign. Members and friends mailed thousands of little bags of rice to the White House with a tag quoting Scripture: "If thine enemy hunger, feed him."

As far as anyone knew, for more than ten years, the campaign was an abject failure. The president did not acknowledge receipt of the bags publicly. Certainly, no rice was ever sent to China.

What nonviolent activists learned a decade later was that the campaign played a significant, perhaps even determining, role in preventing nuclear war.

Twice during that campaign, President Eisenhower met with the Joint Chiefs of Staff to consider U.S. options in the conflict with China, which centered on two islands, Quemoy and Matsu. On both occasions, the joint chiefs recommended the use of nuclear weapons.

Each time, President Eisenhower turned to his aide and asked how many little bags of rice had come in. When told they numbered in the tens of thousands, Eisenhower told the generals that, as long as so many Americans were expressing active interest in having the U.S. feed the Chinese, he certainly wasn't going to consider using nuclear weapons against them.

David H. Albert
Reprinted from "From People Power Applying
Nonviolence Theory"

"Since they installed my new 'Peacemaker'
I've had no heart for war."

My Homeless Man

I hung up the telephone, furious with my friend Neal. He had resigned from a well-paying job in the corporate world because it was not consistent with the spiritual journey to which he was committed. But now, Neal was virtually indigent. He had not been able to pay this month's rent on his modest apartment, and his car was about to be towed out of his driveway. And so, on the telephone, I said some pretty harsh things: How *dare* he go through every penny, believing that faith and meditation will manifest a superior job? How *dare* he make himself so vulnerable? "I just hope you don't find yourself on the street," I said. "This is how people find themselves on the street, you know. Homeless and on the street."

That was on Sunday.

On Monday morning, I found myself on Bay Area Rapid Transit, a passenger on the train that would take me into San Francisco. I was going to spend the day with Sue, to whom I was visiting teacher in a church capacity, and who was in the hospital there for tests. But I was not thinking about Sue as I watched the landscape of the East Bay go by outside the train window. I was still thinking about Neal, and still angry. How *dare* he get this close to the abyss?

Embarcadero, the train station I was told to get out at, soon came into view. I stepped off the train. Now which exit to get to the right bus stop? I looked around for someone to ask. No attendant evident. No one nearby at all except a ragged, bearded man sitting on a cardboard mat, a white patch over his right eye and a red plastic cup in his hand. I walked in his direction.

"Hello," he said, smiling.

"Hello." I fished out a dollar bill and put it in his plastic cup. I had a habit of giving a dollar to the first homeless person I met in the city and sending a prayer for the rest.

"Why, thank you."

"Can you tell me which exit to take to get to the N. Judah bus?"

"Right over there. But where are you headed?"

"Parnassas Street."

"Oh, you're going to the hospital. The N. Judah will drop you two blocks away. Then take the Parnassas Number Six. It'll drop you right in front of the hospital. In fact, I'm going there myself right now. Sometimes I watch TV at the hospital for a bit." He grabbed his cane, folded up his cardboard mat and hid it in a little crevice under the stairs. Before I knew it, we had climbed the stairs and were walking together to the bus stop. What in the world was I doing? I was walking with a street person just as if . . . as if what? As if he was a real human being, as if he was worthy to walk with me, as if he was worthy of doing me a favor. In fact, there he was holding out his hand to me. "I'm Rene," he said.

I shook his hand. "Hi. I'm Carol Lynn. Thanks for your help."

"Glad to."

A neon light began to flash inside my mind. *Wake up! Message from the universe coming through!*

"How are things going for you, Rene?" I asked.

"Pretty good, pretty good. Lost this eye when I was hit by a truck a year or so ago. Couldn't work. Had to sell my house. One thing led to another, and here I am. I was head of a drug-rehabilitation program here in the city. Have a master's in clinical psychology from the University of Minnesota. Everybody is just one step away from where I am now, you know. You can lose everything. Nothing belongs to you. It's just things. The Man Upstairs gives you the opportunity to accumulate things, but they're not yours. They come and they go."

My neon light was flashing very brightly now. Only yesterday I was yelling at Neal for losing everything, and now. . . .

"Yep," Rene continued, "we never know what's going to happen to any of us tomorrow. Now is all we've got. This minute. I just take what comes, and I keep a smile on my face."

"Rene, tell me something," I said, as we boarded the bus. "You have nothing, but you're much happier than most of the people I'm seeing here."

"Happy? Oh, yeah, I'm happy! All that's important is what happens in your heart."

Rene was sitting to my left. An Asian woman behind me was trying to communicate something to me. "Two quarters. Can you give me two quarters for the bus?"

"Sure," I said, opening my day planner to the thin pouch where I keep my money.

Instantly, Rene dumped into his lap the contents of his red plastic cup, a handful of coins and the one-dollar bill I had given him. "Here, I've got it," he said.

Fishing two quarters from his little cache, he reached across me to give them to the woman. "Please. I do this all the time."

Rene never stopped talking. I kept my day planner open and began taking notes as if I had stumbled onto a privileged interview with the Dalai Lama.

"It's like we each have a different thing to do in this world, a different point of view, and nobody can judge anybody else. The most beautiful piece in all of scripture is First Corinthians, verse thirteen: 'Though I speak with the tongues of men and angels, and have not charity, I am become as sounding brass, or a tinkling cymbal.'"

I had heard these words dozens of times recited from behind a pulpit, but never as meaningfully as they were recited by my homeless man with shining eyes on the bus that day in San Francisco.

"'And though I bestow all my goods to feed the poor, and though I give my body to be burned, and have not charity, it profiteth me nothing. . . . Charity suffereth long and is kind; charity envieth not; charity vaunteth not itself, is not puffed up. . . . Charity never faileth. . . . And now abideth faith, hope, charity, these three; but the greatest of these is charity.'"

When the bus began to climb the hill, Rene pointed out the window, laughing. "See? I told you we'll know Parnassas when we get there. Like we'll know heaven when we get there. Up! Up! We need to keep looking up. Up is where all good things are!"

At the Parnassas bus stop, Rene and I got off together. As if we were old friends, this ragged, dirty, generous, happy man of the street held out his arms to me, and I embraced him.

"Good-bye, Rene. See you in heaven."

He grinned. "Up, up where all good things are!"

Neal did lose his car and his apartment, and he is slowly reestablishing himself in the material world. His spiritual journey continues with increasing clarity and peace. Mine does, too. And, I hope, with charity.

Carol Lynn Pearson

The Bath-Time Battle

It's the things you do that say all there is to be said of you.

David Cowan

Chaos, cranky kids and challenges are all a part of a nurse's day in pediatrics. As a student, I learned how to deal with all three. My mentor, Maude Greene, R.N., taught me the importance of a peaceful spirit.

Our biggest problem was our biggest patient. John's body was frail and emaciated, but he was twelve years old. We only had cribs for beds. He was squeezed into the largest one. John was born severely brain damaged and remained an infant trapped inside a growing body. We could not send him to the adult unit; part of him was just a baby.

The nurses always assigned the "challenging" patients to us students. John was definitely a challenge. He hated getting a bath, and he made bath time wartime. We dreaded finding John's name on the duty roster. I prayed he would be discharged before my turn came around. That prayer went unanswered. At bath time, I entered his cubicle with resentment and resolve. Although his eyes did not focus on anything in particular, they seemed to glare at me. His face was constantly contorting. He snarled, snorted and drooled like a mad dog, as he bared misshapen teeth. I moved forward, faking an air of authority, and started to bathe him. He let me wash his face without a fight. But when I tried to scrub away the crusted oatmeal and sour milk smell from his neck, the battle began. He tossed his head from side to side, trying to bury his face in his ratty-looking, smelly old blanket. When I began to wash his chest, he rolled from side to side and arched his back. As I attempted to bathe his arms and legs, he would pull away whatever part I was trying to clean. It was like trying to wash a snake! In frustration, I threw my body across his chest and pinned him down. I finished the rest of his bath as quickly as possible. That drove him into an absolutely frustrated frenzy, and he tried to kick me. He missed me, but sent the metal wash-basin clanging to the floor.

Mrs. Greene came running in to find the two of us whining and drenched. She bellowed, "Joyce, why are you making this so difficult?"

My spirit sagged, and so did my once proudly crisp uniform. "Me?! He won't let me bathe him, and I have four other kids to do before my next class!" I protested.

"He is acting that way because you are not treating him right. Watch how his mother handles him and learn a thing or two, young lady," she scolded, then she took over.

She had never raised her voice to me before. To keep from bursting into tears, I bit my trembling lower lip until I tasted blood. I bathed the other four kids in no time. They knew a bath was just a bath, not a war!

At visiting hours, I dutifully watched the "demon child" and his mother interact. He made a soft cooing sound as she put her arms around him. She was pregnant and could no longer hold him on her lap. Instead, she cradled him in her arms and rocked him back and forth on the bed as she sang to him. She told me that he seemed to miss being held. His whole demeanor changed when she was there. She raked her long fingernails through his lackluster hair. His face softened, and even his breathing was softer, not his usual snorts, grunts and groans. He seemed peaceful.

John's next bath time was revolutionized. I entered the cubicle, whistling. He raised his head and cocked it to the side, like a curious pup. He let me wash his face without a struggle, but when I got to his neck, he started to fight. Instead of retaliating, I made several "raspberry" sounds to indicate my opinion of neck scrubbing. He snorted, but this time it seemed as if he was attempting a laugh. He had difficulty swallowing, so food constantly trickled into the creases of his neck. I gently wrapped a warm soapy towel around his neck and soaked off the crusted food, determined to rid him of that awful smell. Later, I rubbed away the remnants with a thick, dry towel. He responded to my slow, soothing tones—my attempt to imitate his mother's voice. I was very careful not to move abruptly or drip excess water on him because he hated that. When his bath was done, I gave him a long backrub with warmed baby lotion. His spastic muscles relaxed at my fingertips. I ran my fingers through his straggly brown hair repeatedly, the way his mother had. Next, I eased into the rocking chair with him on my lap. We rocked until he fell fast asleep.

We never had another bath-time battle.

Joyce Seabolt

Hagar the Horrible. Reprinted by permission of King Features Syndicate.

Redemption

*O*ur prophet, our messenger, brought us the teaching that all human beings were formed into nations and tribes "so that we may know one another, not to conquer, subjugate, revile or slaughter, but to reach out toward others with intelligence and understanding."

—Azim Khamisa, quoting The Qur'an

"Bust 'im, Bone!" The gang leader's command rang through the night, followed by the sound of shattering glass. A bullet from a nine-millimeter handgun burst through the car window and into the heart of twenty-year-old college student Tariq Khamisa. The footsteps of the four teenagers who had tried to rob him pounded the pavement, their fleeing shadows melting into the darkness.

Across town, Ples Felix watched the TV news bulletin with a heavy heart. His grandson and ward, fourteen-year-old Tony (nicknamed "Bone" by his buddies) had run away from home that afternoon, rebelling against the disciplines of schoolwork and household chores. How much danger might Tony be in tonight? Ples offered up a silent prayer for the soul of the murdered young man and for his family.

For me, Tariq's father, the tragedy began with a note from the police tucked into my front door: "We are trying to reach Tariq Khamisa's family," it read. "Please call." The news of Tariq's murder plunged me into an ocean of grief. The loving support of friends, family and my faith community helped, but the ache of loss could not be assuaged.

Ples Felix's premonition that dark night was the beginning of a nightmare of his own, for it was Tony's hand that had fired the gun.

In the Ismaili Muslim tradition to which I belong, prayers for the dead are said at the funeral and at specified intervals afterward. My spiritual teacher told me, "After forty days, the soul of the dead person moves to a new level of consciousness. Family and loved ones who grieve too much past this time impede the soul's journey. Your son has completed his assignment here. You are not grieving for him—he is beyond this world. You are now just feeling sorry for yourself. Instead, do something good in his name. It will be good for you, good for others and good for Tariq's soul."

His wisdom penetrated my despair and planted a seed of hope. I could not bring Tariq back, but I could do something in his name to stop the violence that had taken his life. I found my thoughts returning to the family of the boy who had killed my son: Their grief must be no less than mine because both of us lost a son that night. Tony would become the youngest person in the history of California to be charged with first-degree murder and tried as an adult. It was the only trouble Tony had ever been in, but he had fallen prey to the appeal of the local tough guys, and in a momentary act of mindless violence, destroyed his own life along with Tariq's. I asked the district attorney to arrange a meeting with the family of my son's killer.

Ples's response to my request to meet was immediate and heartfelt: he said it was an answer to his prayers. From that first meeting, the soul connection between us formed a bond that made us brothers. I told him of my plan to create a foundation in Tariq's name that would help young people reject violence, to choose life instead of death. Together, we would honor Tariq and redeem Tony's one terrible life-destroying act.

The Tariq Khamisa Foundation presented the first of its award-winning programs the following July in the elementary school where Tony had been a student. The response from students and teachers since then has been awe-inspiring. Young people suffer more fear, pain and loss than most adults can imagine. They are hungry for leadership and support in dealing with the miasma of violence that surrounds them. The spiritual spark that brought Ples and me together continues to touch lives all around us. Ples and I look forward to the day that Tony's prison sentence ends, and he comes to work with us at the Tariq Khamisa Foundation. He will be ready to deliver a powerful message to some fourteen-year-old boy who needs to hear it.

Azim Khamisa

The Copper Bracelet

We know that a peaceful world cannot long exist, one-third rich and two-thirds poor.

President Jimmy Carter

The rain poured off the windscreen in a tepid sheet, joining the pools already forming in the reddish ruts of this dusty road. Ethiopia carries few cars on her ancient back once the cities have receded into steaming, sooty blots in the rearview mirror. The rains pour, deep and long, bathing the grateful leaves and petals and faces of children. These children race to the edge of the road at the approaching sound of our Land Rover. A few are clad only with a string around their throat, indicating that they have been baptized. Others wear shorts or shirts handed out of the windows of other Land Rovers by those who have already passed this way. All wave imploring arms out to us in hopes of a handout. Was their condition known as poverty before these Land Rover processions began? All those on this road, both inside and outside our vehicle, feel the pain of their condition compared with ours.

We slow temporarily to a halt, and the real assault of the heart becomes almost unbearable to me as hands and arms reach inside our windows, begging for something to eat or to wear. Shame and pain and impotence drown us all, leaving us feeling helpless in their wake. There is one woman outside my window, a baby hanging from her back, its thin arms wrapped monkey-like around her neck. Suddenly, we really see each other, and her blue eyes lock with my brown ones. The intimacy of personality somehow recognizes and understands instantly our kindred spirits. It slices through this agony, clearing a sacred space wherein only we two exist, nothing but our sudden sisterhood.

I remove my purple scarf, hold it briefly to my heart to imbue my love and respect, then offer it to her. For a moment, our space disappears as her eyes darken with another intent as she snatches at such bounty. I watch as she pauses in this rush-away and slowly turns back to me, self-possession regained. She steps once more to the window, and eyes again turned to mine, she carefully removes her one ornament—a bent bit of copper telephone wire—from her wrist. With great dignity, she passes it through the window and places it carefully into my hand. At this moment, the Land Rover lurches forward again, and as we drive off, I turn backward in my seat to catch and hold this last shared and intense glance with my new sister.

It is now four years since my experience in Ethiopia with Cross Cultural Journeys, and I am sitting in the tension of a major life change. There are many treasures that I shall leave behind since I now must travel light, but the copper bracelet and my bond with this woman from another continent and another life will always go with me.

Belle Star

My Enemy Has Become My Friend

*The time for peace has come, for healing at
last.*
*Let former foes find common ground, put time-
worn hatred past!*
So many precious lives, forever stilled—
*Now let all hearts and minds with harmony be
now and always filled!*
We were meant to live in peace.

Linda K. Williams, in the song
"The Time for Peace has Come"

It was a hot and honest session in that meeting of
Palestinian and Israeli women in Oslo, Norway. The
Palestinian women said that they supported the Israelis'
right to an independent state; the Israeli women said that
they supported the Palestinians' right to resources, political integrity and freedom to live in the land. It was a significant political moment.

Nevertheless, what happened after the conference ad-
journed may, in the end, prove to be even more significant.

On the last night of the assembly, one of these women

went to the other and asked to continue the discussion about what had been lost and what must be gained if the two peoples are ever to live together well. They went out for coffee together. I don't know what was said. I only know that the conversation went on until after midnight.

When it came time to leave, the Israeli woman—old enough to be the Palestinian's mother—decided she would walk the young woman to her hotel. But then the young Palestinian realized how far the older woman would have to walk alone back to her own place of residence and insisted that she walk her halfway back again.

"I've had a wonderful night," the Israeli woman said as they parted. "This time with you was itself worth the conference."

The young Palestinian woman went silent for a moment. "I'm glad for you," she said, "but I'm confused."

The Israeli woman winced inside. "Why? What's wrong?" she asked.

"Oh, nothing is wrong," the younger woman said. "I'm just confused. I don't know what to do now that my enemy has become my friend."

The next day, in the Tel Aviv airport, the Israeli women whisked through customs and baggage claim. The Palestinian women did not. When the Israeli women realized that all the Palestinians had been detained, they turned around, went back and refused to leave the customs hall themselves until all the Palestinians were released.

That, I learned, is what it means to proceed in the "ways of peace." It means having the courage to make human connections with those we fear, with those we hate, with those who think differently than we do. It means refusing to leave the other behind as we go.

Joan Chittister, O.S.B.
Reprinted from National Catholic Reporter *(July 8, 2003)*

A Fire of Peace

All your strength is in your union. All your danger is in discord; therefore be at peace hence forward, and as brothers live together.

Henry Wadsworth Longfellow
The Song of Hiawatha

The celebration was a great occasion. More than twenty thousand people gathered, doubling the size of the legendary city of Timbuktu. The crowd included heads of state, ambassadors and two thousand Tuareg nomads who had come in from the desert on gaily decorated camels. These nomads wore the flowing electric-cobalt robes that earned them the nickname "blue men of the desert." Hundreds of scrubbed and uniformed schoolchildren walked together singing songs and waving flags. Women in headscarves and wrappers of such luminous hue that they brought color to the dull Saharan sun played rhythm instruments and danced and sang traditional songs. Teenage boys raced their camels through the town streets, stirring up heavy clouds of desert dust—and the fierce ire of their elders. Other teenage boys came in tattered army uniforms, having known nothing but fighting since child-hood. They all came to celebrate a special anniversary: It was exactly one year since the *Flamme de la Paix* (the Fire of Peace).

The Fire of Peace happened in this way. Mali, a country in West Africa, is both small (population: about 10 million) and large (land area: about the size of France, Germany and Spain combined). It is also one of the poorest nations in the world. The Tuaregs are an Arabic, nomadic people who live in the northern part of the country. They have seen their way of life slowly disintegrate because of changing economies and nearly fifty years of devastating drought. Fiercely proud and desperately poor, and with their traditions and culture slipping away, they felt essen-tially powerless because their government was controlled by the Bambura and other neighbors to the south. After being heavily armed by neighbors farther north, they became embroiled in a small but vicious civil uprising in the early 1990s that took thousands of lives and created nearly a million refugees. The rest of the world never knew of the conflict because it was lost in the horrors of Somalia and Rwanda.

Alpha Ounmar Konaré, the first democratically elected president of Mali, decided he would do whatever it took to put an end to the violence that plagued his country. In an unusual gesture of humility and openness, the presi-dent asked the United Nations, representatives from sev-eral of his neighboring states, as well as representatives from the "enemy," to come together with the government and help him make the peace. He not only brought together an alphabet soup of U.N. organizations— UNDP, UNHCR, UNPKO, UNDPA, UNIDIR—he also made room in the talks for voices that are rarely heard: women's organizations, youth groups, educators and peace advocates. It was a difficult process to sustain, but with patience, vision and creativity, it began to bear fruit.

After a tentative peace had finally been established in late 1995, the Tuareg rebels began to turn in their weapons, willing to trust the government's promise that in so doing they would be given chances for education and help in starting a livelihood. More than three thousand modern deadly weapons were collected—everything from automatic rifles to small rocket launchers. These weapons were stored in a makeshift armory in Timbuktu.

At this point a new problem arose, a problem no one had anticipated. What should be done with the weapons? The government believed that it should take possession of all weapons of war. The rebels did not want to see the weapons that were so difficult for them to give up going to their former enemy, even if that enemy was also their government. Emotions were raw, and nerves were frayed. The fragile trust that had been painfully established over months of talks was at risk of coming undone because of this difficult issue of what to do with the guns. The weapons, insecurely locked in a mud armory, seemed to have a power of their own to break the delicate peace.

Then a young U.N. officer floated a simple but radical idea: The weapons should be burned. Finally, the government and the rebels could agree on something! It was an idea that everyone hated. The government was desperately poor. Burning more than a million dollars' worth of weapons could almost be interpreted as treason. The rebels, on the other hand, were a traditionally "warrior" people who saw guns as a way of marking the passage from boyhood to manhood. Turning them in was difficult enough; watching them burn was unthinkable.

For nearly a year, the young U.N. officer, in a quiet, humble, persistent manner, negotiated, talked, cajoled, pushed and pulled to reach agreement. On several occasions, it seemed as if it might happen, but then some government official or military officer or rebel leader would subvert the process. Would a banker burn money? Would a professor burn books? Would a farmer burn yoke and plow? How could a soldier possibly agree to burn weapons? At times, it seemed as if violence might break out again. In the end, however, gentle persuasion and persistence carried the day, and everyone came to agree that this fire might be the best thing.

So it happened that, on March 27, 1996, three thousand instruments of war were piled high on a cement platform made for the occasion. They were covered with straw and diesel fuel, and in the ancient, almost mythological city of Timbuktu, a fire was lit that many hope will become a national symbol for the young, struggling, democratic nation of Mali. This fire did not burn saints or libraries. This fire did not burn cities or grain fields. This fire was set not to hurt, but to heal.

There is an image from that fire, captured by a U.N. filmmaker, that has become deeply etched in my heart. It is an image of two soldiers, one black and one white, one government and one rebel, one Bambura and one Tuareg, standing with their arms around each other, gazing almost wistfully into that magnificent flame. In the cool desert night, in the warmth of the burning guns, two young enemies, who had probably known nothing in life other than carrying a rifle, were cleansed of their hatred and freed from a desperate and violent future by a Fire of Peace.

Andrew Murray, D.Min., L.H.D.

Giving the Peace Sign

If you want peace, work for justice.

Pope Paul VI

In 1989, in the Brooklyn neighborhood known as Bensonhurst, an African American teenager named Yusef Hawkins was beaten and murdered by a group of Italian American youths. The incident, which made national headlines for weeks, occurred right in front of an elementary school that had recently become part of the Resolving Conflict Creatively Program (RCCP).

This incident happened because Yusef was in the "wrong neighborhood." He was answering an ad for a used car that had appeared in a Brooklyn paper. The honors student didn't realize that, when he got off the N train at the Avenue U stop, he would find himself in the middle of a very insular and isolated Italian American enclave. Most of its residents have lived there for two or three generations, and many of them—grandparents, parents, children and grandchildren—still live close to their extended families. A group of teenagers saw Yusef Hawkins at the train stop. Their fear and hatred escalated.

They began to beat him with baseball bats and eventually killed him.

I was coordinating the RCCP for the New York City Board of Education at the time. Being the highest-ranking Italian American in the chancellor's cabinet, I was immediately sent to the neighborhood. I convinced an RCCP teacher, Beatrice Byrd, who was then Brooklyn president of the National Association for the Advancement of Colored People, to accompany me. We spent many evenings in Bensonhurst trying to open up a dialogue between two groups of people who shared only a well-defined border: the African Americans who lived in a housing development on one side of town, and the Italian Americans who lived in tenements and two-family homes on the other. To make things more complicated, every Saturday following the incident, several black churches bused in hundreds of parishioners for nonviolent protest marches through the streets. Fear and embarrassment ran high within the Italian American community. We attempted to keep the dialogue open as each march was announced.

The meetings usually went right through dinnertime, so we all were pretty hungry at the end. I had started a ritual of gathering a group of African American folks to go out and get a bite to eat before going home. Once the nightly meetings were over, I couldn't bear to go anywhere near my Italian American brothers and sisters. I was afraid I would hear them repeating the same discriminatory remarks I had heard some of my aunts and uncles make when I was growing up. Keeping my rage inside was difficult enough during the public meetings.

I wished I'd remembered Mahatma Gandhi's example sooner. When violence broke out between Muslims and Hindus on the eve of the partition of India, Gandhi went to the province of Bengal, where the fighting had begun, and spent as much time with those who had committed the violence as with those who were hurt by it. He served both equally.

We were about three weeks into the Bensonhurst incident when I experienced a new awareness of how important it was to fully embrace those of my own ethnicity, in spite of what they were doing and saying. A courageous African American pastor helped me break through my own shadow.

One Tuesday night, during our usual evening meeting, the pastor from Brooklyn was sharing what had happened to him the previous Saturday. He had been chosen to lead the protest march through Bensonhurst that day. Three or four congregations had bused in several hundred people, who got off the bus, and prayerfully and peacefully lined up behind him. The marchers had moved about two blocks when several onlookers began to throw tomatoes and pieces of watermelon at them. Since the minister was right up front, it wasn't long before his crisp, tailored gray suit and white shirt were smattered with red juice.

While he was telling the story, I began to think that I could not go on listening. It disturbed me so much. All my stereotypes about my own heritage were building up inside. But I forced myself to keep listening as the pastor continued:

"When I was hit with the tomatoes, I made the mistake of glancing down at my shirt. Deep humiliation engulfed me, and the pain and despair of centuries began to overcome me. I didn't know how I was going to take another step. I looked back and saw the hundreds of faithful followers being humiliated as well. Feeling I was losing courage quickly, I did the only thing I knew to do: I looked up to the heavens for spiritual sustenance. And when I looked up, I saw an angel disguised as an elderly

Italian American woman. She was probably about eighty years old and precariously hanging out her fourth-floor tenement window, giving me the peace sign!"

At the sight of this woman, the minister's spirit reignited. He pointed upward. The whole group of marchers were now looking upward and walking forward. The old woman had the courage to hold up her hand for several more minutes before she became tired. The pastor finished the march that day, and so did the three hundred people behind him.

The pastor is among those who know that there is a rescuer in every group of oppressors. That night, when he finished his story and it was time to go to eat, I cautiously crossed over to the other side of the room and went out to dinner with the Italian American group for the first time since I had been going to Bensonhurst. At the restaurant, we had Chianti and pasta, and wished for harmony to return to their shattered community.

I'm convinced that we have as much work to do in breaking the cycle of oppression within our own ethnic groups as we have in building bridges to link us with those who are different. I often need to remind myself that not every person in any one group acts, feels, thinks and behaves the same when it comes to issues of prejudice. When I need reassurance of this, I remember the precious old woman who transformed a protest march—and my own thinking—with one kind move of her arm.

Linda Lantieri
Reprinted from Waging Peace in Our Schools

One Child

*L*ive to shed joys to others. Thus best shall your
own happiness be secured.

Henry Ward Beecher

Sorting through my mail while standing in the school
office, I was surprised to see a letter from my previous
principal. I skipped through the rest of the mail and
quickly opened that letter, curious to see why she was
contacting me. Inside the envelope, I found a submission
for a Teacher of the Year award. A Post-it Note stuck on
top bore my principal's handwriting: "How wonderful to
have touched someone's life in this way." As I looked
down to see which student had written the essay, I saw
"Lisa Nicholson*" written in another familiar hand. My
eyes immediately filled with tears. It was late June, the
very end of the school year, and I was in the process of
packing up my room, but not just for summer vacation.
My husband and I were relocating to another state, and I
didn't even know if I would be teaching the following

Name has been changed.

year. I was very emotional as it was and could not handle this, so I stuck the essay at the bottom of the mail pile and returned to my classroom.

As I sat at my desk in my quiet classroom, long after my students had gone home, I began to think about Lisa. I was surprised she had written anything about me, and although I knew how hard I had worked to help her, I didn't think she realized all I had done. I remembered how bitter and angry she was when she first entered my fourth-grade classroom three years before. She was very volatile, oscillating between being withdrawn and sharp; sometimes, she was even warm. I knew something was going on with her, and I tried several times to talk to her to see what was wrong. At first, she resisted, but then, one day, while she chose to have lunch with me in the classroom instead of in the cafeteria with her friends, she burst into tears and told me how her teenage brother had been murdered the year before. I had never encountered such a tragedy, and I didn't even know how to respond. I listened to her, and my eyes filled with tears. Soon, she regained her composure and the rest of the students returned from lunch, but I felt sick all day. I wanted so desperately to help her, to take away her pain, but I didn't know how. I knew that coddling her would turn her away.

For the rest of the year, I did what I could without making it obvious that my heart was breaking for her. I started an after-school club and always had a snack for any of the kids who stayed so that she (along with several other students who were dealing with personal demons) would stick around a little while longer for extra personal attention and academic help. I attended a workshop on helping children deal with grieving and death. I tried to establish a relationship with her mother to work together to help her, but I don't think she was ready for it. I wanted to do more, but I didn't know how. Before I knew it, the school year was coming to an end. As the year progressed, I took every opportunity to spend time one-on-one with Lisa. Sometimes, our time together would leave me feeling optimistic, but mostly I would be an emotional wreck for a week after listening to her pain.

One day in spring, Lisa asked me if she could sing "God Bless America" after the Pledge of Allegiance. I quickly agreed, although I was surprised at such an odd request. After hearing her sing, I was awestruck. I couldn't believe a nine-year-old could have such a voice. She had the vocal power of a gospel singer combined with the sweet tone of an angel. The entire class cheered for her as she quietly took her seat. That same day, I went to the music teacher who was preparing for the summer concert, and I asked her if Lisa could do a solo in the show. She told me that she normally didn't consider fourth-graders for solos, but when I told her about Lisa's voice and about the hard time she'd been having, she agreed to let Lisa audition.

I will always remember how proud Lisa was when she announced that she would be the only fourth-grade student singing a solo at the concert; I will also always remember how proud I was of her when I heard her sing her heart out in front of a huge audience of strangers. I had thought that was the one contribution I had made to her life. I didn't think she would remember anything else about me. Then I read her essay.

I couldn't believe the words that I was reading. Lisa, in very straightforward and simple words, described how she was terribly depressed at the time I taught her, which I already knew, but went on to say that there were many times during that period that she thought of killing herself but resisted because of me. My eyes welled up as I continued to read her account of the way I had impacted her life and prevented her from taking her life by being there for her at such a difficult time. I sobbed for some time after reading her nomination. So many emotions rushed through me at once. I was shocked to realize how desperate she really was, but simultaneously grateful that she didn't act on that desperation. Then I was proud of myself for being such a significant instrument in someone else's life. Mostly, I was humbled at the miracle of our everyday simple efforts. I did work extremely hard to help Lisa, but never did I realize just how high the stakes had been.

If Lisa hadn't heard of the Teacher of the Year award, and if the newspaper sponsoring it didn't forward her nomination to the principal of the school, and if the principal hadn't then forwarded it to me, I never would have fathomed the impact I had on such a precious little girl. I wondered how many other teachers helped students in similar ways, without ever having the opportunity to realize the impact they had. I wondered how many other human beings, who do good every day for the people around them, go unacknowledged, never knowing of the power of their simple acts of kindness and caring.

When I finally pulled myself together enough to gather my things to go home for the night, I looked around my classroom and thought about each of the little lives I had been so blessed to spend the past ten months with. I loved each and every one of them. While I realized I might never see any of them again, I felt such peacefulness knowing that I had given them my best every day we were together.

Regina Hellinger

Guns Are No Match for Gentle Words

The best defense of peace is not power, but the removal of the causes of war.

Lester B. Pearson

There was courage and faith that night in Bogotá, Colombia. And they were enough—again.

About eighty people gathered on a cool Saturday evening in July for Colombia's Independence Day. Glowing candles and the tune of a familiar peace song led two friends and I to the group. State security forces prohibited us from gathering at the capital plaza facing the congressional building, so we created a circle at the nearest intersection. Sympathetic passersby, curious street people and expressionless armed police peppered the crowd. We sang and read litanies that grew out of our vision for a future without violence dominating national life.

A half hour after we started, the inauguration of Colombia's new Congress concluded. Senators and representatives began to leave. We stood aside as the armored SUVs stuffed with soldiers and an occasional dignitary passed by. We kept our vigil, with songs and silence, positioning our banners to keep them visible. The police and soldiers who came to observe us were growing weary of us. Reinforcements with heavier weapons began to arrive.

About this time, I read the first of the messages sent from outside the country. It was a greeting from Boston Mennonite Fellowship:

"On this Colombian Independence Day, we stand with you in spirit as you remind each other, and all who will listen, that peace comes through peacemaking, not warmaking. With you, we long for the day when you, we, and all people everywhere live together in peace instead of war, with joyful anticipation instead of fear, with bellies satisfied instead of hungry or overstuffed, and nurturing instead of plundering the Earth. May you be richly blessed for your creative and courageous efforts toward this."

These words were not well received by the state security forces. Not only were we organized, staying put and brazenly public with our peace stance, but we had international support. I could feel the military monitors of this situation growing more tense. We returned to our song sheet.

Then, to my disbelief, I heard the unmistakable clatter and roar of an armed riot-control tank approaching. "They're going to hose us down!" someone whispered fiercely.

For what? I demanded silently. *Because we are so uppity as to pray for peace?*

I turned to my friend, who read the question on my face. "This," she said with tears welling in her eyes, "is war, Janna."

As the riot police and soldiers grew in number, a pastor urged them and all of the country's armed groups to lay down their guns, abandon their faith in weapons and, instead, seek the nonviolent path of life.

The microphone went to Peter Stucky, president of the Colombian Mennonite Church. When he began to pray, another tank arrived. And then another. As this gentle pastor prayed for food for the hungry, more police in riot gear marched up to him to create a blockade between him and most of the vigil participants.

Peter continued to address his words to our God of life. Except for the occasional revving of a tank engine and the background street noise, it was quiet. We listened and waited. He called for justice where injustice reigns, freedom for the oppressed, regard for life over lust for money and power, return of land to peasants, safety for Colombia's poor who suffer so much, and wisdom for legislators who have not done justice, loved mercy or walked humbly. He exhorted the new administration and Congress to govern in obedience to Jesus' teachings of reconciliation, nonviolence and love.

In the darkness, a fourth tank clanked up the hill and stopped just short of the outermost ring of participants.

We sang another song, praying, "Make me an instrument of your peace." Peter invited us to close in prayer. Then Peter's wife defied all the instructions ever given at direct-action trainings in the United States. She reached out and placed her hand on the nearest riot policeman.

He whispered, "May God bless you," as once more we pleaded for an end to the bloodshed, an end to the fear, an end to this war that threatens the freedom and lives of all who stood and shed tears in longing for peace that night.

Janna Bowman

A Risky Ride for Freedom

I hope I shall never be such a coward as to mistake oppression for peace.

Lajos Kossuth

I watched the TV in horror, thinking, *This can't be happening in America!* In that instant, I decided that I would join the Freedom Riders. That is how, as an eighteen-year-old college sophomore in the early 1960s, I learned that ordinary Americans, getting involved in the political struggles of the time, can actually *change history*. It is never easy—it can be risky and dangerous—but in America, it has always been possible.

My family had taught me early on that racism is the number-one evil in the world, and that, as Jews, we had to combat racism and discrimination wherever we found it— that *our* very existence depended on it.

Similar to many African Americans, I, too, was raised on stories of violent mobs and armed attacks on my people, of vicious prejudice exploding into unspeakable acts of cruelty and horror. These stories were related to me in the relative safety of Pittsburgh and New York, but they conditioned me to regard discrimination and violence by those in power as a threat to all groups and individuals without power.

As a young teen, I was drawn early to the rousing speeches and inspiring writings of Dr. Martin Luther King Jr. His philosophy of nonviolent struggles against racism was not only widely discussed, but actually put into practice—*successful* practice—in the Montgomery bus boycott of 1956, the lunch counter sit-ins of 1960 and then, in 1961, the Freedom Rides.

The Freedom Rides were designed to challenge, person by person, the *local* practices of racial segregation—of lunch counters, restrooms, even water fountains—so that these practices could then be challenged in the *federal* court system.

I can still vividly remember, while studying for my final exams, the incredible pictures on Mother's Day 1961: a Greyhound bus run off the road in Anniston, Alabama, then set on fire, with its Freedom Rider passengers beaten almost to death. These brave individuals—many of them students like me—were putting their lives on the line. How could I do any less? That's when I made the instant decision to stand with them in their struggle as a fellow Freedom Rider. I took my exams the following day, then immediately flew to Nashville, Tennessee, to receive several days of training in nonviolence.

Four of us—two black, two white—then got on a Greyhound bus . . . to where, we didn't even know. Would we face another Alabama mob? Would we make it to Mississippi? Would we end up in jail—or a hospital?

The laws of segregation—and the tactics of the Freedom Ride—meant that we sat separately, each with our own thoughts . . . and fears. Motoring through the kingdom of American apartheid, we encountered fear and hostility on every side. The Alabama authorities had learned their lesson and refused to let our bus even stop in their state. Soon, we were in the very belly of the beast: Mississippi.

As we pulled into the state capital, Jackson, we knew our time had come: A jeering mob of hundreds was waiting. I don't know from where we summoned our courage, but the four of us walked off the bus together to desegregate the Greyhound lobby, coffee shop and restrooms. Almost immediately, as the mob began to close in, officers of the Mississippi National Guard informed us that we were "inciting a riot" and hustled us off to the Jackson City Jail. At a quick "trial," we were sentenced to six months for our crimes, and because cell space ran out in the city, we were eventually sent to isolation cells (on death row!) in the Mississippi State Penitentiary.

Most of us served two months before being released on appeal. Those sixty days were filled with both fear and exhilaration. Many of us were beaten and subjected to psychological torture. But we survived—with dignity— and our lives were changed forever. Hundreds of us— black and white, young and old—filled jails in Mississippi during the summer of 1961. Our actions stirred the conscience of America—and the whole century-old legal structure of segregation came tumbling down in a few historical years of legislative and judicial action. We had, indeed, changed history!

Although I had friends who were killed in the struggle for civil rights, we moved our country forward, and my optimistic belief in social change has remained with me to this day. As Dr. King said, "We've come a long way—but we have a long way to go." Let all of us, together, keep our eyes on the prize.

Congressman Bob Filner

Truth at a Tender Age

We could all learn a lot from crayons: Some are sharp, some are pretty, some are dull, some have weird names and all are different colors . . . but they all have to learn to live in the same box.

Andy Rooney

It happened more than forty years ago, but I clearly remember each moment of the entire frightening episode. I was a small, physically underdeveloped, freckled, blonde seventh-grade girl in an ethnically mixed, inner-city junior high school. A verbally prolific little kid, I had the unfortunate habit of getting into trouble for saying things without thinking. Yolanda, a Latina classmate, was exotically beautiful and well-developed. She had jet-black hair and olive skin, and wore dark-red lipstick, crucifix earrings and lots of makeup. Everywhere she went, she was accompanied by four girls of similar appearance with whom she engaged in a clever mix of Spanish and English. Their partially understandable conversation was punctuated with occasional bursts of sarcastic laughter. Tantalized, I yearned to be Yolanda's friend, but her attitude toward my overtures was disdainful. She scowled at me and my friends, if she looked at us at all.

One day toward the end of the second semester, I confided to a friend that I didn't like Yolanda, unaware of being overheard by one of Yolanda's allies. To my horror, Yolanda approached me shortly afterward and scathingly announced that she and I would "have it out" after school. "Meet me by the tunnel," she sneered. "Be alone, and don't even think about not showing up!" Her friends were beside her, snickering and adding insults.

I was practically paralyzed with terror for the next two hours. Word spread among the students about the upcoming event, and I heard bits and pieces of conversations about bets of how bad I would "get it." My friends felt sorry for me, but were visibly relieved that Yolanda demanded I show up at the tunnel alone.

When the dismissal bell rang, I walked out of the building into a throng of kids jeering in English and Spanish. They followed me as I walked toward the tunnel like a prisoner to her execution. Suddenly, Yolanda appeared with her friends and stopped me on the sidewalk when I was about halfway there. Apparently, she wanted to begin the confrontation where the widest possible audience could look on. There wouldn't be much room for a crowd in the tunnel.

Yolanda began by calling me a stupid little sh-- with a big mouth. Looking at the ground and humiliated to the core, I nodded, and everyone laughed. Next, she grabbed my collar and made me look at her. "You don't like me because I'm Mexican," she announced loudly. An ominous rumbling growl issued from the crowd.

Instantly, I protested in a stronger voice than I expected myself to generate, "No! No, that's not true." And then I shocked everyone, especially myself, by blurting, "That is *not* why I don't like you!"

Seconds of silence that seemed to last forever followed, then Yolanda shrieked, "What? You admit it? You don't like me?" Then she shoved me toward the tunnel and hissed, "Okay, you asked for it. Get going."

Suddenly, hooting and laughter erupted. I heard a boy's voice say, "Hey, Yolanda! You hear that? Who can blame her?"

Another said, "Oh, man, she tells the truth!"

Another taunted, "*¡Ay, Yolanda, posible tiene razón!*" (Maybe she has a reason.)

Others were out for blood: "Give it to her, Yoli!" and *"Que pega la pendeja."* (Just hit the idiot.)

Yolanda gripped my arm as she forced me down the stairs into the narrow pit, reeking of urine, that ran from one side of the boulevard to the other. Every kid who could find a toehold around us crowded in. Yolanda screamed at them to back off to give her some room, and she began to circle me like a hungry wolf. To my surprise, she repeated, "You don't like me because I'm Mexican. That's why you don't like any of us."

Once again, the crowd reacted with a hateful growl.

A deep sadness overcame me. I was quivering inside, but looking her straight in the eye, I said, "I was stupid to say what I said so loudly that your friend heard me. I never wanted you to hear it. But your being Mexican isn't why I said it."

Yolanda objected again. "Tell the truth. You don't like Mexicans!"

Again, I denied it by shaking my head firmly.

"Okay, then, tell her why you don't like her," someone shouted to me.

"Yeah, *gringuita*, tell her the truth," came another voice.

"Shut up!" Yolanda screamed, and her friends gave the crowd menacing looks. But they persisted: "Yeah. Tell her. Do it! Do it!"

I was not relieved by any of this. All I wanted to do was either die on the spot or be magically transported out of there. What to do? Being outnumbered, I would be a fool to fight back. I looked at Yolanda and realized that in a far more serious way she, too, was miserable. I took a deep breath, held her gaze and quietly said, "I don't like you because you aren't friendly. At the beginning of the year, I tried to make friends with you, but you never said hi when I said hi, and when I smiled at you, you never smiled back. I liked you a lot at first, but then I gave up."

Yolanda was frozen in space, staring at me.

After a few moments, I continued, "You think I don't like Mexicans, but you're wrong. You want the truth? I would love to have your hair and your skin. And I wish I could speak two languages like you, and I'm sorry that I hurt your feelings."

Yolanda listened, and her eyes grew larger. She seemed to be amazed, then suddenly swallowed, shook herself and sneered, "Well, look who's kissing my a--!"

At this point my humiliation was overwhelming, and I looked at the floor of the tunnel waiting for whatever would happen next.

"Get away from me!" she screamed. "Just get out of here!" Without looking at anyone, Yolanda gestured at the crowd to part and let me climb the steps. Surprised, but eager to get away as fast as I could, I rushed up the stairs and ran across the boulevard. Thank God, a bus going my way was taking on passengers on the other side. I hurriedly climbed aboard, showed the driver my pass and found a seat. Instantly, I was overcome with racking sobs. Without looking at anyone, I used my dress to sop up torrents of tears.

The end of the term came soon thereafter, and, terrified of Yolanda, I carefully avoided her. There were no confrontations, not even eye contact. Summer came and went. When school started again in September, something happened that still mystifies me: I was seated in a classroom as Yolanda entered. We spied each other, but before I could avert my gaze, she smiled and cheerily said, "Hi, girl, how've you been?" I literally looked behind me and, seeing no one, looked back, supposing that she was baiting me for another confrontation. But Yolanda, keeping her distance, kept smiling an apparently sincere smile. "Did you have a good summer?" she asked. But I was too shocked to respond. During the rest of our eighth-grade year, Yolanda, who no longer hung out with her former friends, went out of her way to greet me with a warm smile. I was still so freaked out that I rarely responded with a fraction of her friendly energy, but it didn't seem to matter to her. We never became close friends, but I lost my fear and actually grew to like her.

Through the years, as I've pondered what happened that day in the tunnel, I've come to an important understanding: Finding the courage to tell the truth opens the heart to the possibilities of peace and reconciliation.

Gerry Dunne, Ph.D.

The Last Day of My Life

Do every act of your life as if it were your last.

Marcus Aurelius

The last day of my life as it had been—or could ever be again—began with the ringing of the telephone calling me out of sleep into the morning.

"Hello, Luv!"

"Tony! It's so early. What time is it? Five-thirty!"

"I'm sorry. I didn't mean to wake you. I miscalculated the time."

My husband, calling from London, was so eager to tell me when to expect him home that night he had forgotten the time zones separating us.

"I don't mind. I'm glad it's you."

"I'm taking the last plane out of London today. We should arrive at Kennedy tonight at 8:40. I'll take a taxi home."

"Alan and I could take a cab and meet you, but it is kind of late."

"Not to worry. I'll take a cab. That will be fine. See you soon, Luv."

"Miss you."

"Me, too. Very much. Looking forward to seeing you tonight."

I replaced the phone in its cradle and hugged my pillow. Knowing exactly when Tony was coming home, I relaxed and tried to sleep again. The clock guaranteed another hour before I had to get up. It was Wednesday, December 21, 1988, and Tony had booked a seat on Pan Am Flight 103.

He had gone to England for a week to take care of some family business. He was booked to return on December 20, but had called to say that things were going slower than expected and he wanted to stay an extra day. I had said that would be all right. Our son, six years old at the time, asked me for years, "Why didn't you say no?" But there wasn't any reason to refuse Tony's reasonable request. I know that; I don't blame myself. But I also know that if I had said, "No, I want you to come home Tuesday," he'd be alive. I will live with that knowledge for the rest of my life.

We were waiting for him to call, telling us he had finished with customs and was about to catch a cab, when the phone rang at nine o'clock. It was Tony's cousin in England telling me that there had been a terrible accident with one of Pan Am's planes, and the family was desperately hoping that Tony had somehow missed his flight. This was how I first learned that my husband and the father of my child was dead—not from authorities, not from the media, but from a relative who wasn't even certain that Tony had been a passenger.

I sent my son to sleep with a story that his father's flight had been delayed for mechanical reasons. I needed to confirm the truth, and I needed time to let it all sink in. As soon as I saw the town of Lockerbie, Scotland, burning on the eleven o'clock news, I intuitively knew that it had been a bomb, not an accident. And though I didn't know any of the details yet, nor how many people had been killed in the plane and on the ground, I knew I wasn't alone. This hadn't happened just to my family. We were connected to a vast tragedy.

I was raised to regard revenge as a primitive response to injustice because revenge fuels the cycle of retaliation. Then a terrorist's bomb ripped my husband's life from him, tore him from our embrace, and this belief traveled from my brain, where I had entertained it, into my stomach where it lodged like a stone-cold truth. I wanted and needed many things: my husband to be restored to me, to howl my pain, to comfort my child, to receive solace from my friends and family, but I never for one moment wanted or needed to inflict this anguish on another human being. I could not believe that anyone who has ever been plunged into this abyss of pain would ever want to create another widow or orphan in the world.

Alas, this is not a universal truth. In most places in the world, revenge continues to be the reason that individuals or governments attack one another. The cycle of revenge and retaliation is, I believe, what killed my husband: Apparently, the Libyan government conspired for two and a half years to destroy an American plane in retaliation for the U.S. government's bombing attack on Tripoli in April 1986. The U.S. attack, in turn, had been justified as a direct response to Libyan agents' deadly bombing of a German disco popular with American military personnel. Libya justified the bombing of La Belle Disco because the U.S. Navy had attacked a Libyan ship in a dispute over Libyan territorial waters.

Watching our secretaries of state and defense reassure the American public on the night of the bombing raid on Tripoli in April 1986 that our "surgical strikes" had hit only military targets, Tony exclaimed prophetically, "Don't they know we're going to pay for this?" It would be Tony and 269 other men, women and children who were to pay.

What I did hunger for was justice. The thought that the men who were responsible for the conspiracy—those who had funded it and those who had assembled the bomb and concealed it inside an unaccompanied suitcase—were free to go about their lives and might not ever be held responsible for their heinous crime was unbearable.

Because my husband had been murdered by terrorists who tried to hide from the consequences of their crime, I could channel my righteous anger against them and against the ineptness and indifference in the aviation industry and our government. Many other relatives of those who died on Pan Am Flight 103 responded to their losses in the same way. We sought out one another and formed an organization within two months. From the beginning, our mission has been to offer emotional support to one another, to find out the truth about what had happened to our loved ones and to work to improve aviation safety and security. One of our most significant achievements has been as a powerful lobbying force with close ties to the U.S. State and Justice Departments. It has been gratifying to see Libya apparently get out of the business of terrorism and begin to comply with the U.N. sanctions of 1991. Our work, which is still unfinished, has enabled me to meet people of goodwill in the highest levels of government in this country and abroad. It has enabled me to feel that I am not powerless.

And because Pan Am Flight 103 was blown up by terrorists from the Middle East, I have become a member of the Dialogue Project, a group of people concerned about the continuing conflict in Israel and Palestine. Jews, Muslims and Christians, Americans, Israelis and Palestinians, we meet one afternoon a month to get to know one another as individuals, to learn about one another's history and pain, and most important, to support those individuals and organizations in Israel and Palestine who seek nonviolent solutions to the dilemmas that prevail in that region. I do this not only for myself as a Jewish woman, but to honor Tony, a Catholic, who was as passionate a supporter of the legitimate aspirations of the Palestinian people for a nation of their own as he was a hater of the terrorists' rationale for murder as a political tactic.

"We may not succeed in making peace in the Middle East," a new Muslim friend and neighbor told me recently, "but we are at peace with ourselves."

Helen Engelhardt

A Bully's Transformation in Room 7

Understand what makes the bully tick;
your brain is better than a big old stick.
Love the doer, but not the deed—
look for the good, the inner seed.

Arthur Kanegis, in "Bullyproof Shield Rap"

"Mrs. Krycia, that song . . . it's about me. I am the bully. Please, can you help me stop?" The class had already been dismissed for lunch, and I was puzzled about why Tommy had made sure he was at the end of the line when he usually jumped up to push his way to the front. Approaching me with a great deal of obvious discomfort, Tommy looked up at me with pleading eyes. I could not believe my ears!

I was teaching a fifth-grade class at the request of the teacher who was at her wits' end with the bullying behavior in her classroom. I had just played a song called "Don't Laugh at Me," sung by Peter Yarrow of Peter, Paul and Mary. The lyrics really could have been written with this boy in mind. The song described a variety of people who had been bullied and how much it hurt.

Tommy laughed at everyone. He was loud and obnoxious about it. He would stand up, point and loudly say something derogatory regarding the person's behavior. It could have been as simple as someone misspelling a word in class, or tripping, or perhaps asking a question he considered stupid. "Ha ha!" he would laugh and point at John. "You are so stupid!" John would hang his head and shuffle his feet. Across the room, Scott would be crying; he couldn't stand conflict. Scott spent a good deal of time crying. Everyone ignored him. Tommy got the attention, and he was, by all definitions, quickly earning the title of class bully. The behavior was contagious. The other boys had picked up on it, and now it seemed that the boys in Room 7 were vying for the title of "class thug." Tommy was not a big boy, but he walked big. His fists were always clenched, and his posture said, "I'll get you if you mess with me." He was eleven years old and appeared to be headed for big trouble.

Perhaps it was not until that moment that Tommy recognized the effect his behavior could potentially have on others. Perhaps he had already noticed that he was being mean and searching for a way to change. Either way, here was my golden opportunity to do something with him. Across the nation, educators had to deal with a huge increase in school shootings, and we were scrambling to stop the violence, but the big question still remained: *How?* So here I stood with a class full of students, and this one boy—who I was very concerned would be at the receiving end of a bullet some day—was asking me to help him stop this behavior that he noticed had spiraled out of control.

I asked the teacher if I could take the boys she considered to be the biggest troublemakers and meet with them twice a week. She was thrilled. She felt when they were gone she could get to teaching. So I began meeting with

the boys and asked them each to make one small, obtain-
able goal—something they could achieve in a week's
time. Tommy's goal was to stop laughing and pointing at
people. He was to make a mark on a piece of masking tape
we had applied to his desk every time he noticed himself
pointing and laughing. I was hopeful. I checked in to the
classroom and noticed a change. The room appeared
calm. The children appeared on task.

The following week, I met with the boys. "How did it
go?" I asked.

Alex, not one to ever be serious about anything,
responded with a tone of combined disgust and joy: "I
can't believe it, Mrs. Krycia! Not only is Tommy not teasing people, he's even getting other people to stop! It's like
we're all being nice to each other. It's weird!"

I looked over at Tommy. He was sitting at the table with
his school lunch in front of him, hands folded in his lap
and looking down as if in prayer. Tommy looked up at me
and smiled. His smile was so innocent; his posture had
changed. He was relaxed. His eyes, no longer little slits,
were wide open and dancing with joy. He reached into
his pocket and pulled out what appeared to be a pile of
trash—and some of it was—but there in the pile was this
beat-up piece of masking tape from the week before. He
held it up to me.

"It was so hard at first! But look, Mrs. Krycia!" Tommy
said proudly as he handed me the tape with the tally
marks. Sure enough, he had tally marks for the first few
days, but they had tapered off. I looked at him and saw a
child—a little boy, not a bully. I wanted to hug him and
run through the halls saying, "He's done it! Look at
Tommy!" But I simply smiled and knew that he, indeed,
had done it.

As the school year went on, Tommy's character continued to be one of leadership and inspiration. Now, when

John trips, or Hannah misspells a word, there is no laughter. There is no hesitation to raise a hand in Room 7. The students know that it is okay to make a mistake and ask questions. Tommy won't allow any teasing.

I was so proud of Tommy that I decided to make a home visit to let his parents know what had been going on at school. I knocked on the door, and his father answered. "I am Tommy's counselor from school. I want to discuss his behavior with you," I said.

His father scowled. "Oh, no, let me get my wife," he started.

I stopped him. "Sir, this is a good thing." Mr. Brown looked at me dubiously. He cleared his throat and called for Tommy and his wife. Tommy came zooming into the room in his stocking feet, took one look at me and smiled. His parents sat down on the couch, and Tommy climbed into his mother's lap. She stroked his hair as I told them what had been happening at school and the changes that had occurred. His mother wiped away a tear. His father proudly said to him, "I knew you could do it, son."

The moment was tender and wonderful. Never again would anyone mistake this boy for a bully! He was kind and compassionate, a born leader who just needed direction. He has been an inspiration to his classmates, to me and to countless others. I am hopeful that Tommy will carry the torch of kindness and pass it on to all those with whom he interacts. Tommy's compassion and kindness certainly proved to be contagious in Room 7!

Kristin Krycia

Peace on Earth, Goodwill to Men

It is through disobedience that progress is made.

Oscar Wilde

[AUTHOR'S NOTE: *The ancient story told by shepherds of angels singing a song of peace on a starry winter night still haunts and inspires us to hope and dream of a better world, a better country, a better neighborhood, a better family. But where do we find that elusive calm, that spirit of "peace on Earth, goodwill to men"? Are we fools to cling to our hope for peace? Recently, a veteran of World War II came into my office and told me a story about himself that renewed my belief that peace can be achieved even in the most incredible of circumstances.*]

The cold winter rain had made their invasion into the countryside of Germany a slow, miserable struggle through quagmires of mud and swollen streams. Private Boyer, an eighteen-year-old recruit from California, longed for the sunny days of home. What he got was a colder day, with no rain and the real possibility of snow. He stamped his feet in his still damp and muddy boots and slapped his hands together in an attempt to shake off the bone-chilling cold. In spite of his misery, Private Boyer was proud to finally be old enough to be in this war and serving his country.

Today, he and his buddy Steve Williams had patrol duty around their temporary encampment. Their unit would be spending the day cleaning weapons, drying out as much as possible and getting ready for a final charge. They all knew the war in the European theater was coming to an end. The Allies were moving with little resistance, the Germans were on the run, and more and more enemy soldiers were giving up and surrendering to the Americans. It was not the time to drop their guard, however. Boyer knew his patrol duty was critically important in assuring the safety of his comrades. He and Private Williams were on full alert with rifles ready for any unexpected encounter.

That unexpected encounter happened in the late afternoon, shortly before Boyer and Williams were to go off duty. They heard him before they saw him, the German accent unmistakable. "Don't shoot! Don't shoot!" They stood immobile, their guns pointed in the direction of the voice, straining to see who had shouted to them. Appearing from the nearby woods was a young boy in the uniform of a German soldier, hands over his head, his eyes wide with fear. He appeared to be around fifteen or sixteen years old.

"Ah, that's a damn shame," muttered Williams. "Those Krauts are so desperate they're recruiting kids to fight their stinking war. They'll have their mothers out here next!" Boyer grabbed the boy, indicated to him to keep his hands over his head, nudged him in the back with his rifle to persuade him to start walking, and said, "I'll take him to the C.O. and see what he wants us to do with him." He marched the boy back to his unit and found his commanding officer.

"Sir, we picked up this deserter on patrol."

"I see." The C.O. looked at the prisoner and then at Private Boyer. Silence followed. Private Boyer stood uneasily, not sure what he was supposed to do. He looked at his C.O. for guidance. Finally, the C.O. spoke. "We have no time or manpower to take care of prisoners here. Take him out five miles and one minute from camp, Private. That's an order."

"Yes, sir!"

Boyer stood stiffly at attention, then turned sharply, motioning his prisoner to start walking toward the nearby woods, his gun prodding the boy in the back. He knew the order meant to take him out five miles from camp and shoot him. But, in spite of his commitment to follow orders, his honor as a soldier and his loyalty to his country, he was conflicted. This unarmed and frightened boy posed no threat to him or his unit. An order was an order, but how could he shoot this defenseless boy? The more he struggled with his C.O.'s instructions, the more he knew that he could not carry out the order. What was he to do? The prisoner and his captor kept walking.

The solution appeared over the next hill. Another unit was bivouacked there. Private Boyer knew immediately what he was going to do. He marched the German into the camp and asked for the C.O.'s tent. Pushing the boy ahead of him, he reported to the commanding officer. Saluting smartly, he said, "Sir, I found this deserter while on patrol. Your unit is closer than mine, so I brought him to you." The C.O. acknowledged Boyer.

"At ease, Private. We'll take him. You better get back to your unit."

The walk back to his unit was lonely. He had disobeyed a direct order. His fate was uncertain. His knees trembling, he reported immediately upon arrival to his C.O. "I didn't hear a shot," the C.O. muttered, not looking up from his maps.

"You didn't hear a shot because I didn't shoot, Sir." The commanding officer looked up and locked eyes with Private Boyer. "I turned him over to the unit that is camped about four miles from here." Boyer did not lower his eyes, returning the steady stare of his C.O. and waiting for his reply.

"Dismissed!" He left the tent on unsteady legs, knowing that he had dodged his own bullet. His duty continued without further incident until his feet submitted to the harsh winter and he was sent to the hospital with frostbite. After his release from the hospital, he was assigned to guard duty at a prisoner-of-war camp in France. On his first day of guard duty, as he was making his rounds, he heard someone in the camp calling his name. "Boyer! Boyer!" Startled, he turned to see who had called his name. He knew no one here and couldn't imagine who would know him. But there, on the other side of the barbed-wire fence, he recognized the young German deserter he had refused to shoot so many months before. An incredible reunion, unlikely at best—and impossible if Private Boyer had obeyed his orders.

Boyer was stationed at the camp for nearly a year. Whenever Private Boyer took prisoners out on a work detail, "Victor" would get in line to go with him. A friendship was formed between the two young men: one a prisoner, the other his guard. Victor told Boyer in broken English that he didn't know if his family was still alive or if his home was still standing. It had been more than a year since he had been conscripted for service in the German Army. But when Private Boyer completed his tour of duty and was preparing to leave, Victor hopefully gave him his address.

Boyer always intended to get in touch with Victor, but time went by and he never did. The memory of Victor, however—and what he was supposed to do to him—has never left his mind. "I just couldn't do it. . . . I couldn't do it," he whispered with tears in his eyes.

And I thought, as I looked at this old warrior: *Yes! Peace on Earth is possible! In the most unlikely of places, this man lived the angel's message of "peace on Earth, goodwill to men" in a heroic act of disobedience.*

Barbara Smythe

Shopping for a New Coat

There is always time for gratitude and new beginnings.

J. Robert Moskin

When I lived in Portland, Oregon, I taught English as a Second Language at a local community college. I had adult students in my class from Vietnam, Mexico, Russia and many other countries. Although they came from many lands, they had one thing in common: a desperate yearning to learn English.

Many of the students worked in a factory for twelve hours through the night and took a bus in the morning straight to our 8:00 A.M. class. They waited until after class to go home and sleep. Sometimes I would see them struggling to keep their eyes open during our class, but they were always there working hard, earnest and eager to learn.

Despite their collective lack of sleep and long hours at work, the level of attendance and attentiveness in class was always excellent. Some of the students had as many as three jobs and took the bus everywhere they went because they couldn't afford cars. Seventy-nine-year-old Valentina from Russia would walk to class every morning, even in the cold or rain.

We developed a wonderful rhythm and rapport during the class. One particularly bright female student from Vietnam later married another student from the class, a young man from Romania.

To teach the course, I needed to use a lot of pictures and hand gestures, since I didn't know all of their respective languages. One of the things I taught was a simple sequence of dialogue called "Shopping for a New Coat." They enjoyed standing up and acting out the gestures that accompanied the text of the story.

Sometimes I second-guessed myself and wondered if I was really teaching my students in the best way possible. But I gave my all to this class, and they gave their all to me. If nothing else, they would always remember what to say if they ever went "shopping for a new coat."

On the last day of class, they threw a terrific party that was brimming with good food and laughter. I was amazed that they had learned enough English to even coordinate such an event with each other. The food was eclectic and delicious, with wonderful dishes from over ten different countries. A Russian woman gave me a dozen roses. A Vietnamese woman gave me a little case of makeup.

Then Alexander from Hungary, one of the most outgoing members of the class, told everyone to be still as he proudly handed me a large, neatly wrapped gift box. After the ribbon was untied and the top was off, I gently pulled back the tissue paper and lifted from the box a beautiful, new, full-length coat.

"We went shopping for a new coat!" they all exclaimed in unison and in wonderfully perfect English. In all my days of teaching college classes, I had never experienced generosity like this. These were people who lived in cramped apartments, sent money back to relatives in their home countries and barely could feed their immediate families. I was simply doing my job, teaching English, and their gratitude was beyond the bounds of what I ever could possibly have expected.

I wear the coat they gave me with pride and gratitude; it's my favorite. Reversible with a drawstring, it is navy blue on one side with a Navajo design on the other. Every time I wear the coat, I think fondly of them—Valentina from Russia, Mai from Vietnam, Maria from Mexico, Vladimir from Romania, Xavier from Guatemala—all of them and their desire and struggle to start a new life in America full of opportunity, hope, freedom and generosity.

Krista Koontz Martinelli

4

A MATTER OF PERSPECTIVE

What is a matter of perspective?

Perspective and viewpoint are miracles that assist us in our lives. We have the opportunity to view a moment and see it from every angle; it is the moment where we get to choose the perspective that will guide us in the future. It is the moment of truth. . . .

I am seeing all the angles in every moment and choosing the one that empowers me, as well as those around me.

Labib's Café

If you want to make peace, you must be peaceful.

Peace Pilgrim

Five nights after September 11, 2001, business is particularly slow for all the Middle Eastern restaurants and shops on Steinway Street in Astoria, Queens. At three o'clock in the morning, Labib Salama, the owner of an Egyptian coffee shop, his friend Nasser and several other men are sitting around the café, playing chess, smoking shisha and talking about the recent attack on the Twin Towers. Suddenly, four young men (two white, two Hispanic) barge into the café. They're turning over tables, throwing chairs around, smashing dishes and a mirrored wall. Labib calls the police. Two cops arrive almost immediately. They snag the four guys, pin them down on the floor and handcuff them. But Labib refuses to press charges. He says he understands. He feels the same rage. "Let them go." The cops are baffled. They tell Labib, "If you don't press charges, you can't collect insurance." Labib shakes his head. "There's enough hatred already. We don't want to make more. Let them go." The cops have no choice but to let the guys go. The cops leave, too, and Labib and his friends start cleaning up the café. There's broken glass all over. Everything's broken. "I'm thinking now we are between the two sides. I'm afraid from the terrorist number one, and now I'm afraid from the American too."

An hour later, at four o'clock in the morning, the same four guys come back to the café. The first thing out of their mouths—they thanked Labib for not pressing charges. Then they helped clean up the cafe. They buy everyone coffee, and these two groups of men talk until 8 o'clock in the morning about their fears, differences and perceptions of each other. As the guys are leaving, Labib tells them, "Next time you want to come and be friendly with us, you don't have to hit us and then say you're sorry. Just come and be friendly in the first place."

We hear this story from Labib and his friend Nasser a week after the incident. Nasser leaves us with this thought. "It's time right now to bring the anger down. You have to inhale everything bad, and forgive the people for the people to forgive you."

Warren Lehrer and Judith Sloan
Excerpted from Crossing the BLVD:
Strangers, Neighbors, Aliens in New America

Hulk Heaven

You cannot shake hands with a clenched fist.

Indira Gandhi

I was a young teacher, the new kid in the department, and so I got to teach the third-period sophomore English C class. Every day, I walked to that classroom with chest tightened, hands clenched and the sternest look I could muster. Period 3 meant facing a class of twenty-five insolent hulks, with a few girls mixed in. Everyone knew that "C" was a euphemism for *bored, intransigent, lazy*—or any combination thereof.

At 10:23 every morning, I sat terrified and sweating as the hulks lumbered into my class. Walt, short and stocky, had a police record. John had been kicked off the football team and now sat with his long legs raising and lowering the desk so that it made intermittent clunks that echoed on the wood floor. Nick sat near the outside wall, twisting the window-blind cord into knots. And Vin kept dropping his books during some of the rare moments of silence.

They talked to each other, called out answers at random and banged knuckles on the desks. When I asked them to write, they dropped pencils, crumpled their notes and sent paper airplanes flying. I set down rules. I pronounced consequences. I gave ultimatums. I told them in no uncertain terms that they had to change their behavior. The daily quizzes I gave to keep them quiet resulted in daily piles of papers for me to correct, but brought no noticeable improvement to their behavior.

One day, the police came to the door to question Walt about something, and that inspired John to clunk the desk even louder. Out of sheer desperation, I ordered John to the principal's office. He looked at me in disbelief, saying, "Why me?" then proceeded to take a full five minutes to unwind his lanky frame from his desk and clomp to the front of the room. When he reached the door, he turned to face the class and bowed while they all clapped.

I left school that day—and every day—frustrated and exhausted. By the time I finished grading all my disciplinary quizzes, I barely had the time and energy to walk my dog. Clearly, I was spending my personal resources and the taxpayers' money on enforcing discipline, not on teaching English. What a waste! I finally got it: The only behavior I could change was my own. What if, instead of acting from fear, I acted from love? What if, instead of standing over them in all my imposing sixty-one inches, I worked side by side with them as a fellow learner? Clearly, the clenched fist wasn't working. Why not open my hands and my heart?

The next morning, I convinced the principal's secretary to give me enough small soft-covered notebooks for my Period 3 class. At 10:23, after giving one notebook to each of my students and one to myself, I announced that we were going to write as fast as we could for three minutes without stopping, and without any regard for spelling, punctuation or grammar. During a moment of stunned silence, I saw a number of sideways glances, raised eyebrows and shrugged shoulders. I said, "Look. I'm working on my writing, too, and I'm going to write along with you. No questions asked. If you don't know what to say, then just write, 'I don't know what to write,' for three minutes without stopping." Nick punched John in the back while John's eyes rolled in disbelief. "Let's go," I said. My heart was pounding as I began to write. After three minutes, I cautiously looked up and saw twenty-five hulks bent over small soft-covered note-books, scribbling away.

We continued this drill every day at the beginning of the class period for the rest of the year. The change occurred slowly. The little notebooks became sources of information and instruction. We started by sharing words that jumped out at us from someone's writing. Then it grew. It became cool to talk about writing, to expand vocabulary and even to spell correctly. We went to the notebooks to use our own sentences for revision, and we learned how to work in pairs and groups. When they wrote, I wrote. I didn't diminish my subject-matter expertise, but I did let them know that I found writing hard work, too. And that was the truth. I read some of my work to them and told them where I was stuck. They offered suggestions and asked helpful questions. When Walt said, "You mean you don't know all the answers?" I realized that this time they were laughing with me instead of at me.

Books stopped dropping on the floor, knuckles no longer banged on the desks, and John's desk stayed miraculously in place. On a memorable Tuesday, I heard Walt call out to Vin, "Hey, what do you think of this description of how the inside of a police car smells? *Pungent.*"

Vin said, "Great word. I've never been inside a police car. What else did you smell and see in there?"

Gradually, Vin started to turn his love of sudden and unexpected sound and rhythm into poetry. Nick disengaged himself from the window cords and became the class vocabulary expert, keeping a thesaurus on his desk for general consultation. On the day John got applause for the piece he wrote on motorcycles instead of his walk to the principal's office, I wanted to dance in the streets.

The notebooks became inspirations for longer pieces. After about six weeks of small daily steps that built on the three-minute writing, I got to class early one day to find Walt writing busily in his notebook. Head down, he said, "Last night I thought of more stuff that I wanted to say about that day in the police car." When he looked up at me for an instant, I saw tears in his eyes. I touched his shoulder gently and said, "Let me know if you want to share any of this with me." He looked up once again, this time with a tearful smile, and we began to share our stories.

From that point on, we all unclenched our fists—and our hearts. The threats and ultimatums were gone. I went home energized instead of depleted, and the taxpayers were finally getting what they paid for. Caring and mutual respect, mixed with a bit of humor, worked every time. It was so simple once I got it. The hulks were really angels at heart.

Dee Montalbano

Roses for Dinner

One spring, I was hired as groundskeeper at the Willcox House Country Inn, a famous bed-and-breakfast located in northwestern Washington state. The mansion, built by Colonel Willcox during the Great Depression, is in a beautiful, isolated setting with a panoramic view of Hood Canal and the snow-capped Olympic Mountains. Many famous people have visited, including Clark Gable, who had his own room there.

The current owners, Philip and Cecelia Hughes, have done a beautiful job bringing the house back to its original condition. Guests are magically sent back in time to the 1930s. However, since most of their efforts had been put into restoring the house, the gardens were very overgrown. Worse yet, there was another problem: a very persistent doe.

Every day when I came to work, there was new evidence of the deer's ravenous appetite. This had been going on for years, and the innkeepers were at a loss for what to do. I, however, was fresh and ready for the challenge, determined to solve the problem. I tried some of the standard deterrents: a mist of ammonia on her favorite choices, human hair, soap, you name it—but none of those things had much effect. We thought of motion detectors that would trigger bright lights or loud noises, but that would disturb the guests as well as the deer. I tried everything I could think of to keep the deer away, but this doe liked it there and was going to stay.

Often when I was weeding, I'd look over and there she'd be, munching some tasty tidbit. I'd growl at her and run her off, but she didn't go far before she ate some more. She knew I wasn't a threat to her well-being, just to her breakfast. Worst of all, she feasted on the roses, in which Cecelia took great pride. Cecelia got very distressed when they were eaten. We put an electric wire around the rose garden, but the hungry deer was not diverted. We were proving to be no match for this animal. I became so frustrated that I named her "Dinner"—and wanted to serve her on one of Cecelia's silver platters.

The driveway at Willcox House has an island, an overgrown deciduous azalea bed with roses, along the front edge. One morning, I was on my hands and knees pulling out blackberry vines and salmonberry bushes when I caught a movement out of the corner of my eye. I looked and there was Dinner, not five feet away, munching a large leaf and staring at me. By the way she looked down her nose, I got the feeling she thought I was a nuisance and she the superior being. I remained on my knees, and we scrutinized each other. As I looked into those big, soft brown eyes, my frustration melted, and I was filled with a deep serenity. I felt a connection with this animal. We did have something in common—we were both mothers. I got the crazy idea of trying to communicate with this creature through mental telepathy. It seemed she wanted the same thing because we were staring deep into each other's eyes.

What's up? I asked her, in my head.

I want to live in peace, was the gentle reply I felt I heard.

I'm here because I feel safe, I have my fawns bedded down nearby, and there is plenty to eat. When the twins are older, I will move them deeper into the forest, and we won't be here anymore.

I understand that, I assured her. *People come here, too, from far away because it is a safe and enchanting place. I promise you that nobody will harm you or your children. I don't mind sharing the vegetation, but Cecelia, the lady who lives here, loves roses, too. She is very upset when they are all eaten.*

A loud clatter broke the magic spell. We both jumped, startled. Our eyes met again for a brief moment before she bounded off across the driveway, disappearing into the forest.

My body tingled as I watched her go. Had I really communicated with this wild animal—or was it just my imagination?

I went into the kitchen where Cecelia was preparing the evening meal. "I just had a meeting of the minds with Dinner in the driveway," I told her. "Maybe we have been looking at this problem the wrong way."

"What do you mean?" Cecelia asked, curious.

"The guests can see roses anywhere. But having wildlife roam around the grounds is something people don't experience very often. It might really add to the charm of the place. Why not include Dinner in the décor? The guests will never notice that flowers are missing."

Cecelia thought about it—and liked the idea. So that's what we did. When guests arrived, they were told that wildlife sometimes wandered around the grounds and that, although the deer looked tame, they were definitely undomesticated—and unpredictable—animals.

For the next few months, Dinner brought her white-spotted twins into the yard. While she grazed, the siblings ran and frolicked around the lawn, just like small children. She knew she was safe and welcome. Occasionally, one of the fawns would fall into the swimming pool or fish pond and have to be rescued by staff, while Dinner pawed the ground and scolded her careless child. Once the crisis was over, she licked her wet offspring dry and cuddled it, just as any mother would. She even seemed to pose so that guests could take pictures. I am sure they'll talk about their experience at the Willcox House for years to come.

I enjoyed watching Dinner with the twins. My presence never bothered her, and the fawns were very curious. They would stare at me through the bushes and jump around like they had pogo sticks on their little legs. Dinner's parenting skills were excellent. I was touched by the gentleness and affection she showed her charges. As summer wound down, Dinner and her children visited less and less. Eventually, they didn't come at all, just like she had said. I would occasionally see them on the long driveway in the early morning, but she was taking them farther into the forest. Finally, they left for good.

So maybe there is a way to live in harmony with these peaceful creatures. Consider who was here first. The animals are just doing what comes naturally to them. If you move into the forest, have some respect and appreciation for the natural inhabitants—after all, you destroyed their yard. Maybe the Golden Rule applies to animals, too. Maybe we should think about what we've done to them, not just what they've done to us.

And, yes, I know that I communicated with Dinner that day in the garden. After that day, she ate only half the roses.

Cathy Som

The Christmas Truce

*May the children of tomorrow
be as shocked to learn of war
as the children of today
are shocked by slavery.*

Linda K. Williams, in the song,
"The Children of Tomorrow"

On Christmas Day 1914, in the first year of World War I, German, British and French soldiers disobeyed their superiors and fraternized with "the enemy" along two-thirds of the Western Front. German troops held Christmas trees up out of the trenches with signs that read: "Merry Christmas" and "You no shoot, we no shoot." Thousands of troops streamed across a no-man's land strewn with rotting corpses. They sang Christmas carols, exchanged photographs of loved ones back home, shared rations, played football, even roasted some pigs. Soldiers embraced men they had been trying to kill a few short hours before. They agreed to warn each other if the top brass forced them to fire their weapons, and to aim high.

A shudder ran through the high command on either

side. Here was disaster in the making: soldiers declaring their brotherhood with each other and refusing to fight. Generals on both sides declared this spontaneous peace-making to be treasonous and subject to court-martial. By March 1915, the fraternization movement had been eradicated and the killing machine put back in full operation. By the time of the armistice in 1918, 15 million would be slaughtered.

Not many people have heard the story of the Christmas Truce. Military leaders have not gone out of their way to publicize it. On Christmas Day 1988, a story in the *Boston Globe* mentioned that a local FM radio host played "Christmas in the Trenches," a ballad about the Christmas Truce, several times and was startled by the effect. The song became the most requested recording during the holidays in Boston on several FM stations. "Even more startling than the number of requests I get is the reaction to the ballad afterward by callers who hadn't heard it before," said the radio host. "They telephone me deeply moved, sometimes in tears, asking, 'What the hell did I just hear?'"

I think I know why the callers were in tears. The Christmas Truce story goes against most of what we have been taught about people. It gives us a glimpse of the world as we wish it could be and says, "This really happened once." It reminds us of those thoughts we keep hidden away, out of range of the TV and newspaper stories that tell us how trivial and mean human life is. It is like hearing that our deepest wishes really are true: The world really could be different.

David G. Stratman
Excerpted from We CAN Change the World:
The Real Meaning of Everyday Life

Christmas in the Trenches

My name is Francis Tolliver, I come from Liverpool.
Two years ago the war was waiting for me after school.
To Belgium and to Flanders, to Germany to here,
I fought for king and country I love dear.

'Twas Christmas in the trenches where the frost so bitter
   hung.
The frozen fields of France were still, no Christmas song
   was sung.
Our families back in England were toasting us that day,
Their brave and glorious lads so far away.

I was lying with my messmate on the cold and rocky
   ground,
When across the lines of battle came a most peculiar
   sound.
Says I, "Now listen up, me boys!" each soldier strained to
   hear
As one young German voice sang out so clear.

"He's singing bloody well, you know!" my partner says to
   me,

Soon, one by one, each German voice joined in harmony.
The cannons rested silent, the gas clouds rolled no more,
As Christmas brought us respite from the war.

As soon as they were finished and a reverent pause was
spent,
"God Rest Ye Merry, Gentlemen" struck up some lads
from Kent.
The next they sang was "Stille Nacht"—"'Tis 'Silent
Night,'" says I,
And in two tongues one song filled up that sky.

"There's someone coming toward us!" the front-line sentry
cried.
All sights were fixed on one long figure trudging from
their side.
His truce flag, like a Christmas star, shown on that plain
so bright,
As he bravely strode unarmed into the night.

Soon one by one on either side walked into no-man's land
With neither gun nor bayonet we met there hand to hand.
We shared some secret brandy, and we wished each other
well,
And in a flare-lit soccer game we gave 'em hell.

We traded chocolates, cigarettes and photographs from
home,
These sons and fathers far away from families of their own.
Young Sanders played his squeezebox, and they had a
violin,
This curious and unlikely band of men.

Soon daylight stole upon us, and France was France once
more,

With sad farewells we each prepared to settle back to war.
But the question haunted every heart that lived that won-
    drous night,
"Whose family have I fixed within my sights?"

'Twas Christmas in the trenches where the frost so bitter
    hung.
The frozen fields of France were warmed as songs of peace
    were sung.
For the walls they'd kept between us to exact the work of
    war,
Had been crumbled and were gone forevermore.

My name is Francis Tolliver, in Liverpool I dwell.
Each Christmas come since World War I, I've learned its
    lessons well.
That the ones who call the shots won't be among the dead
    and lame,
And on each end of the rifle we're the same.

John McCutcheon

Left Foot Forward

Although the world is very full of suffering, it is also full of the overcoming of it.

Helen Keller

In the early 1940s, bombs rained down regularly on Essen, a city in northern Germany. Air-raid sirens screamed of impending disaster without regard for time of day, sending hordes of citizens scrambling to the nearest bomb shelter. After the all-clear signal blew, people emerged, hoping that the very place from which they fled would still be standing. Sometimes, the shells hit one of the multiple munitions factories scattered throughout the city, but often bombs destroyed homes, schools and businesses. Between battles of global dominance, the residents of Essen carried on the ordinary tasks of life. Children played among the ruins, young couples fell in love, and families ate dinners concocted from rationed ingredients.

Perhaps it was because my mother grew up in Germany during unpredictable times that she became a risk-taker. After being raised in an atmosphere of uncertainty, she could easily justify a fear of risk. Instead, my mom lived by the motto that even a small step, taken with courage, is far better than being paralyzed by fear.

Over the years, I wondered about the source of my mother's fearless nature, until one day when I had a crisis of courage. As usual, I picked up the phone to call for advice. After listening to my list of complaints and worries, my mother drew a deep breath, then began to tell me an "Oma and Opa" story. (*Oma* and *Opa* mean "grandmother" and "grandfather" in German.)

I'd heard plenty of "Oma and Opa" stories before and knew my grandparents owned a shoe store in Essen during World War II. Stray bombs and collateral debris had damaged the business many times. As a child, I loved hearing how Opa responded to the destruction by asking his family, "Do you have your arms? Your legs?" After hearing that everyone was well, he declared, "Then we will be fine," and began gathering an armload of bricks for rebuilding. In total, Oma and Opa rebuilt the shoe store seven different times.

With this in mind, I prepared myself for another bomb story. Instead, my mother talked of shoes.

"One morning, after a holiday, Oma and Opa opened the store to discover that every pair of shoes had been stolen. To add insult to injury, the thief turned out to be their business partner, who'd left them with nothing but unpaid bills and left-footed sample shoes . . ."

As my mother spoke, I pictured my grandparents, standing in an empty storeroom, faced with the challenge of feeding their family in the middle of a war-torn city with no merchandise to sell—nothing but a pile of left shoes. My fears began to shrink in comparison. Where would the money come from to pay the invoices and replace the stolen inventory? This was not as simple as picking up bricks and reconstructing a crumbled wall. This was a task that required rebuilding a broken spirit.

Fortunately, my mother comes from a long line of strong spirits.

She continued her story, "Oma and Opa didn't allow their anger to stop them. Instead, they took the sample shoes and created a beautiful display in the front window. That day, they opened for business as usual. Customers came in, attracted by the handsome window presentation, and asked to see certain styles. Oma and Opa greeted each person warmly, took foot measurements and walked back to the cleaned-out storeroom. Once out of sight, they stood calmly and counted to a hundred. Moments later, they returned to the front of the store and announced to the customer that they didn't have the shoe, but would gladly order it. It wasn't a lie. They didn't have that shoe—or any others—but because they held themselves confidently and kept calm, the customers placed orders. After all, it wasn't uncommon for merchandise to be scarce. This time, the war shortages worked in their favor."

As my mother finished, I began to understand that this story was not about shoes.

"Before long, the inventory was replaced with all the money from the orders brought in by the beautiful display. Oma and Opa could've given in to their fears and closed the store. Instead, they opened their hearts to forgiveness. They moved forward and presented what they had—a bunch of left shoes and, most important, a belief in themselves."

I often marveled at my grandparents' courage to immigrate to America long after the war ended and retirement beckoned. Though they brought precious little with them, I realize that they brought all they ever needed—a generous spirit and a deep faith that, when you put your best foot forward, the rest of the world follows suit.

That day, after I got off the phone with my mother, I took a giant step forward—using my left foot . . . of course!

Terri Goggin-Roberts

A Spa for the Heart

Believe what you set your heart upon for it surely shall be yours.

Ralph Waldo Emerson

Sitting in the sun at the health spa, I was surrounded by beauty, yet felt sad and empty inside. I had come to spend the first holiday after my husband's death with strangers. I couldn't imagine spending this Thanksgiving with anyone I knew—giving thanks was completely beyond me. I hoped this week would help me heal. After two years of caregiving and trying to keep my business going at the same time, I felt like a burned-out survivor of war. I was just marking time until I could join Jack, a feeling that seemed common in my recent survivors' hospice group sessions. After all, at fifty-four, what did I have to look forward to? The future was bleak.

The concierge approached my table, asking if I needed anything. To my surprise, I said, "Yes. If you know anyone here who is a recent widow or widower, I would appreciate talking to her or him." Again, to my surprise, she told me about Phyllis, the spa's health director, who had lost her husband several months before.

I invited Phyllis to have lunch with me the next day, and we quickly established some common ground. We were about ten years apart in age, but she had also been with her husband for about fifteen years. She talked of how they met and what their life had been like, and I could tell by her stories and the warmth of her tone of voice that she, too, had a happy marriage. Then it was my turn, and all I could do was cry quietly as I told the story of my own husband's battle with cancer and chronic pain.

As an executive coach, I'm used to asking people what they've learned from their experiences, so it was natural for me to ask her for advice on what had helped her deal with the crushing grief. Obviously, she had been doing something right to be so full of vitality and joy after such a short time. She described her travels around the world with sparkling eyes and her plans for the next year with a joyful smile. What a contrast to how I was! Phyllis had been so open with me, I felt encouraged to ask her, "Did you ever feel like you were just waiting to die? I don't mean suicide. I just mean feeling like all you were doing was going through the motions, with no future and no purpose."

She emphatically stated, "*No,* never." I must have looked incredulous because she shared the following story. When she was a little girl, her family lived in Java, where her dad was an executive with Shell Oil. One day, Japanese soldiers came to the door and took her dad away with a bayonet pointed at his back. Her mother, Phyllis and her little brother all were taken to a Japanese prisoner camp. For three years, they all but starved as they struggled to survive. I listened, open-mouthed, as she told of the horrors her family had gone through. Phyllis finished her story by saying, "Every day, my mother would tell us, 'They can take away our food and our freedom . . . but they can't take away our love of life. If we let them do that, they've won.' That's why, as awful as it was to lose my husband and have to go on without him, I will never lose my love of life."

I felt a rush of awareness inside me . . . a recognition that this was a deciding moment in my life. Here was a woman who had been through so much more than I, yet she had *chosen* to fully live her life. I had a flash of the future—picturing myself at sixty-four, the same age Phyllis was now. Which did I want to be? An inspiring, joyful woman with peace and love in her heart—or a woman in a cocoon, sitting on the sidelines, full of sorrow, not really living but merely existing. Whichever woman I decided to be was totally my choice.

I left the spa radically changed—I had chosen to live life fully, honoring the gift of a good marriage through my remembrance of it, but also moving on to experience life now, as it was, moment by moment. A sense of peace and contentment filled me. And although there are still moments of grief and loss, there are also moments of laughter and enjoyment.

That's life!

Jan Thompson Eve

Beginning Anew

One moment can change a whole lifetime
One life can change eternity.
One stranger befriended,
one broken heart mended
One child loved, one captive set free.

Michael Stern, in the song "One World"

Eight years ago, I organized a retreat for American veterans of the Vietnam War. Many of the men and women at that retreat felt very guilty for what they had done and witnessed, and I knew I had to find a way of beginning anew that could help them transform. One veteran told me that when he was in Vietnam, he rescued a girl who had been wounded and was about to die. He pulled her into his helicopter, but he was not able to save her life. She died looking straight at him, and he has never forgotten her eyes. She had a hammock with her because, as a guerrilla, she slept in the forest at night. When she died, he kept the hammock and would not let it go. Sometimes, when we suffer, we have to cling to our suffering. The hammock symbolized all his suffering, all his shame.

During the retreat, the veterans sat in a circle and spoke about their suffering, some for the first time. In a retreat for veterans, a lot of love and support is needed. Some veterans would not do walking meditation because it reminded them too much of walking in the jungles of Vietnam where they could step on a mine or walk into an ambush at any time. One man walked far behind the rest of us so that if anything happened, he would be able to get away quickly. Veterans live in that kind of psychological environment.

On the last day of the retreat, we held a ceremony for the deceased. Each veteran wrote the names of those whom he or she knew had died and placed the list on an altar we constructed. I took a willow leaf and used it to sprinkle water on the names and also on the veterans. Then we did walking meditation to the lake and held a ceremony for burning the suffering. That one veteran still did not want to give up his hammock, but finally he put it on the fire. As it burned, so did all the guilt and suffering he had held for so long in his heart.

Another veteran told us that almost everyone in his platoon had been killed by the guerrillas. Those who survived were so angry that they baked cookies with explosives in them and left them alongside the road. When some Vietnamese children saw them, they ate the cookies, and the explosives went off. They rolled around on the ground in pain. Their parents tried to save their lives, but there was nothing they could do. That image of the children rolling on the ground, dying because of the explosives in the cookies, was so deeply ingrained in this veteran's heart that now, twenty years later, he still could not sit in the same room with children. He was living in hell. After he had told this story, I gave him the practice of "Beginning Anew."

"Beginning Anew" is not easy. We have to transform

our hearts and our minds in very practical ways. We may feel ashamed, but shame is not enough to change our hearts. I said to him, "You killed five or six children that day? Can you save the lives of five or six children today? Children everywhere in the world are dying because of war, malnutrition and disease. You keep thinking about the five or six children whom you killed in the past, but what about the children who are dying now? You still have your body; you still have your heart; you can do many things to help children who are dying in the present moment. Please give rise to your mind of love, and in the months and years that are left to you, do the work of helping children." He agreed to do it, and it has helped him transform his guilt.

"Beginning Anew" is not to ask for forgiveness. "Beginning Anew" is to change your mind and heart, to transform the ignorance that brought about wrong actions of body, speech and mind, and to help you cultivate your mind of love. Your shame and guilt will disappear, and you will begin to experience the joy of being alive. All wrongdoing arises in the mind. It is only through the mind that wrongdoing can disappear.

Thich Nhat Hanh
Reprinted from Teachings on Love

The Mystery of the Thatch

We should ever conduct ourselves toward our enemy as if he were one day to be our friend.

Cardinal Newman

If Preacher Peter had been awake, he would have heard their quick footsteps as the shadowy figures of the young men made their way down the cobblestone street of the little village of Emmenthal, Switzerland.

Each step brought the young men closer and closer to the darkened home of the old Mennonite minister and his wife. Life for them had been very difficult, for they lived in the eighteenth century when Mennonites were still being persecuted in Switzerland.

"Now we will see what kind of a man he is," muttered one of the young men. "Maybe he won't be so loving after our visit tonight!" he laughed.

"That is the house," whispered another as they slackened their pace. Cautiously they approached the darkened dwelling while their eyes searched the darkness.

"No one is stirring. Let us do our job well."

The men quickly lifted themselves to the roof and soon

the muffled sound of falling thatch blended in with other night sounds. They worked quickly lest someone should surprise them in their treachery.

Inside Peter stirred in his sleep. The strange sounds continued, and Peter sat up in his bed.

"Something is not right," thought Peter. "There are noises on the roof."

Carefully he made his way across the bedroom floor, through the darkened room, and reaching the outside doorway he quietly opened the latch. Peering cautiously into the night, he could make out the figures of several men busily at work.

"What can this mean?" he gasped, as he stared in amazement. "Destroying my thatch!"

Slowly the meaning of their actions became clear to him. He knew that many people in Emmenthal did not understand why he and his people believed it was wrong to go to war. When they had been threatened with imprisonment and death, Peter and his friends would simply say, "We would rather die the bitterest death than disobey God."

"Now they have come to molest me again," thought Peter.

Raising his eyes heavenward, Peter prayed to God to help him do what was right. Then turning, he walked quickly into the little house.

"Mother," he called, "workmen have come to us; you had better prepare a meal."

The strange happenings of the past few minutes had startled his wife, but now she understood. Soon she was busily at work in the little kitchen. And before long a meal was waiting on the neatly spread table.

Opening the door once more, the aged minister called to the boys on the roof, "You have worked so long and hard. Surely you are hungry. Now come in to us and eat."

Hesitatingly they entered the room and stood awkwardly around the table, where lighted tapers gave the room a friendly glow. Peter urged them to be seated, and finally they found their places, where they sat uncomfortably, staring at their plates.

Peter bowed his head and folded his hands, while the guests sat in silence. Then in his kindly voice, Peter prayed earnestly and fervently and lovingly for the guests and for his family. When the last words of the kindly prayer were spoken, the young men raised faces flushed with shame. The food was passed and found its way on to their plates, but it seemed they could not eat. Each sat silent before his well-filled plate.

Suddenly, as if by signal, the men pushed back their chairs and quickly disappeared through the door that they had entered moments before. Once again there were footsteps on the roof, and the shuffle of thatch could be heard. But this time it was not the sound of falling thatch. They were putting it back on the roof! Then, if Preacher Peter were listening (and I think he was), he would have heard the running footsteps of his guests as they disappeared down the cobblestone street and into the night.

Elizabeth Hershberger Baumna
Excerpted from Coals of Fire

Common Ground

*With the gift of listening comes the gift of
healing.*

Catherine de Hueck

It began with an impassioned letter to the editor by a
soldier's mother who was fed up with the "local pacifist
rhetoric" in Goshen, Indiana, which she perceived as a
lack of support for her son, a member of the U.S. military.

> *I would ask all of you to stop and consider what your
> harsh words in the paper mean to a soldier in a remote
> location, reading his hometown newspaper and seeing
> such a painful lack of support for our troops. While you
> enjoy your holiday season, please have some compas-
> sion for those of us who won't be together for the holi-
> days. We would prefer your prayers rather than your
> criticism. (Dana Schmucker,* Goshen News, *
> November 7, 2002)*

A day later, letter writer Dana Schmucker received a
phone call from Carolyn Schrock-Shenk, an organizer of
local war protests and associate professor at Goshen

College, inviting her to meet over coffee so she could understand more fully why the pacifist letters were so painful to read and to hear more about Nick, Dana's son serving in Afghanistan. Carolyn told Dana she committed herself to not trying to convince her of her point of view, and she wouldn't even tell her point of view on a war with Iraq if she weren't asked. Dana agreed to meet.

Nearly half of the two-hour meeting was spent getting to know each other and connecting personally. Then Carolyn asked Dana how she experienced the letters and the anti-war movement as a military mom. Carolyn very quickly realized that the peace protests needed to make the link stronger that opposition to war is actually a support of American troops abroad, not just a support of Iraqi civilians.

After sharing with each other and recognizing that they are both mothers of sons, share religious connections and want world peace, the women decided to write a joint let-ter to the editor. The two wrote about their different views on this war, their commonalities and how talking with each other has "stripped away layers of assumptions and stereotypes."

> We knew that we were on opposite sides when we agreed to meet for coffee, but talking felt like the right thing to both of us. What we both know, at a very deep level, is that we want Nick, and others like him, to come home safely. We believe that our God of love is present with each one of us, all the time, no matter where we are or which side of a war we are on.
>
> We will continue to respond to the current situation in the ways in which we feel called to respond, but we will do so with some differences since our meetings. It is our hope that by writing this letter, we can encourage others to see that it is possible to agree to disagree with-out disrespect or malice.

I (Dana) will respect and understand in a new way those who want to prevent this war. I would ask them to remember our sons and daughters who are trying to do the right thing and who are risking their lives to do so. I believe our troops need to know that we love and support them, regardless of whether we support the war in which they are fighting.

I (Carolyn) will continue to oppose this impending war with a new awareness of how much pain and fear and love military members and their families experience. Nick and his family, and others like them, will be part of my awareness in a new way as I respond to my personal call to peacemaking. I understand more deeply that, at bottom, we want so many of the same things: peace, security, a world of promise for our children. It is these concerns that lead me to oppose this and other wars. (Goshen News, *November 24, 2002*)

The response both women received from the community was "only positive." One community member, Diane Hertzler, followed up their letter with one of her own and referred to their joint writing as the "most important letter of the year."

Soon after, Carolyn planned another local peace protest, and she wrote Dana to ask what she would think about the wording on a sign she wanted to hold: "Support our troops, oppose this war." Dana wrote back to say it wouldn't offend her, or Nick, at all.

Jodi H. Beyeler

[EDITORS' NOTE: *On March 27, 2003, the story of these two mothers appeared on the* NBC Evening News.]

"She's a global peace activist, and
he's a reformed warmonger."

5

ANSWERING
THE CALL

What is answering the call?

Answering the call is heeding the message that is coming from within us. It is a calling that has no explanation, except that it feels right to us. When we answer the call, it is usually an empowering and freeing moment. It is when we are fully empowered, listening to our heart and following its guidance. It is a gift that we give ourselves and those around us.

I am following my heart's desire and answering the call with grace and ease.

Saving Oleg

An avid amateur ham radio operator since age twelve, I have always had an intense desire to communicate with the world—including people I had been taught to think of as "adversaries." During the Cold War, I even taught myself Russian so that I could speak directly with Soviets. I found them engaging and surprisingly easy to relate to. While messages from Russia were not unusual, one was truly urgent: a plea from Igor Korolkov, a Soviet ham operator seeking American medical assistance for his critically injured friend, Oleg Murugov.

Day 1: Oleg's automobile crashed during a torrential rainstorm. His companion died. In a deep coma and with multiple internal injuries, Oleg miraculously clung to life in a rural clinic with no qualified doctor. Amazingly, Igor convinced a Soviet bureaucrat to provide helicopter evacuation to a hospital in Ryazan. Despite surgery, Oleg's prognosis was grim. So Igor did what most of his countrymen would consider unthinkable: He sent out a call on the twenty-meter radio band to America, the "enemy," seeking medical help. His voice was heard in Brooklyn by Ed Kritsky, who happened to be fluent in Russian. Kritsky phoned me (a pediatric dentist) and Lawrence Probes, a physician also known to speak Russian. Kritsky then received a Russian-language fax detailing Oleg's condition. Rita Shkolnik, our neighbor who had practiced medicine in the Soviet Union, worked late into the night helping me translate the detailed medical terminology.

Day 5: Time was short. I phoned Joseph Izzo, a respected neurosurgeon whom I had never met, told him of Oleg's plight and asked for his help. He said he would help, adding, "Oleg's lucky to be alive. The coming two weeks will be critical in determining whether he recovers." Izzo would continue assisting, night after night, for months. Within hours, I organized a network of doctors and hams across the United States. With a similar network in Russia, we became a lifeline for Oleg. Frequent communication began between Izzo and me, and the Russians, through Igor, with translating by Kritsky in Brooklyn and Probes in Michigan. Telexes arrived in English, as Igor translated messages to and from the hospital staff.

Day 7: Three days after Igor's initial call, Dr. Izzo advised Soviet doctors: "A CAT scan would help detect brain swelling. Please keep his head elevated." He prescribed specific drugs and dosages. As exchanges continued, I wrote in my journal: "The relationship between the doctors in America and Russia started to change from one of mistrust and 'why are they doing this?' to one of cooperation. As Oleg lay in bed near death, the doctors and nurses began to follow all instructions."

Day 9: Oleg developed pneumonia. We Americans scrambled to find a broad-spectrum antibiotic. Kritsky radioed New Jersey hospital employee Angel Garcia, who found the medicine and delivered it to Allen Singer, who sped it to JFK Airport for a plane bound for Moscow. Administrative details nearly prevented the shipment from boarding. From my diary: "Only at the last minute was the air-freight agent willing to overlook the red tape and run the package to the plane." Next day, the medicine reached Oleg's bedside after a friend drove all night from Ryazan to Moscow and back. The pneumonia subsided, but Oleg's condition remained perilous. Izzo continued shortwave prescriptions. The patient improved, as did relationships between more trustful Russians and Americans who had never met.

I remember a telex: "Soviet doctors are very grateful for your assistance. Your advice gives them confidence that they are doing the right thing."

Izzo responded: "Please tell the doctors we are thinking about them every minute. We feel a close kinship with them. And you, Igor, are doing a fantastic job!"

Worried by Soviet doctors' discussions about a high heart rate and possible cardiac arrest, Igor asked Izzo, "Doctor, you said it is doubtful to save my friend if there is a cardiac arrest. But have our doctors a chance to save his life if there is no cardiac arrest?"

Izzo: "Yes, there is a chance to save Oleg's life. It is difficult to say at this time about the 'quality' of that life." The telex from Izzo and me that night concluded, "We are proud to work with you. This is a new moment on Planet Earth. Everything we do breathes new life into our relationship and, hopefully, into our brother, Oleg."

Day 14: Our hearts jumped for joy with the news on the telex. "The patient has begun to open his eyes and move his hands; have tried to fix the look and to carry out the commands. Soviet doctors, with your help, believe in success." I'll never forget the sense of relief and rejoicing that night. I could hardly see the control panel through my tears.

Several weeks saw Oleg gradually come out of his coma. He was still critical, yet occasional humorous Russian notes like Day 16's broke the tension: "Oleg passes a stool independently. We celebrate!"

Suddenly, conflicting Soviet and American ideas stalled recovery. Izzo said: "Stimulate him! Get him out of bed as much as possible. He'll be tired. That's okay! Shake him! Talk to him!" The Russians hesitated to move him. They babied him, not knowing how to help patients so injured, most of whom never survived.

But the Soviet doctors did change. And Oleg improved.

Day 31: He sat up in bed and swallowed water. Soon we heard: "Intravenous feeding has stopped. Oleg's mother brings him homemade broth to feed him by tube." A week later he talked, first uttering profanities about his terrible bedsores. We knew he was better!

We newfound partners across the United States kept our vigil for another month, following Oleg's progress through Igor's frequent shortwave broadcasts. By Day 60, Oleg's bedsores were healing, he was eating by mouth, walking twice a day and maintaining conversations.

Then two setbacks stunned us: Oleg's pneumonia and fever returned, and Dr. Izzo underwent emergency surgery for carotid artery stenosis. But within three days, Izzo was again advising the Russian doctors, even as he himself was recovering: "Continue Oleg's antibiotic!" Soon, the pneumonia disappeared, and Oleg strengthened.

Day 80: We soared with elation. Igor's voice on the radio waves: "Oleg is home." He had traveled by train, and friends and family took him to his home and threw him a great party. Across the seas, we celebrated with him like family.

This story is about saving one human life—with cooperation, compassion and marvelous technology. But it means more to me: Whenever I find myself discouraged by "impossible" world problems, I remember those eighty days and the greatness of the human soul that wants to do good if given the chance.

Lionel Traubman

Drafted by Mother Teresa!

*W*here there is hatred, let me bring love;
Where there is discord, let me bring union;
Where there is despair, let me bring hope;
Where there is sadness, let me bring joy.

St. Francis of Assisi

A business acquaintance once characterized my world-view as "distinct," which, when pressed, she downgraded to "incredibly *un*-fun." It was true that I had a unique perspective, perhaps because I was well-traveled in developing countries. So, while others enjoyed cozy dinners for two at fifty dollars, I couldn't help but remember that this was more than most workers in Guatemala earned in an *entire month*. An eight-dollar mai tai translated to sixteen Thanksgiving meals for the homeless in a downtown Los Angeles shelter. Yet another startling truth is that Americans spend about $6 billion yearly on Christmas gifts for their *pets*—roughly equivalent to what the United Nations says it would cost each year *for every child in the world* to be in school! With these facts in mind, I soon realized that I felt most at home in the company of conservative consumers like those I'd met volunteering with humanitarian projects. That good feeling, plus an innate passion for serving, convinced me that this kind of work was where I fit.

When I was in my early thirties, I came across the Missionary Brothers of Charity, a religious order begun by Mother Teresa and devoted to serving the poor. The Brothers ran projects in the Los Angeles area where I lived and soon, I was helping. But I had no formal role since I had been involved with religious groups earlier in my life and had decided henceforth to remain independent. In the next year, I helped organize volunteers to work with the Brothers to distribute food to the hungry, spend time with children in Tijuana orphanages and console grandmothers abandoned in Tijuana by family members entering the United States through the harsh desert. I enjoyed the work immensely—and also enjoyed it being strictly volunteer. My casual involvement took an unexpected turn, however, when Brother Simon, an instigator among the Brothers, invited me to a talk by Mother Teresa.

Thousands of people streamed into the ramshackle auditorium on the outskirts of Tijuana. Simon and I shuffled along within the expanse of Tijuana's devoted nuns, priests and faithful parishioners. We took our seats in an area reserved for clergy, where I felt especially out of place, since, aside from not being a member of the clergy, I was (rather tenaciously) unchurched.

Mother Teresa's small, frail form was barely visible as she entered the auditorium. The mayor of Tijuana introduced her, and then a lineup of mariachis played an over-amplified rendition of "Ave Maria" that sounded like an "uhm-pa" funeral procession.

Clad in her world-renowned white-and-blue-piped habit, Mother Teresa stepped up to the podium. A hush fell over the crowd as she began to speak in her thick

Albanian accent, while an aide translated into Spanish:

"Brothers and Sisters, friends of Jesus, I am so pleased to be with you on this lovely day that God has made. . . ."

Mother Teresa spoke for about ten minutes to thousands who listened so intently that it seemed everyone had stopped breathing.

"In closing," she said, "I must tell you that, all my young life, I was troubled by the suffering of the poor. But now that I am an old woman who has spent many years searching for an answer, I can share with you what I discovered to heal my own troubled heart. It is this:

"Meditate, for in silence you will find prayer, a humble voice in which to speak with God. With God, you will find a boundless love, and the desire borne of this love will lead you to serve the Almighty by serving God's people. In this selfless giving to others, finally, you will find peace. God bless you."

The mariachis blared again, and the crowd stood and cheered. For me, it all seemed to be going on far away; I had been deeply moved by Mother's poignant words. *In this selfless giving to others, finally, you will find peace.*

Simon urged our group to move to where the woman who had often been referred to as "The Living Saint" would be. As we entered an office in the auditorium, I saw Mother Teresa sitting on a plain, metal folding chair. She was surrounded by clergy, and she looked up when Simon approached her.

"Mother," he said, kneeling and taking her hand, which he placed briefly on his cheek. "This is Leslie, who has been helping us in our work with the poor. The Brothers think she would be a fitting coordinator of our coworkers in Los Angeles."

What!?! Since Simon and I hadn't discussed this before, I was taken aback. While I enjoyed volunteering, I hadn't considered a more formalized position within what I

perceived to be a large, bureaucratic religious organization, especially given my own eclectic religious background: a Catholic mother, Jewish father, and twelve
years living in an ashram that combined Buddhist and
Hindu philosophies with those of the West. This conversation would require some full disclosure on my part, I
determined.

Mother Teresa turned to me. "Are you Catholic, dear
girl?" she asked.

"Well, I . . ."

"She is modest, Mother," Simon interrupted, "so instead
of speaking about it every day, she demonstrates her love
for Jesus through her service to the poor."

"And you are willing to make sacrifices in your life to
serve the needs of the poor?" Mother Teresa continued.

"Well, yes, Mother, I'm willing, but I'm afraid that I'm
not—"

"Not worthy?" Simon broke in, knowing what I was
thinking. "Mother, I've explained to her that we're all
unworthy servants of God. . . . I ask that you give her your
blessing."

After being swept along in this unexpected inter-
change, I was momentarily speechless.

Mother Teresa concluded, "Jesus thanks you for your
service to his poor and forgotten, and I will pray for you
as you work with my beloved Missionaries of Charity."

Mother Teresa put her hands together and bowed rev-
erently in my direction. I was overwhelmed with feelings
of joy, humility and, at the same time, anxiety. I felt my
face flush, still unable to utter a word. Brother Simon,
quite pleased with himself, whisked me from the room.

Swallowing hard and regaining my voice outside, I
protested: "But I'm not Catholic!"

"Shhh!" Simon said, his blue eyes sparkling and a vertical forefinger at his lips as he grinned mischievously.

(Who said that monks don't have a sense of humor?)

"You'll do a lot of good work—Catholic or not," Simon declared triumphantly.

It was then I realized that I had been *drafted!*

Meeting Mother Teresa touched me deeply. Through working with the Missionaries of Charity, I was blessed to be able to make a positive difference—albeit in very small ways—in the lives of those less fortunate. There was Lourdes, a single mother of about thirty, and her three little girls. When a Brother and I brought decorations for their Christmas tree, they proudly led us to a droopy pine branch propped in a corner. My heart broke. How profound the depth of their joy with so little, and how humbling the experience. There was an old man who I helped two Sisters carry into a hospital, his leg swollen and gangrenous. He had no insurance and was turned away. The Sisters threw themselves facedown on the floor of the admissions office, begging loudly for mercy until the administrators relented and admitted him. I vowed never again to feel embarrassed about asking for help for others.

Experiences like these inspired me into charitable activities that grew into a full-blown development project in Guatemala that is now in its eleventh year. In doing charitable work, I've received so much more than I've given, leaving me to wonder who among us is the giver and who is the receiver. I cannot claim that I am selfless, although I do aspire to be. Still, I've found a deep and abiding sense of peace through humanitarian service. Mother Teresa's words are even more profound today than when they first touched me more than a decade ago:

In this selfless giving to others, finally, you will find peace.

Leslie Carol Baer

Viva la Huelga on Jicarillo Street

Nonviolence is not inaction. It is not for the timid or weak. Nonviolence is hard work. It is the willingness to sacrifice. It is the patience to win.

César Chávez

Gladden Boaz (appropriately named after the social reformer, Washington Gladden), besides being my father and a schoolteacher, was a very devoted peace and human-rights activist. From the beginning of the migrant workers' public struggle for better pay and working conditions, my father worked side by side with César Chávez as a liaison from his church, the Church of the Brethren, on a national level. My father's heart went out to the hundreds of thousands of farm workers who toiled long, grueling hours in the blistering sun or bone-chilling cold, exposed to toxic pesticides, without sufficient sanitation facilities, and for pay so low that it was virtually impos-sible to afford decent housing—if any housing at all. It was Cesar Chavez's unswerving commitment to pursue only nonviolent means to achieve the farm workers' goals that had especially won my father's heart and established his allegiance to Cesar's cause. And so, there were no grapes or lettuce eaten or brought into our house for years—and that was just the way it was.

One hot summer day, my beautiful and headstrong Puerto Rican mother, Carmen, could not resist a flat of grapes on sale at the market and daringly hid them in our garage of our house on Jicarillo Street. One by one, she lured us to that garage for a grape or two, including Emilia, a fine Mexican woman from Tijuana who helped clean our house occasionally and who was like part of our family. All these clandestine trips to the garage eventually caught my father's attention, and the contraband was exposed and brought into the living room. He did not yell. We would have felt much better if he had. At first, he just looked stricken that his family would eat grapes when the people who picked them were living in such poor conditions and even risking their lives to have these injustices exposed.

A spirited discussion began between my peaceful but principled father and my hot-tempered mother, who was determined to defend her position. How could one flat of grapes make such a difference to the whole cause of the farm workers? When the neighbors could hear the "discussion," Emilia bravely stepped forward and magnanimously offered to solve the whole problem by taking the grapes off our hands.

It was then that my father really got fired up. It was like the "Music Man" singing the song about the evils of playing pool. No evangelist could have been more filled with zeal. He began to tell Emilia about the cause of the farm workers and the sacrifices we all must make so that they could have the possibility of a better life. Then he leaped to the piano and began playing and singing all the farm workers' strike songs from the Teatro Campesino repertoire, and soon we all were inspired, marching around the room yelling, "¡*Viva la huelga!*" [Long live the strike!]. We fell exhausted on the sofa and vowed never to eat another grape.

Emilia finished her work, picked up her belongings and, last but not least, the rejected flat of contraband grapes. Everyone stared with mouths wide open and all eyes on my father. "Emilia, remember your people," he implored.

She smiled and said, "*Sí, Señor* Gladden, but the grapes are already bought, and I am not going to waste them."

Dad slapped his hand to his forehead and fell to the floor in mock defeat. As Emilia trotted happily to the bus stop with the grapes in hand, we could hear her humming the strike song and shouting, "¡*Viva la huelga!*"

Sylvia Boaz Leighton

I Was Ready to Fight

I'm not afraid to go, Mother; I'm not afraid to die.

I just don't want to be the one to make another son's mother cry.

Andy Murray, in the song, "Brave Man from Ohio"

When I turned eighteen, Uncle Sam pointed his finger at me and said, "Palmer, I want you!" The Russians had taken over Eastern Europe. Mao Tse-Tung had conquered China. Vietnam was in the balance. People were saying, "If we don't hold them in Vietnam, we will have to fight the communists on the shores of California." I appreciated my country and wanted to do my part. I didn't want to be a slacker.

But there was a problem. Jesus was also pointing his finger at me, saying, "Palmer, I want you. Christians need to fight evil as hard or harder than anyone else. We need to be ready to die for what is right. But we need to fight differently. I never used a gun, and I never dropped a bomb."

I asked permission to fight communism in a way that

was consistent with my conscience. My wife, Ardys, and I went to Taiwan for four years to overcome evil with good. It was a hot spot—shells exploding across the Quimoi Straits every other day. Even within Taiwan there was internal strife and a lot of anger.

I was put in charge of a mobile medical clinic. We formed a squad made up of a doctor, dentist, nurse and evangelist that went from village to village in the mountains. We often carried forty-pound packs on our backs for three or four hours. One day it was twelve.

But as a result, we had thousands of friends in the aboriginal villages of Taiwan. Even though I was a CO (conscientious objector) in civilian clothes, I served as Sunday school principal for the American military. One day I was telling some officers about the little baby who had been named "America" because of our medical team's help through his difficult birth and delivery. One of the officers responded, "We are losing the war in Vietnam because we can't win the friendship of the village people. You COs could probably win it better than we."

One day just before we left Taiwan, a military Jeep drove up. We groaned and thought, *What have we done now?* But they brought us a large trophy from the local government with the inscription, "For helping us fight communism!"

When we returned to the United States, I prepared a report and sent a letter to my senator expressing appreciation for having the opportunity to fight evil according to my conscience. He read the letter in the Senate chambers, saying, "I believe what you and your team have done has been worth more than millions of dollars of U.S. aid."

Two years later I was serving as a pastor in Oklahoma, and also as part of a team conducting predraft boot camps teaching seventeen-year-old conscientious objectors how to fight God's way. At the same time, a man named Jim Smith ran for Congress in our district and was elected. But on the day of his election, news broke that he was a CO during World War II. The Veterans of Foreign Wars were very upset. They called a meeting to see if they could keep him from getting his seat.

I went and sat in the middle of about 150 veterans. Emotions were running high. About halfway through, I raised my hand to speak. I said, "I consider myself a patriotic American, and I served my country for four years in Taiwan as a conscientious objector." I told them about little baby "America," the thousands of friends we made in the villages and the trophy inscribed, "For helping us fight communism."

"I don't know this Jim Smith," I said, "but I do know that there is another way to fight evil than with a gun. Perhaps Jim Smith also knows of another way. Let's give him a chance." I sat down and all was quiet. You could hear a pin drop. Then, one by one, four or five of those angry veterans got up to say, "This young man has served his country well."

Palmer Becker

A Peacemaker's Journey

In ancient times, there was violence before the Great Peacemaker came, but we had many generations to hand down the wisdoms in the Oral Tradition of story, and we had developed the ability to listen. Because we had listened to the near-silent winds for eons and the subtlest tiny insect calling its mate. And when the Great Peacemaker came, we listened and we heard.

Tandie Mitchell-Firemoon, Ph.D.,
(Assiniboine-Sioux Tribal Member),
From ANCIENT COMMUNION, Guidance from the Ancestors,
"Visions and Stories from the DREAMTIME"

Many generations ago, the Iroquois people lived in a state of perpetual war throughout their homelands in what is now New York state. Even though the Iroquois were the closest of relatives, they were merciless in their battles against each other. The people lived in a state of fear so overwhelming that they refused to leave their palisaded villages without a heavy guard. Hastily planted crops were often left to decay in the tilling fields because

of frequent raids, while ambushes in the nearby forests
prevented the men from hunting, resulting in widespread
starvation. Many Iroquois abandoned their homes, with
some seeking refuge north of Lake Ontario. In one of
these bands of refugees, a very special child was born. The
Iroquois came to know him as Skennenrahowi, which
means "Peacemaker" in the Mohawk language.

When Skennenrahowi grew to be a young man who
stuttered, he informed his family that he was to undertake
the great mission given to him by the Creator: to carry the
Great Law of Peace to all Iroquois people. He was to
return to Iroquois territory with a message of hope that
would end warfare among the People of the Longhouse:
the five Iroquois bands of Mohawks, Oneidas, Onondagas,
Cayugas and Senecas. He departed from the Bay of
Quinte in a canoe he had built, crossing broad Lake
Ontario like a great bolt of lightning. Once he reached the
eastern shore of the lake, he encountered two hunters and
told them that a new day would arrive when warfare
among the Iroquois would end.

He began his travels, soon entering Seneca territory,
where he encountered a powerful female leader named
Jikonsahseh. Through reason and his good mind, he persuaded her to embrace the Great Law of Peace. In return
for her conversion, Skennenrahowi established the role of
clan mother, which gave Iroquois women political and
social power without parallel in the world.

Skennenrahowi made his way east where he met
Aiionwatha (Hiawatha), a leader of the Onondaga Nation.
Aiionwatha, a great orator, was also convinced to accept
the Great Law by becoming Skennenrahowi's principal
disciple. Others were alarmed by the new way, including
another Onondaga leader, Tadodaho, a severely deformed
man who was known for his treachery. Tadodaho decided
to break the spirit of Aiionwatha by having the peace

advocate's seven daughters killed. It is said Aiionwatha's grief over their death was so great that it caused the animals to flee before him.

After wandering mindlessly for days, Aiionwatha came to a small lake. Aiionwatha picked up snail shells that he made into a string, declaring that he would only heal when someone took the string and spoke the words of condolence that he needed to hear. Those words were stuttered by Skennenrahowi, the Peacemaker. With the shells he collected, Aiionwatha developed wampum, a sacred memory device subsequently used to record Iroquois history, which includes their Great Law of Peace.

Relieved of his sorrow, Aiionwatha renewed his efforts to convince the Iroquois to abandon warfare and accept the Great Law of Peace. Gradually, working with Skennenrahowi, the Mohawks, Oneidas, Cayugas and Senecas were persuaded to join together in a league of peaceful People of the Longhouse. Only the Onondagas remained apart since they were under the firm control of Tadodaho. To convince the sorcerer of the power of the Great Law, Skennenrahowi brought together the leaders of the new league to the western shores of Onondaga Lake. Joining together, and with everyone singing a song of peace, they set out in their canoes to challenge Tadodaho. He used every power he possessed in attempting to destroy the delegation, only to see them safely reach his shore. Using their most powerful words, Aiionwatha, Jikonsahseh and Skennenrahowi straightened the crooks in Tadodaho's back, thereby bringing about his acceptance of the Great Law of Peace. In recognition of Tadodaho's peaceful leadership, he was made the central speaker for the league.

Now unified, the People of the Longhouse raised a tall eastern white pine next to Onondaga Lake. This tree was to be called the Great Tree of Peace, the branches of which touched the sky for all to see. Its four gleaming roots extended to each sacred direction around the Earth. Skennenrahowi instructed the Iroquois that any individual or nation seeking an end to war may follow the roots to the Great Tree, where they would receive shelter. On top of the Great Tree, he placed a mighty eagle who was to cry out if danger approached the people. Beneath the Great Tree, the leaders of this Confederacy of Iroquois Nations formed a circle by holding hands, pledging to uphold the Great Law of Peace. Thus, the world's first "united nations" in North America was created by the Iroquois People to promote freedom, liberate mankind from the horrors of war and secure world peace.

Subsequently, the unity of the league inspired the Founding Fathers of the new United States, who saw the Iroquois demonstrate their unity with a bundle of arrows that cannot be broken as a collective. Today, the eagle that sits atop the tree of peace is depicted holding the bundle of arrows on the currency of the United States of America.

Joanne Shenandoah

The Boy Who Believed in Peace Through Love

In a small village of northern New Mexico lived a culturally rich boy with the jet-black eyes of his Latina mother and the drawling speech of his Texas-born dad. Every summer, the boy went over mesas and mountains to his grandmother's home, where he was always captivated by the uniformed pictures of his uncles and his older cousin hanging next to the pictures of the pope, Jesus, the Virgin Mary, President John F. Kennedy and the American flag. He expected that he, too, would go off to war one day and thought about how proud he'd be to have his picture hanging alongside the other pictures on his grandmother's special wall.

The boy was torn by his mixed heritage. During his rocky adolescence, there were gang fights between the Latinos and Anglos in his village. With the last name of Alexander, he hung out with a rough Anglo-cowboy crowd. As a young teen, he began riding bulls, smoking cigarettes and drinking beer. Before long, he was ditching school and stealing to be cool and feel like part of the crowd.

When the boy was fifteen, two men—one from South

Africa and one from Switzerland—came to his high school. The men were representatives of an organization called Moral Rearmament, and they professed their organization's philosophy: that all races and creeds could live peacefully together if they practiced absolute moral standards. The men spoke of the organization's four moral absolutes: honesty, purity, selflessness and love. They were in his town to raise funds to recruit boys from the surrounding pueblos and from his village to join Moral Rearmament. The boy knew he wanted to be a part of this group: He had gone alone to the top of a mountain and heard a voice speak to him. When he came down from that mountain, it was with a changed heart. He confessed to everyone from whom he had stolen and worked extra hours on his paper route to earn the money to pay his debts. He was invited to travel with Moral Rearmament and obtain his high-school diploma through correspondence courses.

The boy packed his bags and spent the next few years traveling throughout Asia, Africa, Europe and America. He lived with families of all nations, learned their customs, ate their food—and shared his dream of world peace. He lived devoutly by the organization's four moral absolutes, with the conviction that all people, no matter what their religion, color or position in life, could live together in peace.

The boy's eighteenth birthday was approaching, and he knew it was his responsibility to register for the draft. His nation was at war, far away, in a country called Vietnam. The boy could not imagine killing another human being, so he registered at the American Embassy in the Belgian Congo as a conscientious objector (CO). He received notification from his local draft board that his CO status had been denied and that he was eligible for the draft. The boy spent the next eighteen months appealing his draft status. He explained his commitment to the four moral absolutes and his mission of world peace. When the draft board asked if he was a Quaker or a Seventh-Day Adventist, the boy replied, "No, I just believe that if you love people, you do not kill people." The interviewer said that the boy either would be prosecuted as a draft dodger or allowed to serve in the military as a CO.

The boy was shipped off to basic training at Fort Ord, where he was harassed for many months. Time after time, his records stating that he was a CO were lost. Time after time, he was beaten for not carrying a rifle in military drills. But the boy held fast to his conviction that killing was wrong. He was trained as a medic and later received orders that he was being sent to Vietnam.

The boy found himself in a strange land, in the middle of a killing field.

A sergeant asked him, "Where is your weapon?"

The boy replied, "I am a CO, and I refuse to carry a weapon."

The boy spent the next year in constant fear as he nursed the wounded in a war without end. He carried a shovel and a hundred-pound backpack through the dense jungle of Vietnam—but he never did carry a rifle. He knew that if he carried a rifle, he would end up killing someone; now, more than ever, he knew that killing was wrong. Too many boys had died in his arms as he tried to stabilize them long enough for a chopper to MEDEVAC them to the rear. Once, in a moment that the boy would relive in incessantly recurring nightmares, he had looked a wounded grunt right in the eye, and the dying grunt's eyes said, "Tell me why, Doc; you just tell me why!" All his comrades called the boy "Doc," confiding in him and trusting him with the treasures of their hearts. In turn, they protected the boy with their very own lives.

The boy's time in Vietnam grew short. Each day, the boy prayed that he would live to see his family and friends again. At last, the day came when the boy took the

"Freedom Bird" back to the "World." The boy, so happy to be alive, also grew confused. There were no parades to greet him, no welcome-home banners in his town. Most people were not even aware that he had risked his life saving those of many others in the jungle of Vietnam. Already heart-wounded by the atrocities of war, the boy felt rejected by his own country. He returned to the mountains of his childhood and went on solitary hikes for weeks at a time with only his dog for companionship. He felt comfortable only when alone in his mesas and mountains and sleeping on the ground.

Finally, one day, the boy cried and cried until it seemed he had no tears left to cry. Then he drove over the mountains to his grandmother's house. A tiny old *abuelita* greeted him at the front door, face covered with happy tears. *"Mi 'jito, ay, mi 'jito* [My little one], I have prayed so hard for your safe return." The boy hugged his grandmother tightly, as a final tear coursed down his cheek. He saw the picture of himself in uniform on the wall of honor, right in the midst of the pictures of Jesus, the pope, the Virgin Mary, President Kennedy and the American flag.

The boy went on to medical school and became the most trusted doctor in his town. He now works endless hours as a small-town family-practice doctor who is once again known as "Doc." While he does not claim to have all the answers, honesty, purity, selflessness and love still radiate from his being. He is fair to people of all backgrounds and religions in his practice, and is the doctor requested to attend both those entering this world and those leaving it.

The boy, Dr. Lonnie David Alexander, is the boy I married at twenty-one, the man who fathered my son and daughter, and the doctor and friend I want holding my hand when I leave this world.

Karen Alexander

The Spirit War Can't Destroy

If we cannot end our differences, at least we can help make the world safe for diversity; for, in the final analysis, our most basic common link is that we all inhabit this small planet. We all breathe the same air. We all cherish our children's future. And we are all mortal.

President John F. Kennedy

Until I was twelve years old, I lived a life of luxury in Sarajevo, the beautiful city that hosted the Winter Olympics in 1984 and the capital of Bosnia-Herzegovina. Our city was filled with trees and flowers and kind people everywhere. We had music and art. And everywhere we looked, we saw the majesty of the mountains all around the city. Sarajevo was perfect to me in every way.

But everything changed on April 5, 1992. That was the day that prejudice and intolerance exploded into bullets and grenades. And for four years, our lives were torn apart by war. My Sarajevo and my childhood were savagely ripped from my grasp. That was the day when hatred poured into our city, when people who had been living together for years in peace could no longer get along. That was the day a minority group of Orthodox Serbs decided that Muslims, like my family, could no longer coexist in peace with them.

I woke up that morning, just like every other day, and walked into the dining room before school. The minute I saw my parents' faces, I knew something was very wrong.

"Nadja, we're sorry, but you won't be going to school today," they said. "Barricades are being set up in the city. The gates are being closed. It's not safe to go outside." Those were the only words they spoke, but their faces said even more—much more.

In those first few weeks, I believed the craziness would end soon. I believed the men with their ski masks and guns would just go away. I believed the sound of gunfire, the terrifying trips to the safety of our cold, moldy basement, the blood I saw in the street with my own eyes would all end soon. But after months, then years, filled with smoke and blood, I felt it would never end.

Before the war, I would have been so happy to have a day without school—just like any child. But when the war started, all I wanted was the normal life of going to school with my friends, seeing my beloved teachers and learning so many wonderful things. Some days, a teacher would volunteer her time to meet with us in the stairwells in the apartment buildings. On other days, we would all risk our lives—teachers and students—to meet together in a small room in a building not far from the school. I didn't want to fall behind the other children of Europe just because of the war. I studied Bosnian, English, French, geography, math, chemistry—and anything else I could get my hands on. I lived through the books I read and the things I learned. That's how I nourished my inner life.

In July 1995, God answered some of my prayers. In response to a letter my mother wrote to the Bosnian

Humanitarian Organization in Croatia, we heard that an American family was willing to host me in their home so I could continue my education. I was endlessly happy. Even knowing that it meant tearing myself from my beloved family, I knew I had to go.

The night my mother and I left for Croatia so that I could take the flight to America, we made our way to the tunnel, the only exit from Sarajevo. I was so torn between my desire to leave the war and my need to stay with my family. How could I go? How could I stay?

As we walked toward the tunnel, grenades were falling about twenty yards from us. And every time the sky lit up, I saw the misery on the faces of the people in line. We were all so frightened, all so tired. The tunnel was dank and narrow, less than five feet high; even children had to stoop to walk through. Mud and water dripped from above, and the whole tunnel smelled of urine. It seemed that we walked forever. Some people passed out as a result of sheer exhaustion or lack of air—or both—and others would pick up the unconscious ones and carry them. A couple of times, I started crying. Then my mother would say, "Remember, Nadja! Remember your dream!" At the end of the tunnel, we walked silently in foot-deep mud. All around us, bombs were exploding, and we knew the snipers could see us. That walk was the longest of my life. Every time a shell exploded, I turned to see if my mother was still alive. And she whispered to me, "Keep walking! Keep walking!"

Two days later, I had to kiss my mother good-bye in Croatia as I boarded the plane to the United States. I arrived in the lap of peace at the home of my host family, the Yeagers in Cincinnati. I was heartsick for my homeland and my family, but the possibilities for my future were in America. The Yeagers loved me, taught me and gave me a chance to live. In America, life has been relatively easy.

I can feel how easy it would be for me to fall into complacency, to take this freedom and this beautiful country for granted. But instead of just living for the easy-going present, I choose to face the past. I choose to speak out about what happened in my country. I choose to speak out about what happens to children when intolerance is allowed to grow until it explodes.

To make sense of my suffering—and the suffering of so many thousands of others—I take the responsibility of learning from the past. And I take the responsibility of teaching others. I speak to schoolchildren about what happens when we don't respect each other's religions. I speak to youth groups and scouting groups about what happened to children their own age in my country not all that long ago. I speak to adults at seminars and organization meetings.

And I find that the children I speak to are anxious to hear this message. They listen and ask many interesting questions. "Does it hurt for you to talk about this to us now?" "Which did you miss more—ice cream or electricity?" And, as children, they always want to know who won the war. I tell them there were no winners. There were—and are—only losers. Everyone loses so much. Children, especially.

But when they press me on it, which they always do, and want to know who won the war, I tell them, "If you really want to know, I will say that we are the winners. The winners are the people who survived and are still not bitter or hostile in the face of intolerance."

I ask myself sometimes why God kept me alive. Why me, when so many others died? To answer that question, I choose to take the responsibility of living for all those who did not live. When I see a beautiful sunrise or the waves in the ocean, when I hear a bird singing its heart song, I pay attention. I pay attention to life for myself. And

I pay attention on behalf of the boy who lay in his mother's arms while I watched his tiny bloody shoelaces swing back and forth as she ran. I listen on behalf of the woman who was murdered in the street while I watched, while she tried to buy bread for her children. I pay attention to the beauty of this world for all the children of my land who will never again see it.

It is painful for me to remember the horrors of my childhood. But if I can help other people understand the importance of love and life, and the need to turn away from the dark natures we all carry within, then my wounds will heal. Then the spirit that war can never destroy will live on forever.

Nadja Halilbegovich
Excerpted from The Courage to Give
by Jackie Waldman with Janis Leibs Dworks

A Beginning

Especially important it is to realize that there can be no assured peace and tranquility for any one nation except as it is achieved for all. So long as want, frustration and a sense of injustice prevail among significant sections of the Earth, no other section can be wholly released from fear.

President Dwight D. Eisenhower

When I assumed the presidency of Costa Rica in 1986, Central America was being ripped apart by three civil wars. Marxist guerrillas were fighting repressive militaries in El Salvador and Guatemala, while the Marxist/Leninist Sandinista government of Nicaragua was under attack by counterrevolutionary rebels. Honduras was being used as a military training ground, and Costa Rica was also under pressure, mainly from U.S. government officials, to become involved in the Nicaraguan conflict on the side of the Contra rebels.

Even though Costa Rica was not at war, we could not escape the consequences of the conflicts going on around

us. Many in Costa Rica were advocating lining up with
the Contras to defeat the Sandinistas, and our declared
neutrality had already been breached by armed groups
staging attacks along our border with Nicaragua. I also
worried about the health of our economy, for I knew that
very few international tourists or investors would want to
come to a country located in a region undergoing major
armed conflicts. Therefore, Costa Rica's well-being as a
nation—economic, social, even spiritual—depended on
pacifying the entire region. From the day of my election,
that was what I set out to do.

The road to getting a peace agreement signed by all the
Central American presidents was filled with potholes.
After I drafted my peace plan, which asked for democracy
as a precondition for lasting peace in the region, I traveled
to the other countries of the region to "sell" it to my fellow
presidents. When I met with the president of El Salvador,
I found that it was not he, but the military officers, who
knew all the details of the plan; at that moment, I realized
that the military there would have the final vote on
whether to accept any plan for peace. In my meeting with
the Sandinista government of Nicaragua, I found that
they were against my "pro-Yankee" peace plan. The fact
that they called it "pro-Yankee" let me know that they had
not even read it, since one of the stipulations of the plan
was an end to outside intervention in the region.
Representatives of the U.S. government were so opposed
to my initiative that they attempted to pressure my colleagues into rejecting the plan. Such was the meddling
that at one of the meetings of the Central American presidents (all Spanish-speaking nations), the government of
Honduras presented an alternative peace plan that was
written in English. This was obviously a plant from officials in Washington, D.C., who had an interest in maintaining support for the Nicaraguan Contras until a

military victory could be achieved, and therefore, an interest in derailing my peace plan. Neither the U.S. nor the Honduran officials had even bothered to translate into Spanish their alternative plan for peace in Central America.

Faced with so many obstacles, how did we succeed? Mainly through perseverance, an essential quality in any negotiation. I made visits and numerous phone calls to all my fellow presidents in the region, allowing my stubbornness to become my greatest asset while I persevered until they agreed to sign the plan. Of course, a measure of compromise and humility was also necessary. Although difficult, I accepted changes to the plan that would make it more palatable to the Salvadoran generals, for instance, or to others who had difficulty with one or another of its provisions.

In the end, we signed the Procedure for a Firm and Lasting Peace in Central America on August 7, 1987. This, of course, was not the end, but rather the beginning of the pacification of the region. The cease-fires stipulated in the plan were not easy to achieve. Each country at war had to come up with its own internal peace accords, and the last of these was signed in Guatemala in 1996. My colleagues and I had taken only the first, but very necessary, step: agreeing that, in order to have lasting peace, our societies must put democracy into practice.

For me, one unforgettable image encapsulates the motivation behind these efforts: that of an indigenous woman who was standing in the crowd that day in Guatemala City, her hair braided, her feet bare, holding her child to her breast. She caught my eye on the way into the National Cathedral for a Mass of thanksgiving after the signing of the plan, and when we came back out and crossed the plaza in the opposite direction, there she was again. She approached me and said, "Thank you, *Señor*

Presidente, for this son and for the one who is fighting." Although there was still much to be done to make our agreement a reality, at that moment, I knew that something new, something positive, something irreversible had begun—and that the remainder of its course would somehow be determined by the people whom this woman and her two sons represented.

Oscar Arias, Ph.D.
Former president of Costa Rica and 1987 Nobel Peace laureate

"I was cooperating with both parties on the peace
initiative bill, and for that, I've been diagnosed
as having bipartisan disorder."

Christian Snyder ©2001.

Not to Bow to Coercion

Courage is not the absence of fear, but rather the judgement that something else is more important than fear.

Ambrose Redmoon

During the days of the Tet Offensive, when fighting raged in the streets of Saigon, people were asked not to leave their homes unless absolutely necessary. People were glued to their radios listening to the latest news. Suddenly, I heard the minister of education on the radio calling "the seventy-one university professors who had signed a petition for peace on January 16, 1968" to come to the ministry "for an urgent national matter."

Then the speaker read all seventy-one names, including mine, not just once, but every half hour. My family urged me not to go, fearing that I would be shot. We had just seen on television Colonel Nguyen Ngoc Loan shooting a guerrilla he had caught. I was very afraid, but I thought that, since the petition had been my idea, I had to take full responsibility and go. If I didn't, it could be all the worse for the others.

Only twenty-one of us came to the Ministry of Education at the time announced on the radio. The minister told us that the National Police suspected we had plotted the Tet Offensive with the communists. He said he wanted to protect us, and that we only needed to retract our peace appeal and sign a new petition condemning the communists. Eighteen professors signed the new petition, hoping to avoid trouble during these tumultuous times. But Father Nguyen Ngoc Lan, professor Chau Tam Luan and I refused. We said that we could not sign the ministry's petition because our students had heard our names mentioned every half hour on the governmental radio and now would hear the same names on the radio for signing this new petition. It would be clear that we had succumbed to the government's pressure to sign. Later, outside the ministry, however, we did offer to draft another petition condemning the violation of the Tet cease-fire.

By refusing to sign the ministry's petition, I was certain I would go to jail. At that meeting, I told my colleagues, "The most important gift a teacher can give his students is dignity. We have always tried our best to be worthy of our students' trust. If we die under violence, our spirits will blossom in their hearts. But if we sign the petition offered by the government today, it means we have submitted to the government's threats. This is not what we want to teach the younger generation." After that meeting, we were all released, but I suspected the matter was not yet over.

When I returned home, I packed my toothbrush, pajamas and a light sweater, so I would be ready to go to jail when the police came. Instead, I received an invitation from the minister of education to come to his office. When I arrived, he said, "You have refused to retract your declaration. I am very busy, but the chief of police has asked me to settle this matter. If you still refuse to retract, I will have to inform the police, and you will be arrested immediately and relieved of your post at the university."

I breathed deeply and said in a very firm voice, "Sir, I came to you today because I know that you were once a professor, my elder brother in teaching. When you speak in such a threatening way, it is impossible for us to have real communication. So do what you want with me. Please send me to jail. If I allow you to coerce me as you suggest, I would be no better than Colonel Lieu, the cherished comrade of President Thieu, who, as soon as he was arrested by the communists in Ben Tre, called upon all South Vietnamese soldiers to join the side of the North."

With tears in my eyes, I continued more gently, "Sir, I am like a bamboo shoot among university teachers. I am young, but my spirit may grow strong and beautiful. I spoke out frankly about the situation of the country, not for my own sake, but for the sake of the nation, even though prison may await me as a result. I appeal to your conscience as an elder brother to help me grow in this attitude, not to bow before coercion. Don't force me to go against my conscience. If I agree to sign your petition under threat of violence, then tonight if unknown men enter my house with guns and force me to sign a petition saying, 'Long live Mao Tse-Tung,' must I not also sign that? If I sign under the threat of guns against my conscience and belief, who will be at fault? Do you really want to teach me that way of coercion?"

He seemed embarrassed, and his attitude changed immediately. He said that I had misunderstood him, that he only wanted to protect me. Then he let me go without signing anything, and apparently, protected me from the police; they never came to arrest me.

Sister Chân Không
reprinted from Learning to Love

Keep Them Alive!

When people recognize that their actions can matter, they nurture a faith that the work of healing the world is worth doing, whether or not they see immediate results.

Paul Rogat Loeb, in "Soul of a Citizen

I had just started a sabbatical in 1989 when some friends came to me with an idea: "A sabbatical is for doing something different, right?" they said.

"That's true," I replied warily, wondering what they had in mind.

"We're opening a new project in Sri Lanka, and we'd like you to be on the first team."

In Sri Lanka, they explained, courageous lawyers were being assassinated for taking on human-rights cases. Small groups of armed men were taking out lawyers who were defending civil liberties in a country where government repression was increasing.

"What do you want me to do?" I asked.

"We're putting together a team of internationals to go to Sri Lanka and hang out with threatened lawyers, to give some protection. You'll be an unarmed bodyguard."

Well, that certainly would be different! I hardly knew anything about Sri Lanka except that it is a gorgeous island nation just south of India and had been embroiled in a raging civil war for years. I knew that thousands had been killed, but I didn't know that hit squads connected with the military were terrorizing human-rights activists. This was 1989, and there was no end in sight. How could a good solution be found if the country was killing off people who cared for human rights and democracy?

I decided to go.

Another friend, who happened to be a civil-liberties lawyer, and whom I thought would understand and support me, challenged my decision. "This is a suicide mission, George," David insisted. "Why should those thugs hesitate to kill you along with the Sri Lankans you're supposedly protecting?"

"Because they would create an international incident," I countered. "It's one thing to kill a Sri Lankan activist; it's quite another to kill an American or European. The other members of the team are from England and Spain. The hit squads are controlled by the government, and the government doesn't want to get in trouble with the international community. Sri Lanka gets foreign aid and doesn't want to look bad to democratic countries."

"Well," David said, "at least let me buy you a gun to protect yourself."

"But this is a nonviolent thing," I protested. "The team is sent by Peace Brigades International, and in PBI's experience, what works is for the bodyguards to be completely nonviolent."

David was completely skeptical. "Where else have they done this?"

"In El Salvador and Guatemala—and you know what those governments are like! They've killed their own people at a greater rate than happens in Sri Lanka. But PBI has been there for years doing protective accompaniment, and it's worked: They've kept alive a lot of people, including activist mothers of those who have disappeared."

"And no PBI people were killed?" David asked, still skeptical.

"Two were knifed, and their project house was bombed, but no one was killed."

"Look," David said, not really backing down, "if you won't carry a gun, I'll get you a bulletproof vest. You've got to have something."

"I do have something, David: my vulnerability. It's like the civil-rights movement taught us in this country. Sometimes it's our vulnerability itself that gives us power. But it is true," I conceded, "that we can't know for sure whether protective accompaniment will work in Sri Lanka because PBI's trying it out there for the first time. But I'm going to join the team and give it a try."

Maybe I showed more confidence to David than I felt inside because on the plane to Sri Lanka I was sweating. This might be the most difficult thing I'd ever done. What I didn't realize on the plane was that this mission would be like some military combat missions—alternating states of adrenaline and boredom. The main thing turned out to be to put one foot down after the other.

Our first lawyer lived in Colombo, Sri Lanka's capital city. He lived an underground life, sleeping in a different house every night to stay alive. His problem was that he couldn't come to his office to meet clients because the office was in an unsafe place. My teammates and I spent hours in his outer waiting room while he was in his office, so that if the armed men came to get him, they would see us first. I was amazed by his courage and that of the others we met who could have gone into exile but chose instead to fight for democracy.

Our second lawyer lived in Kandy, a smaller city where lawyers' offices were all clustered together in the center of the town, a fairly safe place. The lawyers who had been assassinated in Kandy were attacked in their homes. The pattern was that the doorbell would ring in the evening after curfew, the lawyer would go to the door expecting a distraught parent wanting help for a son who'd been arrested, and the lawyer would open the door only to be gunned down in his own entryway.

My job: to sleep in his house and answer the door when the doorbell rang after curfew.

Although my own assignment with the team in Sri Lanka was for three months, PBI remained in that country for a decade, accompanying lawyers, labor leaders, monks and other human-rights activists. Although hit squads remained active throughout that period, not one of the threatened activists protected by PBI was killed.

PBI went on to be nominated for the Nobel Peace Prize for its work. And I hold precious those memories from a time when I helped keep alive some of the most courageous people I've ever known.

George Lakey

Don't Just Do Something— Stand There!

I'm going to stand up, and I'm going to ask why, And if sometime they come for me, I hope there's someone standing by my side.
                    Michael Stern, in the song "Stand Up"

Let me tell you a true story about something that happened last summer when I went into my neighborhood post office. Besides me, there were three other men and a little girl waiting in line. The first man was about my size. The second in line was very big, at least a head taller than me (and also bigger around). I was next. Last was a man with his little girl. He had a colorful little cap on his head, which distinguished his ethnicity and his religion from the other men. He was quite a bit smaller than me, which made him much, much smaller than the guy ahead of me.

This last man was still getting his package ready, so he reached onto some shelves next to the line to get some labels or forms. And then, out of the blue, the big guy started yelling and swearing at the smaller man. He came right up close and leaned over him, saying, "I don't like you coming in here and getting in my way." The smaller man said, "I was just getting something, and please stop swearing in front of my little girl," but the big man just yelled louder and looked like he was going to start hitting.

Now, at my age I don't like to get into trouble, especially when it might be dangerous for me. And besides, I was just hurrying in there to mail off some of my inspirational CDs about helping others, so I really didn't feel I had the time to deal with this right now. I didn't know exactly what to do and, to be honest, I was scared. But it seemed like I had to do something. Without any more time to think, I squeezed between the two of them (which surprised them both) and simply said, "I'm just going to stand here."

Can you guess what happened next? The big guy started yelling at me instead of the smaller guy. But you know what? That first guy in line in front of the big guy then turned around and said in a calm voice, "Why don't you just be quiet? Nobody did anything to you."

Now the big guy seemed confused about which of the three of us he wanted to bully the most. And the most amazing phenomenon happened—he didn't seem quite so big anymore. Instead of yelling at any one of us, he just muttered and mumbled and swore—at no one in particular—until he left the post office.

Now, I thought about this whole thing for a long time and, of course, wrote a song about it. I could hardly believe that someone with so much hatred was right there in my own neighborhood. I thought about that little girl and how wide her eyes were as she watched what was happening. I wondered if I could have done something differently or what else might have happened with someone that crazy. But one thing became clear to me: I knew how I would have felt if I hadn't done anything.

Michael Stern

The Dress

The security clerk pretended to check tickets on the dress rack nearest the door. Her eyes carefully scanned a woman who stood hesitatingly just inside the boutique door. The clerk took a quick mental snapshot—old shoes with run-over heels, a small run in her right stocking, out-of-style leather handbag, crinkly black nylon dress at least fifteen years old and straggly hair. Not the image of this store's usual clientele. She approached the woman, asking the mundane, "May I help you?"

The elderly woman smiled and whispered, "Yes, I need a dress." The surprised security clerk quickly signaled a nearby salesperson who hurried over to the waiting customer. Store policy toward the less desirable was, "Wait on them quickly; get them out of sight."

"How may I help you?" the salesclerk asked. This would only take a moment, and then she could go on her morning break.

"My only granddaughter is getting married. I need a complete outfit for the wedding. I want her to be proud of me. Just tell me what I should wear."

"You mean you want to see a bridal consultant?" the clerk asked incredulously. The woman nodded her head and followed the clerk to a small oval room filled with fancy clothes.

"Why did you bring her in here?" the consultant whispered angrily.

"She wants to be outfitted for a wedding," the clerk said as she laughed and walked away.

The bridal consultant had been a model in her younger years and still affected the haughty look she believed implied sophistication. She asked the woman to sit down at the small desk opposite her and took out a pad and pen.

"First, I must know how much you are prepared to spend," she asked. She was eager to get this over with and might as well cut to the chase.

"I have been saving my money for this outfit ever since their engagement was announced last spring. Annie sent me an airplane ticket so I can spend it all on something nice to wear." Her slightly palsied hand pulled the envelope from her handbag. "I think there is seventy dollars here. You may count it if you like. I can spend it all if need be."

The consultant quickly counted the money. "Actually, there are seventy-two dollars. Perhaps you should visit our basement thrift shop. They have a few dresses for around fifty dollars."

"I went there first. They suggested I come to see you," she said smiling. "They said you would be glad to help me."

(*Oh, that Miriam. She loves a good joke. Wait until I get the chance. I will pay her back for this*, the haughty one thought to herself.)

Just then the elderly woman spotted a powder blue dress on a nearby rack. She stood and walked quickly toward it. Before the consultant could stop her, she held the dress before her in a mirror. "Now, this one I like. It is beautiful, but not too showy." It was a plain dress with a long-sleeved jacket edged with just a touch of matching lace. "I should have matching shoes, of course. I will wear my strand of pearls. Afterward, I will give them to the bride as a wedding present. They belonged to my grandmother. Look, the dress is just my size."

The consultant gulped. She was suddenly feeling a mix of frustration, sympathy and anger. How could she tell this sweet old lady that the price of the dress she wanted was three hundred dollars? Matching shoes would be another seventy-five dollars. Sometimes life just wasn't fair.

A young, beautifully dressed bride-to-be stood nearby watching the scene. She had just picked up the custom veil she had ordered for her own wedding next week. Her family was well-off and had told her to spend whatever she wished on her wedding. She interrupted the consultant before she could speak to the grandmother about the dress.

"Excuse me a moment," she said as she led the consultant aside and whispered. "Let her have the dress, shoes, whatever else she needs. Just add it to my bill. Tell her they are on sale. Just take fifty dollars of her money. That will leave her with a little spending money—and her pride."

"But why?" the consultant asked. "You don't even know her."

"Just call it a wedding present to myself. I never knew either of my grandmothers. As I walk down the aisle, I will think of her and pretend she is my grandmother, too."

Lee Hargus Hunter

6

INSIGHTS AND LESSONS

What are insights and lessons?

Events occur daily in our lives. Some we understand even in the moment they are happening, while others take some time. Insights and lessons are whispers of knowledge that come to us about each event. Sometimes the knowledge comes as a big bang, while, at other times, it can be fleeting.

I am seeking, with grace and ease, the insights and lessons that are assisting me to be a powerful force for change in my life, my family, my community and my world.

Innovation 101

What can one little me or you do?
What can one little person do to help this
*   world go round?*
One can help another one, and together we
*   can get the job done.*

Sally Rogers, in the song
"What Can One Little Person Do?"

When I heard the back screen door bang, I gathered up the stack of unpaid bills I was staring at and tucked them back in the manila folder. My ten-year-old daughter Tiffany rushed in and plunked her backpack down on the table beside me.

"Sorry I forgot and slammed the door again, Mom, but wait till you hear this. We had an assembly and a film about world hunger at school today."

She reached into the cookie jar as I opened the fridge to pour her a glass of milk.

"Do you know that, with a hundred dollars, we can help feed a family of six for a whole year?" she continued with her mouth still full of cookie.

This kind of enthusiasm wasn't typical of my steady-as-she-goes oldest daughter. Something had clearly ignited her imagination.

"So, can we give a hundred dollars, Mom?" she asked, pushing straggly brown bangs out of wide blue eyes.

I opened my mouth to say what I was thinking, what I'd heard throughout my childhood, probably what my parents heard throughout theirs: "We can't afford it." Then something, like an invisible hand on my shoulder, miraculously stopped me.

Suddenly, my thoughts drifted back to words I'd read an hour before. I'd been researching materials for a workshop that I was preparing on the topic of innovation. Mired in background information and possible approaches to take, my mind became a blur. My eyes and spirit grew weary. I took a break and sat down with a cup of Earl Grey tea and a book on prosperity, one I liked to turn to when I needed inspiration. The book reminded me that habits of thinking become beliefs that are more limiting than any force in the world. Like the short chain and stake placed around the ankle of a baby elephant in the circus, by the time it reaches adulthood and could easily break the chain and go free, the elephant has stopped trying. It reminded me of how I stopped asking my parents for things as a kid.

I believe that desire is healthy; indulgence is not. I didn't have the means to indulge my children with many extras, but their minds were another matter. I wanted to lavishly encourage them to use their intelligence and passion to reach for the best life has to offer.

Moving the folder out of sight to the chair on the other side of me, I sat down next to Tiffany, thinking, *I want to support her dreams; I need new words.*

"That's an interesting idea, Tif. I wonder what it would take for us to be able to do that."

Her visionary ten-year-old mind and generous heart went to work on the problem immediately. "How much can we give?" she asked.

I thought back to the argument my new husband Ted and I had the night before. Our bank account was overdrawn—again. I'm a worrier by nature; a saver, not a spender. Our new home had stretched our finances as tight as a rubber band.

Tiffany recognized the look on my face before I realized it was there. The years when I was a single mother had bonded us to the point where I could hide little from my wise daughter.

"Okay, how much do we spend on groceries for the five of us—everything, including juice, snacks, meals out and Ted's glass of wine?"

"Our budget is $150 a week. That usually covers it," I said, feeling the role reversal.

The next night at dinner, a rare silence fell over the table as Tiffany unveiled her plan. She'd enlisted the help of her seven-year-old sister Anna and nine-year-old step-brother Mike.

She began slowly, "Mahatma Gandhi said, 'Live simply that others may simply live.'"

Tiffany explained that by reducing our grocery bill from $150 to $50 for a week, we'd be able to donate $100 to help feed a family in need.

By the end of the meal we'd each signed handwritten contracts prepared by Tiffany, Anna and Mike. We agreed, in writing, to consume no more than $10 each in groceries for the coming week. I insisted we look at the Canada Food Guide to make sure we made healthy choices.

None of us will ever forget that $10 week. We were quite a sight at the Grant Park Safeway in Winnipeg. Two elderly women spoke in hushed tones after Anna wheeled her cart up next to mine as I reached for a dozen eggs.

"Mom, don't get eggs. Go thirds on a jar of peanut butter with Tiffy and me."

I half expected someone from Family Services to be waiting for me when we left the store. At the checkout the five of us lined up like ducks in a row with our carts of carefully planned purchases, each clutching a $10 bill.

I hoped to lose a few pounds that week as a bonus. It didn't happen. None of us lost an ounce. The image that's etched most clearly in my mind is our dining-room table at the end of the week, piled high with all the food we'd purchased, but not eaten. Like Jesus' tale of the loaves and fishes, we started out blessing a little and ended up with way more than we needed.

I learned more from my ten-year-old about innovation that day than from all my management experience and research. Tiffany's fresh idea, propelled by a heartfelt vision and passionate commitment, was a powerful creative force—an unchained elephant.

I also learned that whether managing my household food budget or an organization, a vital leadership task is removing fear-based roadblocks and limiting beliefs. Worn-out words, thoughts and actions must give way in order to offer new ideas a path to run on.

I treasure the gift I was given to stop autopilot words like, "We can't afford it," and ask the right question to fan the flames of creativity that gave our family life-enriching new possibilities.

When one of us wants something that may seem impossible, I've come to love the question, "That's an interesting idea. I wonder what it would take to be able to do that?"

Joanne Klassen

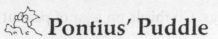

Pontius' Puddle, Joel Kauffman ©2004 Joel Kauffman.

One Cookie at a Time

I expect to pass through this world but once. Any good, therefore, that I can do or any kindness I can show to any fellow creature, let me do it now.

Stephen Grellet

I began baking with my grandma, Edna Boaz, a Church of the Brethren minister's wife, at three years of age. We brought cookies to sick, elderly and lonely people. I noticed that this always made them smile.

In college I baked cookies for the dorm during finals, and I've continued ever since. I usually get up early, pray for the people I'm baking for (even though I may not know who will receive them) and watch the sunrise. People have encouraged me to go into business, but I only get up at 4:00 A.M. for love, not money. A friend pointed out that my cookie "hobby" was really a cookie "ministry." A neighbor crowned me the "Cookie Fairy," and now I have cards that say, "Spread the sweetness of God's love to everyone you meet, a caring ministry to encourage smiles on faces and joy in hearts."

My mission in life is to share love and encourage others to find out what they can do in their everyday life with their gifts and talents to achieve a better world. My husband Harold had our kitchen remodeled to accommodate two ovens. He purchases the ingredients, delivers and assists wherever needed. We call him the "Sugar Daddy."

"Hilarious" is one word to describe a fifty-six-year-old "Cookie Fairy" walking around in a pink and gold princess dress, complete with wings, crown and wand. This has led to many memorable adventures and blessings. I could fill a small book with "Cookie Fairy" stories. Amazing as this may sound, I am very serious about changing our world one cookie at a time. The experience I am about to share with you actually inspired me to create the card that I hand out with every cookie.

I love taking walks at work, and when I set out, I look rather strange. I resemble a cross between Greta Garbo, Annie Oakley and Olive Oyl. I wear a big black hat (Annie Oakley), gold and black sunglasses (Greta "Dahling"), and size 11 shoes that scream Olive Oyl (Popeye's girlfriend).

As I was walking one afternoon, I ran into a group of about twenty high-school students attending a special program at the university. As I briskly approached the group, they started to laugh and ridicule me. I work with youth a lot and I'm a mother, but my face felt hot from embarrassment as they taunted me. Shaken, I reached the sanctuary of the library where I work. For the rest of the day, I couldn't get those young people out of my mind. Suddenly, I realized it wasn't me they were ridiculing. They didn't see me as a person, but a foil for their jokes.

I thought about other people who might walk by and where this kind of hostility could take these students in adult life. Suddenly, they were everyone's children—my children.

Despite my coworkers' protests, I decided to return the next day, and in the same getup. I wanted them to accept me looking a little unusual. My hope was that they would learn to be accepting of others as they are.

As I approached their bus stop, the hoots and whistles were deafening. The girls sat in a huddle and looked a little embarrassed. I waved to the group and said, "Hi, I'm Sylvia, and you really hurt my feelings yesterday. I'm an old lady trying to keep in shape. You should be encouraging me, not putting me down, and you'd better hope that your future wife looks as good at my age." (The girls cheered.) Then I asked if they would be there tomorrow because I would have a surprise for them.

One of the boys yelled, "She's probably bringing a gun."

I replied, "I'd never hurt anyone, especially my new friends."

What kind of surprise did I bring the next day? COOKIES! Two kinds wrapped in individual bags for each person and tied with ribbons. The people at work thought I was nuts. One friend offered to go with me, but I wanted to go alone. This time at the bus stop, the students were very quiet. With a big smile I handed out the cookies and asked their names. I suggested they encourage people and make a difference in the world.

As I walked away, one of the more vocal boys called out, "What's your name again?" I answered him, and he gently said, "Thank you, Sylvia."

Sylvia Boaz Leighton

Their Bullet, My Life

The strongest principle of growth lies in the human choice.

George Eliot

Entering the large assembly room, the motor of my powered wheelchair humming in my ears, I could feel the eyes of every boy, all local gang members, staring at me. I wondered how they would react to my computer-activated voice. Would they listen to what I had to say? Would they understand the violence and pain they were causing? Could I really make a difference?

"Hello, I'm Cruz Carrasco," I began. "As you can see and now hear, I am unable to walk or talk by myself. I wasn't always in this wheelchair, and once I could speak as well as any of you. In fact, up until I was seventeen years old, I lived a life probably very similar to yours. My dream then was to play pro football. I loved it! I started as a sophomore for East L.A.'s Roosevelt High School Rough Riders and was soon their star running back.

"By the time I was in the twelfth grade, UCLA had offered me a full scholarship, and I was ready to take it. I was going to be the first college graduate in my family. I promised my mom I would buy her a big house with a pool when I was a star. And then, without warning, my plans and dreams were literally blown away. I don't remember that day now, so what I am going to tell you is what my family and friends have told me.

"November 4, 1986, was a normal school day. After football practice, I headed home, had dinner with my mom, and then went up to my room to do my homework. I heard one of my football buddies calling to me outside my window. My friends knew Mom couldn't hear them back there. I sneaked out the window to go for a ride with him on his new moped. If I had asked my mom, she wouldn't have let me go. We rode around and stopped to hang out with another football buddy at his house, even though we knew his neighborhood was heavily infested with gangs and drugs. Unfortunately, before we arrived at my friend's house, a bad drug deal had gone down in the neighborhood. Little did I know that this would be the last time I would walk by myself, talk by myself, have normal vision or live the life of my dreams.

"Once the gang realized the cocaine they had bought was really soap, they came back, armed with a .44-caliber Magnum, driving down the street and spraying bullets into the neighborhood. In sheer panic, we started to run for cover. My two friends fell as bullets ripped through their legs. My terror was ended abruptly when a bullet exploded in my head.

"For the next four and a half months, I lay in a coma, machines feeding me and making me breathe. There was not much hope that I would recover. Can you imagine what it was like for me to awaken to the helpless horror of what had become of me?

"The two years after the shooting are a blur to me now. I do know that, throughout the seemingly endless year and a half that followed, I was in rehab; my mother refused to give up on me and vowed to eventually bring me home. Her determination was contagious, and in spite of my suffocating despair, I clung to hope.

"I was nineteen when I finally returned home. I had not become the college football hero I had dreamed I would be. Instead, I was having to start over from infancy, physically. I was filled with grief over the life I had lost. It was agonizing to realize that my friends had all gone to our prom and graduated from high school. Some had gone on to college; some were working; some were living in their own apartments; some were even married with kids. Once home, my mother did what she knew how to do best: She loved me. She enrolled me in a program for disabled adults, and I finished high school. But I still couldn't communicate or move my own wheelchair; I was trapped in my own body. I was filled with anger and frustration. I realized that Mom's love wasn't enough. It was then that Zoe came to work with me.

"Zoe began as my occupational therapist and became first my friend, and then my partner in life. With Zoe, I finally had someone listening to my dreams rather than focusing on my disabilities. Zoe made sure I received the voice-output computer to speak with and the power wheelchair so I could get around independently. Once I realized I could again interact with people, I wanted to find a way to keep what happened to me from happening to anyone else.

"That is why I am here today, eight years after I was shot, to let you know about the effects of the choices you make. Before you make those choices, I hope you will take the time to think about how they will affect your life and the lives of the people around you. They never caught the guys who shot me, although I did learn a most painful truth: One of the men in the car was my best friend from elementary school! I never dreamed that the boy I loved like a brother would take away my life as I knew it. I'm sure he didn't, either. What a cruel result his choices and mine made on my life. While I had been pursuing football, he had joined a gang. I never thought it was cool belonging to a gang, but I did think it was okay to be friends with gang members. I never realized that simply associating with gang members would change my life forever."

I spoke for about fifteen minutes and showed them a video of myself before and after the shooting. When I was finished, they shared with me that they had never met someone who had been affected by gun violence like I had. They knew they had affected a lot of lives through their violence, but they had never seen the true impact of their actions. When we were finished talking, they all came up to shake my hand. I was filled with hope.

A few weeks later, I received letters from some of the boys thanking me for coming and vowing to get out of the gang. Some even said they wanted to look for a more peaceful way of life. I was ecstatic. What had happened to me finally had some meaning. I would never play football, but I could make a difference in young people's lives.

In May 2000, Zoe and I adopted a child. As I see the wonder and hope in my son's eyes, I dream of a future when the only gun violence he will know about is the cause of my disability. I'll never be the same as before, but we all have to be the best we can be. When I look out into the audience during a presentation, I hope that this won't happen to any of them. I beg them, "Please stay away from guns, drugs and gangs. Stop the violence! It is the only way we can all live together in peace."

Cruz Carrasco and Zoe McGrath

From Packin' to Preachin'

There is a destiny that makes us brothers. No one goes his way alone; all that we send into the lives of others comes back into our own.

Edwin Markham

I started running away from home when I was eleven years old. Home was thirteen brothers and sisters, all of whom ran away from our crazy, abusive father by the time they were fourteen. Our mother had been murdered. I was desperate for attention, for a sense of who I was and what I was supposed to be, for a place where I felt safe. The gang found me. They took me in, taught me who I was to be, gave me protection, and filled me with pride and a sense of belonging. What do you have to give the gang in return? You have to give them all of yourself, and you never get it back completely.

The gang became my family for the next seventeen years. It was a family of drugs, guns and jailings, but I belonged, and that was my security. During those seventeen years, nearly fourteen of them were spent in foster homes, jail or prison. When I was twelve, I tried to kill my father. The charge was attempted murder. I was held, without remorse, in the juvenile justice system until I was eighteen. By this time, I was a drug addict.

The next ten years were filled with jailings, carrying guns, not having enough money for my drug habit and constant paranoia. The only women I knew were gang chicks. I knew I would just make more gang members with one of them. I had already gotten a fourteen-year-old girl pregnant when I was eighteen, married her (I didn't want to add statutory rape to my rap sheet), and then couldn't keep the relationship together. My life was going nowhere. I was tired. The gang offered me no way out. I wanted to get away, become a member of the "middle class." I figured I could accomplish this by pushing drugs in a bigger arena. I walked away from the neighborhood. I can never go back. There would be blood if I did. I know where I can go and where I'm not supposed to be.

Though leaving the neighborhood and the gang was not for honorable reasons, it was the first step that was to change my life forever. I was headed for redemption, although it was going to be a long journey. Too soon, I was serving five years in a federal prison for transporting drugs across the border. But when I got out, the first real sign of change happened.

I met some amazing people through a chance encounter. They took me in, and they loved me, unconditionally. I learned what love was about from these two people. They allowed me to call them "Grandma" and "Grandpa" and loved me, just as I was.

I quit the drugs except for Sundays. On Sunday mornings, I smoked a joint and then went to church with Grandma and Grandpa, relaxed and happy. I had no idea where this was all heading. How was I to know that God was not going to leave me alone?

The old ladies in the church knew that I had musical talents. One of them came to me and asked me to lead the morning worship service. I didn't want to, but I would do anything for those old ladies, so I did it. The next Sunday they asked me to lead the worship service again, and then the next Sunday, and the next. I gave up my Sunday joint. It's hard to lead a worship service when you're high!

I still carried a gun, but I was beginning to feel safe. One particular day, I just wasn't paying attention. I was enjoying a walk at the beach with my baby. I was pushing the stroller, head down, when I bumped into another stroller. I looked up into the face of the one man I had vowed to kill. The last time I had seen him, he had pistol-whipped me, hung me from a balcony and left me for dead. Now we stared into each other's eyes, instinctively reaching for our weapons. A bizarre coincidence. Two innocents, a moment away from the shattering blast that would make them fatherless. There was no movement, no sound; even the babies were quiet, as though waiting for a signal. And then a peace came over me. I dropped my hand from my weapon and extended it to the man I had hated. He reached out his hand to mine, and we shook hands. No words were spoken. I have never seen him again.

By this time, a landscaping business I had started was successful, I was still going to church with Grandpa and Grandma, I had put down my gun, and the Lord was still "bothering" me. The church had been without a pastor for months. One day I heard the Lord's voice saying, "I called you, Gilbert." I went to Grandma and Grandpa and said, "I think I'm supposed to be your pastor."

They just smiled at me and said, "What took you so long?"

I've been their pastor for twenty-five years now. Fifteen years ago, we established the Bittersweet Ministries for drug and alcohol rehabilitation. Over three thousand people have gone through the program to date. Our Bittersweet Gospel Band performs all over the country as ambassadors for our programs.

My life had really changed, but I didn't know how much until one night in Chicago. We were there with the band. My friend and I were standing outside the home of our host talking before we went inside. Two guys came up to us and asked what time it was. I looked at my watch and immediately felt a gun on my neck. The other guy was restraining my friend with a knife. I knew I could take the kid, but instead I started telling him that God loved him. His hand began to shake. I reached for his arm, saying, "Look, I'm not going to take the gun, but I'm afraid you're going to shoot someone if you don't stop shaking. I'm a pastor, and I want you to know the Lord loves you." I just kept telling him, "God loves you, son. God loves you." The boy looked into my eyes for a long moment, reached for the money I offered him, and then disappeared into the night with the other kid.

I don't know if his life was changed, but I sure realized at that moment how much mine had! I had been loved into a new life—a life of peace instead of paranoia, happiness instead of heroin, a life of preachin' love instead of packin' death.

Gilbert Romero
As told to Barbara Smythe

Peace at Work

My humanity is bound up in yours, for we can only be human together.

Archbishop Desmond Tutu

Being a consultant to businesses of all shapes and sizes, I have been amazed at how much conflict there can be in the workplace. The accumulated stress and tension of being angry at a boss or coworker take their toll daily, as people quit, are fired, are talked about or have heart attacks—on Monday mornings, especially. For many, the workplace is nothing short of its own kind of war zone, and I have ventured into it, attempting to share tools that will make for peaceful and contented hearts.

One particular event that stands out in my mind took place at a mountain resort on a beautiful snowy day. The executive team of a very large hospital system had gathered in their sweatshirts and blue jeans to address leadership issues and to discuss the year ahead. Before the event started, one of the staff members took me aside and said through clenched teeth, "I just want you to know that I will be resigning on Monday. I've already written my letter of resignation. I just didn't want you to hear about it later and think it was a result of anything that happens here this weekend. I am fed up with that man!" she pronounced, glancing in the direction of the CEO. "And I am not alone, either. He has been terrorizing us since he came on board nine months ago. I'm not going to work in an atmosphere of distrust and tension. My health means more to me than that."

As I was moments away from walking up to the podium, there was nothing I could do but simply listen to her. In that instant, from her words as well as the grim expressions on the faces of the rest of the team, I realized that I had my work cut out for me. *This is going to be one long weekend,* I thought to myself as I silently prayed for guidance.

The principles of teambuilding that I teach and write about are rooted in scripture, and I have been amazed to see how simple principles, put into practice, can bring about great changes in productivity. One of the key principles is *transparency*. Everything hidden will soon be revealed, and people cannot thrive in an atmosphere of secrecy and covert agendas. So I decided to open the meeting with an exercise in transparency.

"Name the thing that you are most afraid of." (When I did this exercise with a group of military leaders, it flopped. Believe me—"flopped" is an understatement. But this time, I really prayed for guidance, and the exercise worked.)

Interestingly enough, the person who most quickly embraced the concept of transparency was none other than the CEO himself. Let's call him "Charles."

Charles stood up, looked around the room at his team, and said, "The thing that terrifies me the most is failure." Every head snapped to attention. Could this be their fearless leader? The man nicknamed "Attila the Hun"? Was this same man admitting vulnerability? He paused for a moment, then said, "I know I've been really rough on you since I came on board, and I guess that is the reason why. I am afraid I will fail." His honesty opened up the group, and one by one, they each began to share their individual fears. By the time the exercise was complete, there were tears in more than a few eyes.

The weekend continued, with people sharing their individual hopes and dreams as well. Bonding can only take place when the rough edges of each snowflake melt together, and that process was happening before my very eyes.

In the final day's exercise, I said, "Right before Jesus left, he prayed to his Father, thanking him for giving him his disciples. He said, 'They were your gifts, and you gave them to me.' I have always been struck by how, at the end of an incredible life, filled with awe-inspiring events, he saw the imperfect, sweaty and still-not-quite-getting-it crew of his as God's gifts to him!" I continued, "I would like each one of you to tell the people seated at your table two things: first, how they have been a gift to this hospital, and, second, how and why they have been a gift to you."

It just so happened that Sheila, the executive who had earlier warned me of her impending resignation, was seated at the CEO's table. To my surprise, he got on his knees and said to her, "Sheila, you are God's gift to this hospital because you are ready to take on any task that comes, and do it with excellence and thoroughness. You have never shirked from responsibility, and you are an example to all of us of someone who truly cares for the patients." He paused, swallowed hard, then said, "And Sheila, you have been a gift to me because, no matter what was going on, or how upset I got with everyone, you always maintained a sense of calm and joy. As soon as you walked into any setting, I knew that light and fairness had come into the situation. I don't suppose I have ever

told you this, but I considered you from the start as one of
my champions, and I do to this day." By this time, Sheila
was reaching for a Kleenex box, as was everyone else at
the table.

He then did the same with each leader there, and they
were speechless in the wake of his words. We then ended
the session with a prayer from the chaplain. There were
hugs all around. As I was gathering up my things and
finally heading out the door to catch my plane, Sheila
came up to me and whispered simply, "I'm staying."

I turned to her and smiled, whispering back, "I know."

Laurie Beth Jones

"This is why our production level is up.
Less stress and more peace and tranquility!"

Christian Snyder ©1997.

Forgiveness Is Not a Legal Matter

What you will do matters. All you need is to do it.

Judy Grahn

"In America we have the right to hate, but not hurt," says Morris Dees, executive director of the Southern Poverty Law Center in Montgomery, Alabama.

But walking that fine line requires more than justice. It takes guts.

In 1971, Dees was determined to continue the work of the civil rights movement. Dees, who grew up in Montgomery, organized a small group of attorneys to serve the underdog: victims of civil rights atrocities and their survivors.

Today, this nonprofit law center, which operates solely on private donations, is internationally known for its legal victories against white-supremacist groups, and for Teaching Tolerance, an extension of the center's educational effort to prevent violence. Armed guards swarm like honeybees outside the Southern Poverty Law Center. Why? Because in 1983, the center was firebombed by members of the Ku Klux Klan. In the guardhouse, we were asked why we wanted to visit the law offices. Generally, tourists come to see the Civil Rights Memorial, which was sponsored by the center in 1989 and is located directly in front of the law building.

Unable to flash a *Sun Newspaper* press card, we simply shared our journey of hope. It worked. Like Dorothy of Oz being welcomed into the Emerald City, we were graciously escorted up the steps and into the contemporary building full of angles and light.

"We monitor the activity of hate groups," said our tour guide, gesturing to a wall map forested with pushpins. "Each pin represents a pocket of 'anti-something' activity in the U.S."

"Look at Ohio," whispered Bruce, rolling his eyes. A cold chill ran down my spine as I counted the pins.

"We publish information about their activity in our magazine, *Intelligence Report*," she said, handing us a copy. On the cover of *Intelligence Report*, a militia group touting a Confederate flag prepared for war. White neo-Nazi skinheads, their right arms raised in a stiff salute, eyes glazed, jaws clenched in rage, veins bulging, were ready to release their venom. I cringed.

That evening, I read several bone-chilling, eye-opening stories. One opened my heart as well: In the spring of 1981, two Klansmen heard on the ten o'clock news that the jury was deadlocked in a case of a black man charged with the murder of a white policeman. Enraged, they decided to kill a black man that night—any black man. Armed with a .22-caliber pistol and a rope tied in a hangman's noose, the two Klansmen—James Knowles, seventeen, and Henry Hayes, twenty-six—drove to a black neighborhood where they found Michael Donald, nineteen. Donald was a masonry student at Carver State Technical College and the youngest son of Beulah Mae Donald. They beat him, cut his throat and hanged him from a tree. Despite the evidence, the district attorney said that neither race nor Klan activity seemed to be factors in the death.

When a thousand blacks marched in protest, Dees stepped into action. As Luke Skywalker wielded his light saber, so did Dees wield his own instrument of justice: the law. Helping Beulah Mae, the Center filed a civil suit against the United Klans of America. Dees changed history: Never before had the Klan been held responsible by a jury for its policy of violence. The force was with them. The multimillion-dollar judgment bankrupted that Klan faction, the first in a series of victories Dees would have over tyrannical hate groups.

However, Dees says the real victory came when Knowles, who plea-bargained and was sentenced to life, asked to make a statement in the civil case: "I've lost my family, and I've got people after me," he said. "I was acting as a Klansman. I hope people learn from my mistake, learn what it cost me."

Then he turned to Beulah Mae and told her that he had nothing to pay her, but if it took the rest of his life to make amends, he would. Sobbing, he asked if she could find it in her heart to forgive him.

She softly said, "I have already forgiven you."

Julie Madsen
Excerpted from InnerViews: Stories on
the Strength of America

[AUTHOR'S NOTE: *Just after the Oklahoma City bombing, my husband Bruce and I sold our belongings, packed up a twenty-six-foot trailer and a pickup truck, and began a "journey of hope" in America. That 150,000-mile journey covered all fifty states. This is one of the ninety-five stories of hope chronicling our adventures.*]

Just That Simple

Six months after the terrible events of September 11, my husband and I went off on a long-anticipated trip to Kenya and Tanzania. We went not only to visit Nairobi and the animal parks but to meet the people of those two nations, learn how they live and get to know our fellow inhabitants of this small planet just a little bit better.

Of course we reveled in seeing so many lions in their homeland, listening to the cries of beautiful birds, watching amazingly tall giraffes ambling along in front of our safari vehicle and falling in love with the little warthogs who stood up to elephant and cape buffalo alike.

But meeting the people of Kenya was the most wonderful treat of all. The houseman at Sweetwater who proclaimed to us that all Kenyans love Americans, the guide who took us to his home to meet his family and give us a gift of Kenyan coffee and the fast talkers who were anxious to sell us anything Kenyan. And of course the noble Masai who lived in clanlike villages carrying on their old ways with the cattle (which is their wealth), and yet abandoning their old nomadic life, as their government encouraged them to do.

We visited a Masai village, which was just a circular

enclave not far from the banks of a river. The houses were round, constructed of dried cattle dung, twigs, wooden poles and thatch for the roofs. The cattle brought home in early evening were left in the center of the circle of houses, but some of the calves were brought into the houses with the people. We were invited into one home, shown how the people lived, cooked, made beer and spent their time. Not one modern amenity. No electricity, radio, television. No music except for their traditional songs and instruments. Lots of red tunics, skirts and shawls since red is a color lions can see.

Masai life was explained to us by John, a young man who spoke English well, having been educated for seven years in the West away from family and village. The entire the clan observed us listening as we observed them. Nowhere on the rest of the trip through Kenya or in Tanzania did we ever get to know people quite so well as the Masai.

Back home again it was time to resume life. In early June, there appeared in *The New York Times* an article about the Masai of another Kenyan village learning about the attack on the World Trade Center nine months after the event. It was a difficult concept for them to understand just how tall the buildings had been since tall was more or less the height of a giraffe or acacia tree. The Masai were saddened by his tale of fire and smoke and brave people trying to save others. Yet they were happy because their student had made it home safely from his visit to New York on that September 11.

Now they wanted to do something to bring peace back to the city and its people, but what? Through careful negotiations and political connections the village presented fourteen head of cattle, a good-sized herd, to William Brancick, the deputy chief of mission of the United States Embassy in Nairobi. This gift of specially blessed cattle represented great wealth and the most significant gift the Masai could give. Mr. Brancick thanked the donors and explained how difficult it would be to transport the cattle to America, but he would gladly accept them, sell them, buy Masai jewelry and present that gift to the American people.

The Masai are a peaceful people whose lives, simply lived, have rhythm and grace. They accepted their government's insistence that they stop slaying lions and develop other means to show that a young man was ready to take a bride. They also learned to settle down to raise their cattle, abandoning their traditional nomadic lifestyle. The description given to them by their returning student had to have shocked them to their very hearts, for if they could change their ways and live in peace among people and animals, there had to be a way for other people of the world to do the same. Just that simple.

Marilyn Savetsky

Nonviolence: The Gentle Persuader

I'll pay 'em back with a blessing—
do the unexpected; I'll return good for evil—
catch 'em by surprise! I'll be creative, not
*   violent—*
use my brains, not my brawn; I'll tap into the
*   connection of their humanity!*

Linda K. Williams, in the song
"Pay 'Em Back with a Blessing"

I had a friend who was not at all convinced of the efficacy of nonviolence, but his wife worked in the office of the Fellowship of Reconciliation in Nyack, New York. She was familiar with the rationale and had discussed it many times with her husband.

One night, the two of them took their daughter into New York City to see a show and for dinner afterward. It was a cold winter night, and two or three inches of snow lay on the streets. My friend suggested that his wife and daughter remain in the warm restaurant while he went for the car. It was late, and there was little traffic. Turning a corner, he saw three men in the middle of the sidewalk between him and his car. Not until he came closer did he begin to suspect that trouble was brewing, for the men spread out across the sidewalk as if to deny him passage.

I'm going to be held up, he said to himself. He thought of turning around and going in the other direction, but he was too close to them by now. He thought to himself, *I wonder if there is anything to what Dorothy has been telling me. And besides, what have I got to lose?* He had almost reached the men, who had spread out their arms to show clearly that they planned to detain him.

When he came within a few feet of the larger man in the center, he spread out his own arms, smiled and greeted the man as a long-lost friend, giving him a tight embrace and slapping him on the back. In the embrace, the man whispered to him, "You stupid SOB! Don't you know this is a stickup? Those other two dudes are apt to kill you. Give me all the money you have."

"I don't have any money," my friend whispered truthfully. "I just ate at a restaurant with my wife and child and paid by credit card. I have eighty-five cents, but I live in Nyack and need fifty cents to get across the George Washington Bridge."

"Dammit!" the man said. "Then give me the thirty-five cents."

George did so, and the three men let him pass without incident.

So does nonviolence work? It certainly did this time, and maybe—just maybe—if it were tried more often, it would work more often.

Glenn Smiley

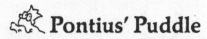

Pontius' Puddle, Joel Kauffman, ©1990, reprinted by permission of Joel Kauffman.

Losing It, Finding It

*Forego your anger for a moment and save
yourself a hundred days of trouble.*

Chinese Proverb

The mall was particularly crowded and noisy that
Sunday afternoon. My son, a very high-energy six-year-
old, pulled us into every toy store to check out the newest
action figures or anything else that caught his eye with
the single-mindedness that only a six-year-old can
muster. My brother was content to be out of the confine-
ment of the depressing facility for adults with retardation
that was then his home. He wanted to talk, drink coffee
and smoke. His goals also included getting some cool sunglasses, but he was generally enjoying just being with the
family. I needed a watch battery and a few other necessities. My grandmother, visiting from Florida, probably
wanted to just sit down and relax and not do the mall
crawl as we plodded on, attempting to meet all our diver-
gent needs. My wife stoically endured as she kept our
human caravan together amidst the crowds. But I was in
charge. The mall excursion had been my idea. I thought it

would give all of us some quality time together. But the only quality that we all seemed to share was that our nerves had begun to be a bit frayed by the strain and tedium of the overall experience.

As we ended the long afternoon and headed for the exit, my son burst between two adults lost in talk, causing them to stop and stare at the little person who had interrupted their conversation. The tension I had been carrying was quickly intensified and found a righteous focus. I didn't snap—I boiled over. As a conscientious father, I chose to stop, confront my son, and demand that he return and apologize to the strangers for his rudeness. I spoke to him in a harsh, judgmental tone. Frozen, he gazed at me, unblinking, in embarrassed silence. I could feel my internal-intensity ratchet tighten as I insisted that he make amends at once to the two people who now stood in silent witness to our confrontation. My wife quietly suggested that we take up the matter later. I flatly stated that this was the time, and mine was the way. I went back to insisting that my son say he was sorry to the strangers. I bore down heavily as his gaze dropped to the floor. My grandmother made a small, worried sound as she frowned and twisted her purse strap nervously. With anxiety, she witnessed her grandson's wrath and her great-grandson's humiliation.

One of the strangers stepped forward, offering that it was okay and no apology was needed. I refused his offer and tersely stated the obvious. I needed, for his own good, to have my son, now shamed in freeze-frame, do the right thing—my way. Scorched by my fiery intensity, the gentle stranger pulled back and helplessly watched the stalemate deepen. A silent gathering of passersby had formed, watching my unbending demand go unheeded. All were silent except for me. I was vaguely aware of the spectacle that I was creating, and the real discomfort and strain that I was causing everyone, particularly my own dear son.

My brother, whose intellectual ability is measured in the early preschool range, stepped silently to my side. He gently put his hand on my back and said to me in a low voice, "Peace, brother, peace." The dark spell was shattered. I reached out and touched my son's shoulder. I looked down and read the emotional wreckage from my anger storm on my child's upturned face. In a trembling voice, I told him that what he had done was wrong, but that what I was doing was worse. I apologized to the strangers, to my family and, most earnestly, to my son. I took my boy by the hand, and we left the mall.

My brother, like all people, has the capacity for wisdom. Today, he lives in a regular suburban home with two other guys. They receive the support they need and enjoy the pleasures of privacy, quietude and a home with dignity and individual respect. But twenty years ago, when he lived in a crowded, depersonalizing facility, he was a genuine peacemaker and a man of gentle and clear wisdom. He said three words to me that cut through my intellectual and moral conceit and resolved an intractable dilemma that had ensnared many in my anger and self-righteousness.

Jeff Moyer

The Gentle Art of Blessing

Many years ago, I was put into a Catch-22 situation in my work: I was forced to choose between staying at a job I loved—where I had great freedom and felt extremely useful to society—on the condition that I accept something highly unethical, or quit my job. Because I did not wish to commit a moral hara-kiri, I chose to leave.

In the coming months, I developed resentment toward the people who had put me into this situation, especially one man, and it was literally killing me. I felt victimized, and the problem became, in psychological terms, an obsession: I was ruminating over it literally day and night.

Then one day, reading the Sermon on the Mount in the Bible, I had a breakthrough: *Bless those who curse you.* The darkness lifted. Then and there, I started blessing the people who "cursed" me. I blessed them day and night.

Suddenly, a few months later, in the street, I started blessing those around me. I did this in shops, on the train, in parks—everywhere. It became such a vibrant, powerful and beautiful activity that I would walk the whole length of a train just for the sheer joy of blessing people. And a few months later, while preparing a talk on the theme of "Healing the World" for an international youth meeting, the following text came to me in a moment of total inspiration. I felt like a scribe under dictation, and my hand could hardly follow the ideas that flowed into my consciousness.

On awaking, bless this day, for it is already full of unseen good, which your blessings will call forth; for to bless is to acknowledge the unlimited good that is embedded in the very texture of the universe and awaiting each and all.

On passing people in the street, on the bus, in places of work and play, bless them. The peace of your blessing will companion them on their way, and the aura of its gentle fragrance will be a light on their path.

On meeting people and talking to them, bless them in their health, their work, their joy, their relationship to the universe, themselves and others. Bless them in their abundance and their finances. Bless them in every conceivable way, for such blessings not only sow seeds of healing, but one day will spring forth as flowers in the waste places of your own life.

As you walk, bless the city in which you live, its government and teachers, its nurses and street sweepers, its children and bankers, its priests and prostitutes. The minute anyone expresses the least aggression or unkindness to you, respond with a blessing. Bless them totally, sincerely, joyfully, for such blessings are a shield that protects you from the ignorance of their misdeed, and deflects the arrow that was aimed at you.

To bless means to wish, unconditionally, total unrestricted good for others and events from the deepest chamber of your heart. It means to hallow, to hold in reverence, to behold with utter awe, that which is always a gift from the Creator. He who is hallowed by your blessing is set aside, consecrated, holy, whole. To bless is yet to invoke divine care upon, to speak or think gratefully for, to confer happiness upon—although we are never the bestower, but simply the joyful witnesses of life's abundance.

To bless all without discrimination of any sort is the ultimate form of giving because those you bless will never know from whence came the sudden ray that burst through the clouds of their skies, and you will rarely be a witness to the sunlight in their lives.

When you pass a hospital, bless its patients in their present wholeness, for even in their suffering, their wholeness awaits in them to be discovered. When your eyes behold a man in tears or seemingly broken by life, bless him in his vitality and joy.

It is impossible to bless and judge at the same time. So hold constantly as a deep, hallowed, intoned thought the desire to bless, for truly then shall you become a peacemaker, and one day you shall behold, everywhere, the very face of God.

P.S. And, of course, above all, do not forget to bless the utterly beautiful person YOU are.

I began to share the text in letters with friends, and the most amazing thing happened: I started receiving letters, phone calls and faxes from all around the world—and later e-mails, when various people started posting the text on the Internet. Typical is this response from Mahmoudou, a peasant leader in West Africa: "I have started to turn blessing into an everyday experience, in all situations. It has become part of my very marrow. And each day, it fills me more and more. May Allah reward you." The Mother Superior of a Catholic convent was so inspired that she made copies for all her nuns. Roger, an inmate on death row in Texas, has been using it. Perla, a woman from the Philippines, e-mailed it to friends all around the world.

People wrote to share the healing impact of the text in various situations. Karen, from Australia, e-mailed recently: "This Gentle Art of Blessing is so beautiful and represents everything that has been held in my heart for years." And days ago I received a touching message from Delice, an Alutiiq [Eskimo] grandmother from Afognak Island in Alaska, sharing her enthusiasm for the text.

It appears that this enthusiasm about the practice of blessing is due to the fact that *it works*! Since discovering the "gentle art" sixteen years ago, I have never been faced with a difficult human relationship, deep anger, resentment or other challenging situations that did not yield to blessing.

Blessing enables one to say YES to every single situation, event and encounter that presents itself in our lives. That does not mean we necessarily approve of the situation—one cannot approve of child abuse, for instance—but that we believe in the healing power of blessing to correct the situation. Blessing is also a wonderful tool to remain open to the present moment—one of the most fundamental spiritual practices that exists, and one that is more sorely needed than ever.

For me, one of the greatest blessings happened three years ago, when I unexpectedly encountered the person who had masterminded the situation for me at the office. We met and had dinner together, and I cannot find words to express the incredible joy, and especially *gratitude*, I felt for the man. This person, whom I had seen as my tormentor and enemy, suddenly appeared as what the universe had always intended: my teacher on the path of greater love.

So, friend, try The Gentle Art of Blessing. And, above all, start by blessing *yourself*, constantly, sincerely and joyfully, for one cannot give to others the good one would withhold from oneself.

Pierre Pradervand

I'm Gonna Write It on the Agenda!

The pen is mightier than the sword.

Edward Bulwer-Lytton

"Theresa, would you rather talk about this now or at the family meeting?" I asked.

"At the family meeting? Dad, give me a break!" she cried. And she stomped into the breakfast room to write "quit piano" on our family meeting agenda. This was all preceded by a mini-explosion as Theresa, then seven, was practicing the piano after school one day. She slammed her hands on the keys and shouted, "I quit!"

I stormed into the room, saying, "You can't quit. It's the beginning of the month, and we've already paid for all four lessons. Besides, my mother let me quit the piano, and I regret it. And furthermore, quitting is irresponsible behavior, and irresponsibility is not tolerated in the McGinnis household!" Suddenly, I heard myself ranting and stopped. That's when I caught my breath and put the question above to Theresa: "Would you rather talk about this now or at the family meeting?"

Thank goodness, at the time of the outburst, our family

had been using this alternative forum for conflict resolution and decision making for about three years. We had found a workable alternative to my authoritarian outbursts, to my need to control family decisions, to the kids' sense of powerlessness. Since friends had introduced us to this decision-making mechanism, it had served us well. Not that we were doing our family meetings "perfectly," whatever that means. And not that we still didn't have outbursts like the one above. But Kathy and I had gotten in touch with our "nonnegotiables" and "bottom lines," and had articulated those to our three children. And now, we as a family had a way of correcting ourselves and mutually working through problems and disagreements.

Our children (now adults) convinced us of the truth of all this on a number of occasions. Perhaps the most memorable example and testimony to the value of family meetings happened when Tom, our oldest, was thirteen. One Sunday afternoon, he informed me that he was putting "cable TV" on the next night's family meeting agenda. When I told him he was wasting his time because we had decided only six months earlier that we couldn't afford cable TV, he said calmly, "Dad, let me worry about that."

The next night at dinner, which is when we had our weekly family meetings, Tom's "cable TV" was first on the agenda. When eleven-year-old David, as leader that night, asked him what he wanted to say about cable TV, Tom pushed his plate aside, stood, gathered some paper from the counter behind him, turned back to us and said, "Twenty-six reasons why our family should get cable TV."

What a shock! No one had ever written out a statement in five years of meetings; no one had ever stood, either. To give a sampling of his twenty-six reasons, he began with, "Mom and Dad, you value family togetherness. If we got cable with one of the movie channels, we could watch more movies together as a family." Next he stated, "You're concerned about the quality of the TV we watch. Well, I've researched the three movie channels and find that most of those X- and R-rated movies you don't like are on the other two channels. I think we should just get HBO. And you're concerned about how we spend our family recreation money. HBO and the works cost $13.90 a month. David, Theresa and I are willing to kick in $6 a month out of our allowances. That leaves $7.90. I'm sure you realize that you go to at least one movie a month and pay $4 each. If you would stay home that evening with your children and watch a cable movie instead, your $8 and our $6 each would mean we could get cable without spending any more family recreation money than we do now." He went on through his list of twenty-six reasons, then he sat down—and stared at Kathy and me.

Kathy looked at me, sitting there somewhat shell-shocked, and asked what I thought. I stammered at first, saying something like I couldn't think of any reason why not. Then David asked if we had a decision. Each one of us said we would be willing to try cable for a few months to see if it would work. Tom, with tears in his eyes, proclaimed, "This is the most emotional day of my life. This morning after the dentist pulled out five teeth, I thought I was going to die at school. But tonight, I've persuaded the family to buy cable TV. This is the most emotional day of my life!"

Kathy and I love to share this story, not because we are convinced of the value of cable TV, but because it convinced us of the power of the process of the family meeting. If a "recovering authoritarian" like me can do it, almost anyone can!

Not only did family meetings offer a corrective for an authoritarian father, it provided an outlet for an impulsive child. Contrary to the impression that family meetings may only work for highly verbal, well-behaved children, both Theresa and David were diagnosed with ADD (Attention Deficit Disorder), David's manifesting itself in volatile impulsivity. As a four-year-old, in the heat of rage, he punched out our dining-room window. At twelve, he destroyed his bike because it wasn't working as he wanted. So when I heard his full-volume outburst coming from the bedroom that he and Tom shared, I raced upstairs hoping to save the second story of our home.

David was storming around their room, cussing out Tom because he had apparently taken one of David's things. "I can't stand living with that *#@%&! I'm so ^%$#@! angry, I'm gonna, gonna, gonna WRITE IT ON THE AGENDA!!!!!!" With that declaration, he stomped downstairs and into the breakfast room where he grabbed a pen and wrote "TOMMY! NOW!" on the family meeting agenda.

David had found a way of dealing with his issues besides punching out a window—or his brother. He was putting the issue on our family meeting agenda and calling for an emergency meeting that night. In our family, writing "NOW" after an item signaled that the person couldn't wait until the next regular family meeting and needed a resolution right away. We were so proud of David for being able to take this approach. Eighteen years later, as a thirty-year-old, David looked back on that episode as a real step forward for his ongoing efforts to channel his anger and impulsivity in constructive ways. I can't help but think how different the news headlines would look today if only all the angry people in our world would . . . could . . . WRITE IT ON THE AGENDA!

James McGinnis, Ph.D.

A Veteran Against War

*The ultimate measure of a man is not where he
stands in moments of comfort and convenience,
but where he stands at times of challenge and
controversy.*

Martin Luther King Jr.

I joined the U.S. Army Air Corps in early 1943. I was
twenty years old and eager to get into combat against the
Nazis. I could not bear to stay out of a war against fascism.
I saw the war as a noble crusade against racial superiority,
militarism, fanatic nationalism and expansionism. Without
my parents' knowledge, I signed up with the air corps.

Before officially becoming an aviation cadet, I had to go
through the four-month basic training of an infantryman
at Jefferson Barracks, Missouri—forced marches with full
field packs and equipment, lots of calisthenics, and learning how to fire pistols, rifles, carbines, submachine guns,
and how to distinguish the smells of poison gases. Then
on to an airfield outside Burlington, Vermont, where I
learned to fly. After that, on to Nashville, Tennessee, for a
whole set of classification exams to decide if I was best

fitted to be a pilot, navigator or bombardier.

I did very well on the math tests for navigator and on the reflex-coordination tests for bombardier, so I wasn't surprised when I was classified as a bombardier, but also scheduled to get some navigation training. We were all put on a troop train headed for preflight training in Santa Ana, California. After Santa Ana, I spent six weeks at a gunnery school outside of Las Vegas, Nevada, then four months in the desert country of Deming, New Mexico, learning all about the famous "hush-hush" Norden bombsight—both in theory and practice. We flew at different altitudes and dropped bombs on little huts set up in the desert. I was good at it, had a low CE (circular error, or number of feet from the target), and graduated from bombing school with the gold bars of a second lieutenant on my shoulders and bombardier's wings pinned on my chest at graduation.

The Allied invasion of Europe—D day—was already under way. I was so anxious to get into combat that, twice in the next months, I traded places with other bombardiers to get on the short list for overseas. Finally landing in England, we were transported to our air base in East Anglia, which bulges eastward toward Holland and Germany. Then it was life in a Quonset hut—sleeping bags, cold water, rationed food—and flying what turned out to be the last missions of the war.

It was not like the movies, with Robert Taylor leaping out of his bed into the cockpit and flying off. It was five hours between waking and the takeoff at dawn. The briefing officer told us about the mission. We were going to bomb a little town named Royan, near Bordeaux, on the Atlantic coast of France. (After the war, I learned that it was a resort town for French vacationers; Picasso swam there.) The explanation: There were a few thousand German soldiers holed up near Royan, waiting for the war to end, and we were to take them out. Each bomb bay would carry something new: thirty one-hundred-pound canisters of "jellied gasoline"—sticky fire. They didn't use the word, and I only realized long after the war that this was an early use of napalm.

So we destroyed the German forces (twelve hundred flying fortresses bombing several thousand German soldiers!)—and also the French population of Royan. After the war, I read a dispatch by the *New York Times* correspondent in the area: "About 350 civilians, dazed or bruised, crawled from the ruins and said the air attacks had been 'such hell as we never believed possible.'"

At our bombing altitudes—twenty-five or thirty thousand feet—we saw no people, heard no screams, saw no blood, no torn limbs. Up there in the sky, I was just "doing my job"—the explanation throughout history of warriors committing atrocities. The war was over three weeks later. I heard no one question that raid on Royan. Why were we killing more people when the war was about to end? I didn't question it either.

After victory in Europe—V-E Day—my crew flew back across the Atlantic in our battered B-17. We had a thirty-day leave before going to the Pacific to take up bombing again: this time, on Japan. We passed a newsstand around which people were gathered, and there was this huge headline: "ATOMIC BOMB DROPPED ON JAPANESE CITY OF HIROSHIMA. WAR'S END EXPECTED." We were simply happy. Now, I wouldn't have to go to the Pacific, and the war would be over—total victory over fascism.

It was John Hersey's postwar report, *Hiroshima*, that first made me aware of the horrors we visited on that city, made me see what we had done to a city of civilians, to old people and to schoolchildren, made me see the Japanese as human beings, not simply a nation of ferocious, cruel warriors. It led me to match the infamous "death march" on Bataan, that Japanese atrocity, with another kind of death march in Hiroshima, this time *our* atrocity, when dazed, burnt civilians—their flesh hanging, their eyeballs out of their sockets, their limbs torn from their bodies—walked in a stupor through the eerie remains of their flattened city under a miasma of radioactive vapor.

In 1966, I traveled to Japan at the invitation of a Japanese peace group. We all met in Hiroshima, rebuilt now except for a few things deliberately left standing to remind people of what had happened. We were invited to a "House of Friendship," a kind of community center for survivors of the bomb. We were expected to say a few words of greeting to the people there, and when it was my turn, I started to say something, but then I looked at the men and women sitting on the floor, their faces turned to me, some without legs, burns on their faces and bodies. My mind flashed back to my work as a bombardier, and I choked up, unable to speak.

Hiroshima and Royan were crucial in my gradual rethinking of what I had once accepted without question: the absolute morality of the war against fascism. There is no war of modern times that has been accepted more universally as just. The fascist enemy was so totally evil as to forbid any questioning. They were undoubtedly the "bad guys," and we were the "good guys," and once that decision was made there seemed no need to *think* about what we were doing. But I had become aware, both from the rethinking of my war experiences and my reading of history, of how the environment of war begins to make one side indistinguishable from the other. I became convinced that the atmosphere of war brutalizes everyone involved, begets a fanaticism in which the original moral factor is buried at the bottom of a heap of atrocities committed by all sides.

War is not inevitable, however persistent it is, however long a history it has in human affairs. It does not come out of some instinctive human need. It is manufactured by political leaders who then must make a tremendous effort—through enticement, propaganda, coercion—to mobilize a normally reluctant population to go to war.

We must look for negotiated solutions, even at the expense of national pride. We must consider human life more important than boundary lines. And we must buy time for the achievement of justice without war.

I see this as the central issue of our time: how to find a substitute for war in human ingenuity, imagination, courage, sacrifice and patience.

Howard Zinn, Ph.D.

If You're Angry and You Know It . . .
Remember Henry!

Anger is like a warning light on your car's dashboard —if you attend to it promptly you're more likely to get where you want to go. Stop, look under your hood and into your heart to find out what needs attention.

Shari Klein and Neill Gibson, in "What's Making you Angry?"

1. I hit myself.
2. I hit my sister.
3. I hit my brother.

I sighed, shook my head and rolled my eyes as I read fourth-grade Henry's answers to our "School Family" activity sheet on "Three Things I Do When I Am Angry." Henry, who often enjoyed being the class clown, had been in rare form that day, and obviously had carried his silliness over into filling out the activity sheet.

So, right before giving our good-bye hugs for the week, I called to Henry in a none-too-pleased tone of voice, "Henry, stick around for a few minutes." With an innocent look on his face—as if he had no idea what he'd done wrong—he shrugged and nodded an okay.

At that point, my disappointment became irritation—the nerve of him! For, during our "School Family" hour just that day, my sixteen kindergarten through fifth-graders had sung and energetically enacted the lyrics to this song:

If you're angry and you know it, **talk it over**—(I'm angry!),
If you're angry and you know it, **talk it over**—(I'm angry!),
If you're angry and you know it, that's okay, you can control it!
If you're angry and you know it, **talk it over**—(I'm angry!).

And we sang and acted out the other verses, too:

Count to ten—*(One, two, three . . .)*,
Stop and think—*(Hmm!)*,
Pound a pillow—*(Whap, whap!)*,
Take a walk—*(Step, step!)*
Just relax—*(Ahh!)*.

We also had a lively discussion of the topic, with eager hands flying in the air, sharing when and why they've been angry, and we brainstormed many additional ways of dealing with that potentially explosive emotion. They were so into it! After hearing all their creative, diverse and effective ways to deal with their anger in positive ways, I looked proudly and lovingly at my kids with a definite lump in my throat, and said, "If only everyone in the world would deal with their anger in the smart, self-disciplined and kind ways that you've all shared here . . . well, we certainly wouldn't see the horrible headlines in the daily newspapers that we do now, would we? And this would be such a better world!"

Yes, the lesson had gone even better than I'd hoped!

And then Henry had to go and spoil the moment for me. He sure had managed to burst my bubble, pretty much obliterating my sense of accomplishment at how beautifully the lesson had gone. Here he was, being disrespectful and a real smart aleck about something he knew darn well I felt passionately about. For heaven's sake, we'd been together for five full years!

So, with the other students now gone, I was face-to-face with Henry and just about to address him with stern admonitions of "When I give the group a written activity like this, I expect your thoughtful, serious responses! No wasting time or paper; no being silly and disrespectful!"

Was I in for a surprise! He looked up at me with a solemn face, utter sincerity in his big brown eyes, and said sadly, "But that's what I really do when I'm angry!"

What a false judgment I had made! I suddenly saw him in a totally different light. Yes, silly though he could be at times, here was a sweet young man willing to share openly with me something that he knew without question I'd view as a BIG problem. I felt honored that he trusted me with his cry for help—and regretted having been so quick to react negatively.

I said, "Henry, I'm really sorry I misjudged you; I had no idea you were being serious with those answers. I want to thank you for your honesty. It's very important to me that you're willing to share this concern with me. I'd really like to talk with you for a few more minutes. I'll send your classroom teacher a note to let her know that I've 'borrowed' you for just a bit—okay?"

With a sigh of relief, Henry responded, "Yes, I *do* need some help!" He actually seemed eager to explore some ways to channel his anger into more positive directions. His cooperative attitude and interest were such a relief for *me*.

Together, we brainstormed some anger-control ideas

on the spot, and I gave him another copy of the activity sheet. Instead of asking for just three options, I added more lines, saying, "You and your family can work on these together. I'm sure they'll be happy to help you try to find different ways to deal with your anger."

"Without beating up on them, huh?" Henry put in, true to his class-clown nature.

We shared a chuckle at that.

Also, I changed the wording to read, "HELPFUL Things I CAN Do When I Am Angry." Henry gave me a hopeful smile before happily heading back to his classroom.

As I watched him leave, I wondered what the result would be. But of one thing I was certain: I would never again sing this song without remembering this crossroads moment with Henry.

On Monday, Henry bounded to my room, beaming with pride as he handed me his newly filled-out sheet:

HELPFUL Things I CAN Do When I Am Angry
- Play soccer
- Play tag
- Watch TV
- Tell my mom and dad what I am mad at
- Talk with my friends on the phone
- Play outside
- Play inside
- Help people

I filled with joy and pride as I read his answers, and the last one melted my heart. From now on, if you're angry and you know it, remember Henry. I sure do, and I always will.

Linda K. Williams

The Rosenstrasse Prison Demonstration

In Berlin, on a gray weekend at the end of February 1943, police and Gestapo swept through the cold streets and arrested the remaining Jews, mostly men, who had been left more or less at large because they were Jews "of Aryan kin" (i.e., married to non-Jewish women or having non-Jewish mothers). As may well be imagined, there was little resistance to the unannounced roundup. Without incident, the arrested men were brought to a large, recently converted building on the Rosenstrasse, a few blocks from a major Gestapo headquarters.

However, the "Jewish Radio," as the still-remaining Jews' informal phone network was called, was buzzing. Within hours, the wives and, in some cases, mothers of the arrested men learned where they had been taken. What then took place was like nothing that had ever happened under Nazi rule. By the following morning, from every part of the city, "as though in answer to a call, as though prearranged," the women converged on the Rosenstrasse detention center, demanding the release of their loved ones. All day, they defied repeated orders to leave. As their numbers swelled to more than six thousand, the prisoners themselves took courage and began clamoring through the barred windows to be released. It was an acutely embarrassing display, especially since Gestapo headquarters was but a few blocks away. One or two machine guns could have swept the street clear of these troublemakers—if violence were the only kind of force in the world.

For many years, this episode provided an answer to the inevitable "it never would have worked against the Nazis," because, in fact, the demonstrations *did* work. They created an impossible dilemma for the regime, and within a few days, the Gestapo, not the women, blinked. By Sunday, the men were free. Some, who had already been deported to concentration camps, were hastily put on trains to Berlin—many so hastily that they couldn't get back their own clothes and were told never to talk about what they had seen there.

Until recently, most people who knew about the episode, even most Germans, thought that the "Aryan-related" sons and husbands were no doubt quietly rearrested later in twos and threes, and this time there was no one to save them. So the demonstration was a spectacular but not a lasting success. It "worked," but it also did not work. It did not have much lasting effect on the whole system. Or so we thought.

Finally, in 1996, a full-length study appeared: *Resistance of the Heart* by Nathan Stoltzfus, documenting what actually happened, not only in Berlin, but also in Paris and other cities that also had the *Mischling* ["mixed-breed"] problem—and where the local headquarters were watching anxiously for guidelines from Berlin. There are fascinating details about the insanity of Nazi logic and the contradictions of violence. The Führer himself refused to make a decision. He, whose "fanatical will," he once boasted, had "rescued the German nation," was paralyzed. Nonviolence paralyzed him.

The big surprise, however, is that virtually everyone snatched back from the jaws of death by their loved ones out in front of the Rosenstrasse detention center survived the war, as did their counterparts in Paris and other European capitals under Nazi control. Tens of thousands of people were rescued by this impromptu demonstration of untrained women who had been living for more than a decade under a regime of authoritarian terror the likes of which the modern world had rarely seen. Nonviolence was almost never tried against the Nazis, but when it was, it scored a resounding victory.

Michael N. Nagler, Ph.D.

Choosing Your Attitude

Some time ago, my family built a large deck and pool, which we happily enjoyed for several years. The pool was set in a private area and had views of the lake and mountains beyond. We had no idea that this pool adversely affected anyone, or that our next-door neighbors loathed this new pool and the resulting activity it brought to our yard. It was not apparent to us until much later that our neighbors felt that their peace and harmony—indeed, their entire quality of life—had been compromised. They never said a word.

We were totally taken aback one day when a huge plywood wall appeared between our homes. The wall was more than 8 feet high and 150 feet long—and strategically placed to block our views of the lake and mountains. All we could see was plywood.

Both my husband and I are negotiators at heart, and it had never occurred to us that we couldn't work things out with people. We called the neighbors and said, "It appears you must be very angry to have built such a wall, so let's try to work this out. Why don't you come over and we'll come up with a solution? We really want you to know that when we built the pool, we had no intention to purposely hurt you. We didn't discuss it with you because we didn't think it would interfere with you in any way."

My neighbor's answer still rings in my ears. "Who cares what you think? You ruined things for us, and we don't want to talk to you."

I got off the phone, visibly shaken. "I don't understand this. Why won't they work with us?" I asked my husband.

His reply was simple, "They're angry. They don't want to work things out; they want revenge. It happens all the time. Solving the problem isn't the only issue anymore. They want to hurt us the way they perceived we hurt them."

After a few more tries, it was clear that negotiation was no longer a possibility, so we considered all the alternatives that people usually consider when they're angry. We thought about all the awful things we could do to get even with them.

It was my fifteen-year-old son who brought us up short, although I like to think we would have come to our senses very soon anyway. "You know," he said, "if we try to get revenge, we are just going to live in the middle of a war. We will do things to them from now on, and they will do things to us. None of us will ever have any peace."

"You're right, of course," I said, and felt myself pulled back to what I hope is my true self. "Let's think about this in a different way."

Our neighbors had made their decision, and now it was time for us to make our own.

So we considered the wall from different perspectives. True, it did block our view, but the most upsetting thing about it was the feelings it invoked. Every time we looked at it, we felt a sense of loss and frustration and that uncomfortable feeling that comes of knowing someone really dislikes you. The wall stretched all the way across the property outside our living-room window. Before its existence, we would sit and drink coffee in the morning and look at the views, feeling at peace with the world. Now when we looked out, we felt a bleak chill. One day, as we looked at the wall and considered our possibilities, my husband said, "You know, if we were creative, we could use that wall as a backdrop to create a pocket garden. It could be beautiful. Maybe something good could come of this."

We didn't realize how good. We began work to transform the wall. My husband and our sons built a lattice structure to provide a place where plants could grow and eventually hide the plywood. I watched as they worked together, whistling, talking, helping each other. Friends began to get into the spirit of this wall as well. They knew the story and rallied 'round to help. Soon we had a community of people cooperating to transform something ugly into something beautiful. Ideas, time, flowers and plants were all contributed. Many of our friends were artists. Some brought over original artwork, birdhouses, butterfly houses and birdbaths. One of our friends even made a wonderful clay birdhouse that looked like my husband! Together, we all selected vines that would cover the lattice.

By the end of the summer, the wall—and all the anger and negativity it had represented for us—was giving way to the new garden, which was becoming a symbol of love, friendship and coming together through peaceful actions.

Living with my beautiful little garden provides special moments of pleasure and insight, the most important of which is that I can choose my attitudes, and by doing so, gain great power to live a peaceful life. I try to remember that what is important is to turn away from anger and reach out and pull in the peace and goodwill that abounds in the world.

Ellie Porte

Puddles After the Storm

Our U.S. Navy ship had been at sea during a training operation with some of our allies in South America. Our time at sea was marked by endless hours of flight operations as we launched aircraft after aircraft and then ninety minutes later retrieved them on the pitching deck of our aircraft carrier. The Gulf War had just been declared, and our ship and accompanying air-wing were preparing to engage in the war effort. Hour after hour the flight deck bristled with aircraft moving to the catapults and being launched on practice bombing runs. There seemed to be no letup in the intense pace of preparation for war.

Forty days at sea with flight operations beginning in the early morning and concluding near midnight when the last aircraft returned had tested man and machine. Making a port visit in Chile was a welcome and much-needed respite.

Our entry into port was met with a severe storm that lasted throughout the night. The morning dawned with gray clouds and a drizzling rain. I was responsible for organizing a visit to an orphanage as part of our Operation Hand-Clasp effort, a program developed to encourage understanding between nations and to provide military men and women a way to contribute to the lives of children in the foreign ports we usually visit. At the appointed hour, one hundred sailors turned out to participate in our visit to the orphanage. When we arrived, we were greeted with breaking clouds, sunshine and the silent, shy faces of the children.

In no time at all, the sailors were actively engaged in repair work to the buildings, cleanup of the grounds and sports activities with the children. Everywhere you looked you saw sailors with children sitting in their laps, hanging on their arms, and clamoring for more and more attention. Everywhere you went you were surrounded with the sound of laughter and the shouts of delight. Clearly the sailors and the children had bonded, and much-needed attention was being shared in both directions.

Puddles were scattered around the grounds from the rain, and it didn't take long for the sailors and children to begin splashing through them, each attempting to make a bigger splash than the other. When our visit to the orphanage drew to a close, a tough, quiet Aviation Boatswain's Mate, who was known more for his crude language and sullen demeanor than anything else, approached me.

"Chaplain," he said, "I want to thank you for inviting me and pushing me to come when I didn't really want to. I haven't played in mud puddles like this since I was a kid myself. It was always the one thing about thunderstorms I liked. When the storm was over, we could play in the puddles, and the fear caused by the storm would be forgotten."

I was reminded in this touching way that even though the clouds of division and conflict fill the skies, when the storm is over, there will be puddles in which to play. What a world it would be if we could all remember to take time to splash in the puddles we find in our lives and to remind ourselves of how much joy we can find by indulging in simple acts of caring and sharing.

Reverend Wollom A. Jensen

Pets Teach Peace

Violence is the last refuge of the incompetent.

Isaac Asimov

I grew up on a farm in New Jersey. We had two hundred chickens, fifty pigeons, five pigs, three dogs, three cats and a cow. As a teenager, I had many soulful moments in the chicken pen, where the chickens would cluck to me and I would pour my heart out to them, expressing all my adolescent frustrations—at my parents, who wouldn't let me do whatever I wanted; at my friends, who scorned me; at my teachers, who didn't appreciate my efforts; and at the world, so full of injustices.

We physically punished our dogs when they were bad. The standard response to a soiled rug or chewed slipper was to hold it against a dog's nose and beat her with a newspaper or a hand. My favorite dog was Vixen, a collie/German shepherd mix. When Vixen would do something bad, I would let out my repressed adolescent fury at her, yelling, "You bad, bad, #$%^! dog! You're so #$%# bad." Vixen would sulk away, head lowered. Such events were an emotional release for me, and now that I reflect on it, probably confusing for her.

Many years later, I was living in the city with my wife Sara. At that time, I was starting a "Peace Studies" program at the University of Wisconsin–Milwaukee. I had been reading Dr. Martin Luther King Jr., Mahatma Gandhi and other proponents of nonviolence. I was very impressed by the promise that nonviolence would help create a better society, and I was starting to teach it to my college students.

In 1985, we acquired a puppy named Simone. I took Simone to the vet to get her first puppy shots. While I was waiting in the veterinary clinic, I picked up a pamphlet, "Caring for Your Dog." The pamphlet said in no uncertain terms, "Never hit your dog!" The reason it gave was that if you hit your dog, your pet could never be sure whether you were going to pet or beat it when you extended your hand.

Here is the perfect opportunity to test my commitment to nonviolence, I said to myself as I read that pamphlet. *We will raise Simone nonviolently!*

When I went home and told Sara about my desire to put the theory of nonviolence into practice with Simone, she enthusiastically agreed, saying, "We don't spank our children, and they are not badly behaved."

We never hit Simone. Instead, when she did something we didn't like, we would change the tone of our voice, telling her that her behavior was bad. She became so sensitive to our verbal commands that all either Sara or I had to do was lower our voice, and Simone knew she had done something bad. Everyone who knew her said she was the most well-behaved dog they have ever seen. Simone never begged at the table because I would lower my voice and tell her, "No begging!" In fact, sometimes I didn't even have to say anything; just scowling was enough to get her to behave.

Both Sara and I teach adults nurturing parenting skills. It is very hard to convince parents that they shouldn't spank their children. Eighty percent of parents in the

United States think it is all right to hit their children, in spite of solid research that shows that children who are physically punished earn less money, don't achieve as much education and are more likely to be incarcerated than children who are raised without spanking. Arguing with parents that spanking is a bad practice is fruitless. Parents insist that as children they were spanked, and they are all right. They can't imagine how a child could be raised without spanking. They say things like, "How else can you teach right and wrong to a young child? After all, a pat on the backside does not really hurt."

Often, telling parents that you don't spank your own kids doesn't help because parents tell you that maybe your kids don't need discipline, but theirs do. Instead, I always counter with the story of Simone, who is perfectly behaved and has never been hit. I tell my students, "If I can raise a dog to be compliant without hitting her, surely we can raise our children nonviolently. After all, we have the gift of speech to communicate with children. It is much better to tell children what we want, set clear limits for their behavior, let them learn from the natural consequences of their actions and reward them for positive behavior. For, like Simone, our children want our approval. They want to please us."

Many students have told me that this story makes a positive impression upon them, more so than my citing statistics about how damaging corporal punishment is for children. One, a Baptist minister and an officer in the reserves, now preaches about nonviolent parenting in his sermons. As an adult, I use my peacemaking skills to resolve conflicts so that I am no longer a tinderbox of repressed emotions like the teenager who used to hurl obscenities at his dog.

Dr. Ian Harris and Sara Spence

7

ON WISDOM

What is wisdom?

Wisdom is knowledge; it is a knowing, a sharing of insights and lessons, thoughts and ideas. Wisdom comes at all ages and stages in life. We gain wisdom from others as well as from our experiences. We are blessed to be wise and courageous in sharing our thoughts and words.

I am courageously sharing my knowledge and wisdom through my words and actions.

Taxi!

A moment's insight is sometimes worth a life's experience.

Oliver Wendell Holmes Sr.

I eagerly positioned my cab at the end of the taxi lineup outside the fancy marina resort hotel. It was a good location, and I was sure to get a passenger who would tip well. While I was waiting my turn to be first in line, I wondered if the other drivers in this lineup were as thankful as I was to be in this land of freedom and opportunity. I doubted that any of them had planned to be taxi drivers. I certainly had not.

My thoughts wandered over the long journey I had made to be here. I had grown up in Somalia, in eastern Africa, and dreamed of becoming a businessman. After graduating from the university, I had started an import/export business where my ability to speak Italian, Arabic and some English was useful. Soon my business was flourishing. Unfortunately, Somalia erupted in a civil revolution, and I found myself in danger. To stay in Somalia would have meant certain death. There was no choice but to abandon my business and flee with my young family to America, seeking political asylum. We arrived with very little means. I quickly took a job driving a taxi, something I could do immediately, in spite of my limited English. We were doing all right now, with the second job I got at AT&T, and finally I was able to tell my wife to relax and stay home with our three children. I was filled with a sense of well-being.

"Taxi! Taxi!" The voice of the hotel doorman jarred me out of my reverie. I put my cab in gear and pulled up. The doorman opened the back door of my cab and held it as a fair-haired, young businessman got in.

"Good day, sir." I smiled as the man settled himself in the back seat. "Where would you like to go?"

The man looked up and stared at me. "Where are you from?" he bluntly asked.

"I'm from Somalia, sir."

The man continued to stare at me. "Are you Muslim?" he asked suspiciously.

"Yes, sir," I answered politely. "I am Muslim."

The man abruptly opened the car door, got out of the cab and called to the doorman. I was startled by his behavior, but I was interested in this man now. I wanted to talk to him, to understand him and his fear. I pulled my cab out of the drive-through line.

The doorman looked at the young man and asked, "What's happened, sir?"

"I don't want this guy," he said pointing at me. "Please call me another taxi!"

The doorman just stood there, not knowing what to do. At this point, I jumped out of my cab and approached the now visibly agitated man, saying, "Sir? May I talk to you?"

I gestured to the cabs waiting in line. "Look. All these cabbies are Muslim, sir. None of them will hurt you, but please ride with me. I will give you a free ride wherever you want to go! Ask the doorman; I am a dependable driver. You will be safe."

The man looked at me with distrust, then at the door-man for reassurance. The doorman nodded his approval. He shrugged and warily got back in my cab. "Oceanside," he directed, somewhat defiantly, but with a questioning look on his face.

"That's okay, sir. I said I would take you for free, and I will." I smiled, even though I knew the drive to Oceanside was a hundred-dollar fare and would take nearly two hours of my time. "Please be comfortable, sir. Would you like a cigarette?"

The man accepted the cigarette and appeared to relax a little. We drove in silence for a few minutes. Then I asked, "Why didn't you want to ride with a Muslim, sir?"

As I expected, the man began to talk about the September 11 terrorists' attacks and the thousands of innocents who had been killed. He concluded this litany with an emphatic declaration: "That's what Muslims do!"

Even though I had expected the response, the words still hurt. Ever since September 11, I had felt shame that men claiming to be Muslims had committed such terrible acts. I wanted this man to understand that those men were not behaving like Muslims, that they were crazy.

"Sir? You have ten fingers on your hands. Right? Each finger is different from the others. Right? People are like that. Whoever was involved in September 11 was against Muslims, against Christians, against Jews. No religion in the world says that violence is the right way." There was silence in the cab as I negotiated the traffic on Interstate 5. Then I asked, "What about the bombing in Oklahoma, sir? Was that a Muslim?"

"No."

"Where was he from, sir?"

"America."

I persisted with my questions. "What religion, sir?"

"Christian," my passenger reluctantly responded.

"Did the Christians agree with what he did, sir?"

"No!"

"It is the same with Muslims and these sick, crazy guys that did this terrible thing on September 11!" I felt triumphant. "Please, please, please don't think every Muslim would do what those crazy men did on September 11. You know that Christians do not do what that crazy man did in Oklahoma. Let's go forward with that reality."

There was a moment of silence.

"Yes. You're right, you're right," came the soft and thoughtful reply from the back seat.

"Okay! Okay!" I eagerly responded. "I'm Muslim. You're Christian. We're brothers. If you were about to die right now, right here, I would not let you die. I would help you. And you would do the same for me, right? So we are brothers! It doesn't matter what religions we are; we are Americans. We can help each other that way when we forget about the religion. We are Americans—that's it!"

"Right! Right!"

We arrived, and the man attempted to pay the fare.

"No, no, sir! I told you that this would be a free ride, remember? Here is my card. I am Nur Ali. Please call me when you need a ride. You can pay me back that way!"

About three hours later, I got a call from the man to pick him up and bring him back to his hotel. The fare was $98, and the man gave me $128. He was staying at the hotel for three days. For all three days, he faithfully called me to take him wherever he needed to go.

The last day of his stay, I took the man to the airport. As he got out of the cab and paid me his fare and a tip, he said, "Good-bye, Nur. I am sorry. Please forgive me."

"Of course, of course," I told him. I couldn't stop smiling, which I'm sure left no doubt in his mind that my forgiveness was sincere. "We are brothers. We are Americans. We must forgive each other."

I was still smiling as I returned to the resort hotel and maneuvered into the taxi lineup. I was glad to be in America. I was free. I was at peace.

"Taxi! Taxi!" It was my turn. I looked expectantly at my next passenger.

Nur Ali
As told to Barbara Smythe

Pontius' Puddle

Pontius' Puddle, Joel Kauffman, ©1990, reprinted by permission of Joel Kauffman.

No More Meanness

*B*e *kind to one another, tenderhearted, forgiving one another . . .*

Ephesians 4:32

It was parent night at the end of our week of Vacation Bible School at the Sweet Fellowship Baptist Church. After much practice, each child's group was prepared to act out for the parents a dramatic presentation of a Bible story. One group consisted of four lively five-year-old boys prepared to act out the story of Moses and the Hebrew slaves leaving Egypt.

Wielding their plastic swords, the boys especially liked playing the mean Pharaoh and his army who would not let the people go.

At the appropriate time, I nudged our Moses to stand before Pharaoh and say, "Pharaoh, the slaves are all tired and they don't want you bossing them around anymore. Let the people go!" Pharaoh, sitting on his throne and twirling his plastic swords, responded—with prompting—"Never, never, never!"

Young Moses then left the room only to return within

seconds. Once again, he approached Pharaoh: "Pharaoh, my people are really tired of being beat up. Now will you let the people go?" Once again, I whispered into our Pharaoh's ear: "Say 'Never, never, never.'" But Pharaoh had had enough. He jumped down from his throne and said, "I don't want to be mean anymore. All of you can go! Just go! You can all go home now." Then he threw his sword on the floor and walked off with his arm draped around Moses.

Has the world grown tired of being mean? Can we listen with our hearts and be at peace? If we adults all took the time to listen, really listen, might we not also really hear and decide to let go of our own meanness?

Nancy Hastings Sehested

A Lesson in Forgiveness

The best way to destroy an enemy is to make them a friend.

Abraham Lincoln

A few years ago, my son Jihan, while visiting his dad, Steve, called to ask me to bring over the jacket he'd forgotten to pack. When I arrived, Steve was agitated, angry and grumbling about being wakened earlier by a loud leaf-blowing machine. He said when he had gone out and complained, the leaf blower insisted he was only doing his job and continued his noisy work.

Just then the doorbell rang. There stood a man who identified himself as Reggie, the leaf blower's supervisor. Steve stepped out onto the lawn and soon their disagreement got heated. Angrily, the supervisor turned away and mumbled under his breath, "Stupid nigger!"

Steve sprang to react and, foreseeing a potential fistfight, Jihan and I jumped between them. I angrily told Reggie to leave and steered my family into the house. We were all angry and frustrated and hurt. I soon had to leave for work, but the toxic effect of the incident hung over me for the rest of the day.

When I returned home that afternoon, there was a phone call from Steve, who told me the following story:

"After you left, Jihan and I talked about racism and anger and self-image. I shared stories of growing up black and the survival skills I developed to succeed in the world. It was an important but painful lesson for our son to witness today. I drove him to a friend's house to play, returned home, and on my porch I found a bottle of wine, a business card and this note:

'I am so ashamed and embarrassed about my behavior today. I feel especially bad that I behaved so horribly in front of your son. I grew up in the South as a privileged white man. When I left home, I vowed to shed all my family and community's racial prejudices. But today, in my anger, I was shocked to hear myself revert to using the N word. I certainly should know better. You see, I am a gay man, and I know firsthand the pain of hurtful names. Please forgive me and tell your son that I am sorry from the depths of my heart for what I did today.'"

The note was signed by Reggie.

Steve said he put the note in his pocket and went into the den. He selected a carved figure from his African art collection, picked up the gift of wine and walked down the street to the address on the card. He knocked on the door, and when it opened, Steve saw fear in Reggie's eyes. Steve, gift in one hand and the wine bottle in the other, smiled and said, "Let's share a glass together."

The men hugged, their eyes filling with tears, as they experienced the truth of two hearts merged with love.

That evening Steve and I shared this powerful story of reconciliation with Jihan. Its profound and moving message of forgiveness still resonates with our family, and continues to make an impact in the heart of those who hear this story.

Adrianne Bowes

Too Many Children?

Don't spend your precious time asking, "Why isn't the world a better place?" It will only be time wasted. The question to ask is, "How can I make it better?" To that there is an answer.

Leo Buscaglia

I work for a very large company with many employees, most of whom I do not know. As I was walking in one morning shortly after Thanksgiving, I overheard two ladies talking about the needy family that had been "adopted" for Christmas by her husband's company. She was very upset over the family that had been selected because they had "too many children"—they should not have had that many if they couldn't take care of them.

My blood was boiling, but I bit my tongue.

She continued to relate that she and her husband decided not to give anything this year because they didn't want to help a family that "just didn't know when to stop." The second lady agreed.

I couldn't help myself. I turned around and, as calmly as I could, I asked them what they really knew of this family.

The lady who had been doing most of the talking explained that there were seven kids, the oldest of which was only ten. The parents were only thirty and "obviously they started too young, instead of getting an education to provide for their family." She knew their first names, their ages, favorite colors, and the items they needed and wanted for Christmas. The list of wants/needs was pretty basic: hats, mittens, coats, a doll for little Susie, a truck for Joe, etc.—nothing extravagant at all. The "problem" was just that they had "too many children."

At that point, I introduced myself, explaining that I was also in my early thirties and had "too many children." I had seven children, and my oldest was only eight.

The women decided my situation was different because I was working and providing for my children and that they were not being "adopted by strangers for Christmas."

I then told them that most of my kids also had their names on Christmas want lists and would very desperately love to be adopted for Christmas—permanently adopted by a "real" family. You see, six of my seven children are *foster* children.

They stammered, stuttered and apologized; they had never thought of that. I gave them a few other possible instances of how a family can end up with "too many children." It could be anything: death of the parents, blended families, grandparents raising grandchildren, and on and on. After hearing this, the ladies said that they wished they would have done something to contribute, but it was too late because the collection already had been completed and turned in.

I knew that they could see things differently now. I explained how I often got rude comments at the grocery store when I took my kids and used government vouchers (subsidies for food for low-income families and for kids in foster care). We heard cruel comments like, "You shouldn't have so many children if you can't afford to feed them." One day after hearing this, my oldest asked me, "Mom, can we afford all this food?" She was truly bothered by these comments (we routinely spend three hundred dollars a week on groceries, after the vouchers). I don't explain it to strangers in the store because it would only hurt the kids even more. They all have come to dislike the "F word" (as in, *foster*), which not only makes them different, but also gives them a feeling of being unwanted or unloved. But many of our family and friends are teaching others not to be so quick to assume and judge.

The ladies and I continued to talk for a while, and I showed them pictures of my seven kids. We talked about the number of children in foster care in the United States, as well as in overseas orphanages, waiting to be adopted. It's incredible that there are so many children in need. In some way, she was right: the "problem" is that there are just "too many children"; too many who need to be loved and cared for—even adopted, not just for Christmas but forever.

The following morning, when I arrived at my desk, there sat two bags of Christmas gifts for "my" kids. It's amazing how much people really do care when they really know.

Kathy Gerst

A Peace of Pictures

Let us pray for our children.† Our children deserve a world without end.† Not a war without end. . . . Let us recommit ourselves to the slow and painstaking work of statecraft, which sees peace, not war as being inevitable.† Let us work for a world where someday war becomes archaic.

Rep. Dennis Kucinich, author of
Department of Peace proposal

Shortly after my inauguration in 1977, President Anwar el-Sadat of Egypt came to visit me in Washington. He was interested in bringing peace to his own people and strengthening friendship between Egypt and the United States. However, he saw no chance to make real progress on resolving basic differences with Israel anytime soon. On several issues, he responded, "Maybe in my lifetime." I told him that I was prepared to use my full personal influence, and that of my country, in support of any effort he was willing to make. Later, during our private talks upstairs in the White House, he agreed to take major strides toward peace in the long-standing conflict between his country and Israel. This was very much in the interest of the United States. (The last Israeli/Egyptian war had been the most recent time the Soviet Union and United States military forces had gone on nuclear alert.) Later, I met with Israeli Prime Minister Menachem Begin and found him willing to consider the initiatives Sadat and I had discussed.

In November 1977, Sadat made a dramatic trip to Israel to call for peace and to explain the demands of the Palestinian people living in the occupied territories. Although Begin and the members of the Israeli Knesset [parliament] listened politely, and although Begin personally repaid Sadat's visit, there were no concrete results from these overtures. I was disappointed at this lack of progress. One day, Rosalynn and I were walking down a woodland path at Camp David, the secluded presidential retreat in Maryland, talking about how beautiful and peaceful it was. Rosalynn said, "Jimmy, if we could only get Prime Minister Begin and President Sadat up here on this mountain." That gave me the idea, and a few weeks later, I invited both men to join me for a series of private talks.

In September 1978, they both came to Camp David. On the agenda were several issues. Among the most important for Sadat were the Israeli occupation of Egyptian lands and the rights of Palestinians to their own homeland. Begin was most concerned about Israel's national security, about gaining formal diplomatic recognition from the Arab countries and about the particular fate of Jerusalem—a holy place for Jew, Christian and Muslim— if the occupied territories were to be relinquished or shared in some way. I hoped that, in the process of the discussions, we would answer many, or even all, of these questions.

Rosalynn would be at Camp David with me, and our advisers, personal physicians, cooks, secretaries and other assistants prepared to come for three days, or a little longer if necessary. We never imagined it would take thirteen long, hard days and nights before an agreement would finally be reached. The small mountain camp was not designed to accommodate so many people, particularly for such a length of time, and many special arrangements had to be made. The staff even had to prepare three different types of meals at each sitting—kosher food for Begin and the Israeli delegation; special food for Sadat, which his own personal chef would cook; and other food for the rest of us! We also planned to have three different religious services, using the same small room—for Muslims on Friday, for Jews on Saturday, for Christians on Sunday.

President Sadat was the first to arrive for the peace talks, and I was pleased to discover that he seemed quite flexible on most questions. He said he was firm on the two issues of taking care of the Palestinian people and getting all Israeli settlers off the land in Egypt's Sinai Desert. In everything else, he would be willing to trust my judgment, and he agreed to stay at Camp David as long as necessary. Sadat voiced strong doubts about Begin's willingness to compromise. I urged him to consider the Israelis' caution in light of their special situation as a very small country surrounded by powerful and hostile Arab neighbors. When Prime Minister Begin arrived later, he and I also had a private discussion about the major issues.

From the first day, we worked on the problem of the West Bank and the Gaza Strip. We had to discuss the Israelis' claim that they had occupied these places in 1967 in an attempt to defend themselves against a war the Arabs had started, and that they were therefore entitled to keep at least part of the area. Egypt's argument was

that the territory had been seized illegally, and that all of
it should be returned to its original owners, the
Palestinians. If Israel did agree to release the land, we also
had to discuss how the Palestinians could then govern
themselves without threatening Israel's sense of security.

As we discussed these and other emotional issues, I
soon realized that Begin and Sadat were personally
incompatible. The sometimes petty, sometimes heated
arguments that arose between them when we were all in
the same room convinced me that it would be better if
each of them spoke to me as the mediator instead of
directly to the other. Each of the two leaders accused the
other of trying to destroy his country's economy and
even deliberately encouraging the illegal trade in hashish
and other drugs. For the last ten days of the Camp David
negotiations, the two men never spoke to or even saw
each other except for a Sunday afternoon trip to the
nearby Civil War battlefield at Gettysburg, although their
teams of advisers did continue to meet face-to-face.

I went back and forth between the two leaders and
their advisers, constantly seeking approval on the wording of each point of a comprehensive agreement. It was a
slow and tedious process, and all of us were often discouraged, seeing little or no chance for success. Each day,
I would write down a list of the points on which agreement had been reached, with a separate list of outstand-
ing differences. Slowly but surely, the second list got
smaller and smaller.

Day after day, assisted by my American advisers, I
revised and presented new drafts of the agreement to
both negotiating teams. On the eleventh day, however, I
finally realized we faced failure because of just two issues:
the dismantling of Israeli settlements in the Sinai and the
status of the city of Jerusalem. We had negotiated a good
paragraph about sharing control of the holy city, but it

was such an emotional issue for both Jews and Muslims that both Begin and Sadat became nervous about how their countries would react if they included the paragraph in the final document. Even if we compromised by leaving the question of Jerusalem out of the agreement, it was apparent that neither man intended to compromise on settlements in the Sinai. At this point, I had been away from Washington and the nation's business for a long time. I informed everyone that I would have to return to the White House on Sunday, the thirteenth day, and this ultimatum fixed a final deadline for our talks.

In the end, something unexpected almost miraculously helped to break the deadlock. We had taken some photos of the three of us, and Begin had asked me to sign one for each of his eight grandchildren. Sadat had already signed them. My secretary suggested that I personalize them, so on each photograph I wrote in the name of one grandchild above my signature. Although Begin had become quite unfriendly toward me because of the pressure I was putting on him and Sadat, I decided to take the photographs over to his cabin personally. As he looked at the pictures and read the names aloud, he became very emotional. He was thinking, I am sure, about his responsibility to his people and about what happens to children in war. Both of us had tears in our eyes. He promised to review the language of my latest revisions.

Shortly thereafter, Begin called me. He would accept my compromise proposal, which was to leave the decision about dismantling the settlements up to the Israeli parliament. I had thought of this as a way out for him. He would not have to back down on his promise not to dismantle any Israeli settlements but could shift the burden of the decision to the parliament. It worked. The American team struggled frantically to get a final draft of what would become the Camp David Accords, incorporating all the last-minute changes, which Sadat and Begin finally both approved. This was, indeed, a framework for peace, as we called it, laying the foundation for a future treaty between Israel and Egypt.

With the final document approved, Begin walked over to Sadat's cabin, about one hundred yards away, and the two men met again for the first time in days and shook hands as friends. That afternoon, Begin, Sadat and I left Camp David in my helicopter and flew to the White House for the signing ceremony. Six months later, after Israeli settlers had begun withdrawing from Egypt's Sinai region, a formal treaty was signed between the two countries—the first treaty ever between Israel and an Arab nation.

I know how difficult it is for nations in dispute to agree to negotiations once a confrontation exists and abusive public statements have been made. As with Begin and Sadat, extraordinary courage is often required on the part of political leaders to speak out against what might be perceived as a wave of popular sentiment in favor of war.

President Jimmy Carter
Reprinted from Talking Peace

The Music Bus

I was just getting back from touring Alaska, ready to fly home out of Bellingham, Washington. Once I started checking in at the airport, I noticed there was a big problem. The counter person was throwing up her hands as she had to tell everyone that all the planes were having problems and they would not be able to fly! You can just imagine the stress in that room. Then it was suggested that a bus would be provided to take us to Seattle, and perhaps some of us would be able to make our connections. Everyone was worried, as we only had an hour and a half to make the connecting flight, and the bus was not even at the airport yet.

Finally, the bus pulled up, and the driver said in a nasty tone, "They just pulled me out of bed after an all-night shift, and they expect me to perform a miracle and get you to Seattle in time to catch your flight. Good luck!"

Needless to say, everyone was in a really bad mood. I was loading my equipment into the bus and had slung my banjo over my back when the bus driver said, "What? Are you going to play that in my bus?"

"Well, I really did not plan on it," I replied.

"I was only kidding," said the driver. But I started thinking about it, and I reached inside my case and pulled out the banjo.

A worried, angry woman said, "Well, what if I don't like it?"

"Then tell me and I'll stop," I replied.

We drove off, and the tension inside the bus was horrendous! Then I started plucking the old standard "Blue Skies" (a neat version I learned from Pete Seeger). In a few minutes, I noticed everyone was humming along. A few more minutes went by, and I heard a few voices singing. I started to sing, too, and before long, the whole bus burst out in song. Even the driver sang along, his big bass booming through the bus.

One song led to another, and everyone seemed to have a request. "Do you know 'You Are My Sunshine'?" Soon, photographs appeared—pictures of vacations, family members, newborn babies and old friends. Everyone laughed and sang, with food being passed around the bus, and before long, the airport was in sight.

The bus driver called, "We made it!"

With time to spare. Everyone clapped their hands. Then he said, "We never would have done it without the help of our banjo player." Shouts of approval rang through the bus. The bus stopped, and we all got out; people exchanged addresses and invitations to visit, a few exchanged hugs, and we all went our separate ways.

As I was leaving the bus, the driver said, "This was the best ride I ever had. Thanks for your music!"

A few weeks later, back in the hills of old Vermont, my mailbox was filled with letters from my new friends. Their letters reminded me of how, by reaching out with just a song or a bit of friendship, you can turn a very tense situation into a peaceful experience—a magical, musical bus ride.

Rik Palieri

Breaking the Cycle of Violence:
A Decision of Faith

During his eighteen-month stay in the hospital, NYPD Officer Steven McDonald had lots of procedures and therapies that were necessary to save his life, but what he did during his son Conner's baptism celebration led to the deepest healing of all. He decided to forgive the fifteen-year-old who had fired gunshots into his head, then shot him twice more as he lay on the ground. One of those bullets had gone through his spinal cord.

Many wonder how he could forgive young Shavod Jones. In Officer McDonald's own words: "I often tell people that the only thing worse than a bullet in my spine would have been to nurture revenge in my heart. Such an attitude would have extended my tragic injury into my soul, hurting my wife, son and others even more. It is bad enough that the physical effects are permanent, but at least I can choose to prevent spiritual injury."

Officer McDonald was responding to a routine call when this horrible incident occurred. Since that day, he has responded to many more calls—from a high-school principal worried about the effects of bullying or a counselor who wants to help her client deal with personal trauma, from organizations in Northern Ireland dedicated to the hard work of reconciliation, and most recently, from peace groups in Israel/Palestine.

So Officer Steven McDonald travels to many different settings—with the wheelchair he needs to get around and the ventilator pump he needs to breathe and, most importantly, with his powerful message of forgiveness. Often, he teams up with Bruderhof leader and author Johann Christoph Arnold who included Steven's story in his book, *Why Forgive?* These tours have evolved into an entire program, Breaking the Cycle, which is designed for schools and other youth organizations. Johann and Steven speak at assemblies and also set up smaller group exercises tailored to develop each person's innate capacities for love and forgiveness. The team has been invited into dozens of schools in the New York area. They are certain that young people trained with the powerful tools of nonviolence offer the world the best hope for stopping the cycle of violence.

Steven explains that prior to being shot, he did not consider himself to be a religious person. He was newly married and about to become a father. Suddenly, while discussing his future with his wife and surgeon, his faith took on new importance. Many messages were delivered to him during his long hospital stay, and many people of all faiths were praying for him. He says, "It was God's love that put me back together."

Steven was aware of the impact his story was having on high schools and with young people. He knew that reconciliation could work in other places and among groups of people as well as individuals. His own Irish identity was part of his motivation to be part of a "Journey to Forgiveness" in Northern Ireland in 2000. He went back again and again. Inspired by his three trips to Ireland,

Steven turned to another part of the world where sectarian hatred and bitterness are causing tremendous suffering: he wanted to offer his message of reconciliation to people in Israel/Palestine. Arrangements were made for the Breaking the Cycle duo to visit with peace activists and others working to heal this broken land. Steven was also eager to visit the sacred places of his Christian faith. He found, to his delight, that many holy sites and areas of the Old City in Jerusalem had been made wheelchair accessible as part of the preparations for a visit from Pope John Paul II.

Although Steven McDonald's body no doubt still suffers pain, he is not troubled by the agony of hate and revenge. He has freed himself of that burden. Often, he is asked if he regrets forgiving Shavod Jones. Steven says this: "Months and years have come and gone, and I've never regretted forgiving Shavod. Back then, we never imagined it would carry any importance in other people's lives. We did it for ourselves. . . . It helped us, but more important, it has helped others as well. Popes, presidents, heads of state and ordinary people have invited us into their offices or homes to tell our story.

"So God has turned something terrible into something beautiful. I think God wants to use both our abilities and disabilities. God needs our arms and legs and minds and hearts—all that we have—to let others know that God is alive and well, and wants us to love each other. . . . Forgiveness is really about our own healing. We may experience slight offenses, or they may be profound. But in the end, it is our choice—and it is the survival of our own souls that is at stake."

Jo Clare Hartsig
with Steven McDonald

The Angry Man:
A Soul Searching for Peace

Every judgment, every criticism, is the tragic expression of an unmet need.

Marshall Rosenberg

I became acquainted with a seventy-six-year-old retired teacher at a very difficult time in his life. During his years as a teacher, he had given himself completely to his students, guiding them and sharing with them his wisdom. He was a good father to his own children as well, teaching them all that he knew. Finally, his children were grown and started making successful lives of their own. It was time for him to retire from his great love, teaching.

He and his wife immigrated to Australia where he found himself unable to make the cultural adjustments to his new country or to accept his own aging. He became very frustrated and angry. He began to take out his fury on his wife, blaming her for everything that he thought was wrong. His wrath was relentless. He was losing control. His family didn't know what to do. The children feared for their mother's safety. They called the authorities for help and had him moved to a separate apartment to protect their mother. Alone in the new apartment, he threatened to kill himself. His fear and rage were soon targeting his entire family. "I'm going to kill all of you!" he screamed at them over and over. "I'll kill you first and then myself! You'll see! You'll see!" His wife and children were very frightened. This is when they called me to come and speak to their father.

My own heart was filled with apprehension when I was taken to meet this man. He was very agitated. I sat quietly and listened to his cries of despair and hopelessness. His face was distorted by anger. His eyes were wild and had no clarity. His thoughts were violent and incoherent. I understood why he frightened his family. I wondered how I could help him. Then I remembered having been told that he was a gifted sitar player. I wondered if he would consider coming with me to Plum Village, our Buddhist retreat and monastery in France, to teach the sitar. I quietly proposed the idea to him, and he agreed to come with me.

He was not instantly transformed at Plum Village. He was still very angry and disturbed. He did teach some students the sitar, but he took no joy in his own efforts or those of his new students. It was then that I told him my story:

I was born in the Mekong Delta region of Vietnam. It is a simple, rich land—but a land that has been ravaged by foreign oppression, revolution and natural disasters. My people have suffered great injustices, many losing their property and their livelihood, many others losing their lives. This suffering is part of who I am. I could be very angry. Instead, I choose to give up my negativity to the Earth as I meditate. Each day, I practice The Five Touchings of the Earth, and through that practice, I find peace. Here are some of the things I say as I meditate:

In gratitude, I bow to all generations of ancestors in my blood family.

I see my mother and father, whose blood, flesh and vitality are circulating in my own veins and nourishing every cell in me. Through them, I see my four grandparents. Their expectations, experiences and wisdom have been transmitted from so many generations of ancestors. I bow deeply and allow their energy to flow through me. I ask my ancestors for their support, protection and strength.

In gratitude, I bow to all generations of ancestors in my spiritual family.

I see in myself my teachers, the ones who show me the way of love and understanding, the way to breathe, smile, forgive and live deeply in the present moment. I see through my teachers all teachers over many generations and traditions, going back to the ones who began my spiritual family thousands of years ago. I vow to practice to transform the suffering in myself and the world, and to transmit their energy to future generations of practitioners.

In gratitude, I bow to this land and all the ancestors who made it available.

I see that I am whole, protected and nourished by this land and all the living beings that have been here and made life easy and possible for me through all their efforts. I vow to contribute my part in transforming the violence, hatred and delusion that still lie deep in the collective consciousness of this society, so that future generations will have more safety, joy and peace.

In gratitude and compassion, I bow down and transmit my energy to those I love.

All the energy I have received I now want to transmit to my father, my mother, everyone I love, and all who have suffered and worried because of me and for my

sake. I know that I am not separate from them. I am one
with those I love.

In understanding and compassion, I bow down
to reconcile myself with all those who have made
me suffer.

I open my heart and send forth my energy of love and
understanding to everyone who has made me suffer, to
those who have destroyed much of my life and the lives
of those I love. I do not want them to suffer. I channel
my energy of love and understanding to them and ask
all my ancestors to help them.

"You can do this, too, my friend," I said quietly to him.

The man was weeping. Through his sobs, he pleaded, "Teach me, Sister Chân Không. Please teach me."

His transformation was not immediate, but after three months of focusing his pain and anger on gratitude and compassion, he was at last experiencing peace within himself. He told his story a little at a time during this period of meditation. It seemed that his father had always been very angry and had targeted him with that anger many times. He became aware that he had become the continuation of the circle of suffering that his father had begun. He was eager to return to his family and share his new outlook on life.

He died several years later, a peaceful death, having reconciled with his family and having had the opportunity to teach his grandson, with love and joy, what he had learned. He had broken the circle of suffering. He asked me to tell his story of how the angry man found peace, so that others could break their circle of suffering.

Sister Chân Không
as told to Barbara Smythe

[AUTHOR'S NOTE: *The Five Touchings of the Earth were excerpted from* Creating True Peace *by Thich Nhat Hanh.*]

Reaching Out for "the Other"

We've got to believe we can build a better world, trade this way of hatred for peace; the common ground between us is the hope for you and me.† Until its time has come, we've got to believe.

Leslie C. Baer, in the song "Got to Believe"

For centuries, social and economic discrimination by the British state against Irish Catholics resulted in deadly cross-cultural battles. More recently, the bloody struggles known as "The Troubles" in Northern Ireland have affected everyone there on all sides of their political, ethnic and religious divisions. Physical and social boundaries are the outcome of conflicting goals and identities. For over twenty-five years, Loyalists who wished to maintain Northern Ireland as British territory and Nationalists who sought the removal of British control from Northern Ireland were engaged in armed conflict.

Many citizens experiencing The Troubles did not take up arms. They sought shelter in their homes situated in culturally segregated communities demarked with murals of their cultural icons, heroes and martyrs. However, their insular neighborhoods became targets for armed opposition positioned on the other side of their society's geographic, economic and political divisions. Random attacks on "the other" in their community were retaliatory outcomes of an undeclared war on identity difference.

Regardless of the spreading violence that Sean*, a young Catholic man, witnessed, he was shocked and overcome with grief when his apolitical, nonviolent and handicapped sister and her husband were gunned down at home in front of their two infants. Their identities as Catholics in a Nationalist community caused their targeting by Loyalist paramilitaries. The premise of such intimidation is that people will not risk crossing cultural boundaries if they are in fear of their lives. At least they wouldn't dare do it without taking up arms. The tactic did not have the predictable effect on Sean.

Sean anguished over his family's losses, but restrained his instinct to drown his pain and anger in pints of ale. He also refused to arm his own household in preparation for a possible attack. Yet Sean realized that a passive nonresponse to violence sustains it as much as picking up a weapon to strike back. He recalled from history how violence was stopped when the conflict that caused it was constructively addressed. He also knew that peace grows from within, which meant he would have to deal with his current psychological problems before constructively building peace anywhere else.

Sean faced the challenge that all people encounter when their loved ones are murdered: he had to reduce, and hopefully overcome, his anger and anguish. This was particularly difficult for Sean due to his deep affection for his murdered sister Rosaleene. "She was so special. She

*Names have been changed.

was born with a disability that almost killed her as a child. Rosaleene's doctor predicted early that she could never lead a 'normal' life. Well, she proved them wrong with her determination and strength of character." In reflecting on Rosaleene's courage and strength, Sean realized that he could use those qualities in his current location, the cross-road between revenge and reconciliation.

Sean understood that he needed to do more than avoid revenge and forgive the killers, who were never arrested and convicted. He knew about their paramilitary group and their continued presence in the region. As dangerous as it was, he realized he must heal himself and others by reaching out to those who assassinated his dear Rosaleene.

With the help of his understanding family, Sean decided to change his career from manual work to social work. To learn how he might facilitate social reconstruction with community members on all sides of the group divisions in Northern Ireland, he turned to peace-building organizations. His new career entailed forgiveness and reassurance that he, as well as those he helped, could reach out for and work with the culturally different others in their community.

Thirty years after Rosaleene's murder, Sean still feels the loss and pain. He accepts the ongoing danger of an attack when he ventures into communities of "the other" to work with them. Yet he is focused in his goal "to build peace through contact, assistance and understanding." When I joined him in his cross-community work with Belfast teenagers, he gave me pointers on the careful use of identity labels, including Irish and British, that when misused could result in offense or even violence. Clearly Sean had developed essential skills, such as sensitivity to cultural identity, for establishing an integrated community with diverse youth groups.

Last week, Sean began carefully teaching ex-convicts in

the community of "the other" conflict resolution and other interaction skills. He demonstrated perception differences and communication problems that lead to misunderstanding. Some of his trainees are former paramilitaries and supporters of the group that killed Rosaleene and her husband.

Says Sean, "I could not come into this area unless I was trusted and given permission. But it's still scary being in 'their' community where recognition of and aversion for my identity difference can be deadly." But, he maintains, "We need to go beyond forgiveness. We have to reach out for those that we see as the enemy; understand those histories and reasons that make us value and strive for different goals and aspirations. If we stay fixed in our own physical, mental, emotional, social and cultural silos, we will also be viewed as the 'other.' When that happens, we lose our common humanity."

How can you reach out to "the other"? You start with two open hands.

Candice C. Carter, Ph.D.

A Gesture of Peace

I am a Cheyenne Indian and a Mennonite Christian. I am also a Cheyenne Peace Chief, committed to living a life of peace, no matter the cost. Peace Chiefs are not to engage in quarrels or take sides in a dispute. Their task is to promote peace and harmony within the tribe, as well as in the wider society.

"Even if your own son is killed right in front of you, you are to do nothing," one ancient saying instructs us. "If you see your mother, wife or children being molested or harmed by anyone, do not take revenge. Take your pipe, go sit and smoke, and do nothing, for you are a Cheyenne Peace Chief," says another teaching.

This ethic comes to us from our ancient past. Like other tribes, we had developed sophisticated methods of conflict management and resolution. The teachings of tribal hero Sweet Medicine guide the chiefs in being peaceful servants of the Cheyenne people. As European settlers invaded Cheyenne territory in the mid-1800s, Cheyenne chiefs worked for peace with U.S. soldiers, often with tragic results. Today, Cheyenne chiefs help to mediate tribal conflicts.

In 1968, the town of Cheyenne, Oklahoma, wanted to celebrate the centennial of the Battle of Washita. This so-called battle was actually a deliberate attack by Colonel George Armstrong Custer and his Seventh Cavalry on a peaceful village of Cheyenne governed by Peace Chief Black Kettle.

The townspeople invited the Cheyenne people to join in celebrating the hundred-year anniversary of this event. Initially, we responded: "Celebrate? Celebrate the destruction of a peaceful village where women and children were killed? No, thank you!"

But the townspeople persisted in trying to convince us to join them. The Peace Chiefs thought about it. "How can we inform the well-intentioned townspeople that we cannot celebrate? If we do anything, we will commemorate, not celebrate. But how?"

The Peace Chiefs wrestled with this question and finally found an answer. The bones of one of the Cheyenne killed in that attack were on display in a museum. We decided to make the following proposal: we, the Cheyenne, will come and be part of the centennial activities if the townspeople allow us to bury the remains of our ancestor.

The townspeople were approached. They agreed to our conditions. A ceremony for this moment was planned, and it was to be the last event of an entire day of celebration.

November 27, 1968, arrived; everything was in place. A tepee village had been set up at the actual site in preparation for one of the main events of the day, a reenactment of the attack. Hundreds of spectators and participants arrived.

Among those arriving were the grandsons of the Seventh Cavalry. They called themselves The Grand Army of the Republic, Grandsons of the Seventh Cavalry. They had come from California, and neither the townspeople nor the Cheyenne knew they were coming.

Dressed in authentic uniforms with real weapons and sabers, these Grandsons of the Seventh joined in the mock attack. They approached the Cheyenne village in the same flanking movement used a hundred years before.

The scene looked so real to me. Hatred for these men began to rise within me. My feelings were intensified because my own children were in that village and would be shot down as rehearsed. I reminded myself that I was a Peace Chief, committed to nonviolence in action and thought. I remembered Peace Chief Black Kettle and the way he sought to live in peace. I resolved to do the same.

The attack took place. True to history, women and children were shot. Finally, it was over, and we could proceed to the Black Kettle Museum. There we were to bury the hundred-year-old remains of a victim of that massacre.

We left the museum carrying a special bronze coffin and singing a Cheyenne song. Just like that day so long ago, it began to snow. As we passed through the crowd, a Cheyenne woman took off her blanket, a very beautiful Pendleton blanket, and draped it over the coffin. It was a gesture in keeping with our tradition.

Then, to my dismay, a command rang out: "Present arms!" I heard weapons being handled. The Grandsons of the Seventh were there. I didn't want them to be there, but they were. How dare they salute a victim of their fore-fathers' actions? I was not responding like a Peace Chief.

I was asked to be spokesperson for the Peace Chiefs, to explain the next part of the ceremony to the crowd. The blanket would be given away to someone who would be honored by the Cheyenne people. As I approached the podium, I knew the Peace Chiefs would be making a decision about who would receive the blanket. I told the crowd what was happening, and the chiefs made their decision.

I thought perhaps the chiefs would choose the governor or some other official. Instead, they asked me to announce that their choice was the commanding officer of the Grand Army of the Republic, Grandsons of the Seventh Cavalry. Captain Eric Gault stepped forward in sharp military fashion. The chiefs handed me the blanket. When the captain approached and came near me, he stopped, drew his sword and saluted. As he replaced his sword, I asked him to turn around, and I draped the blanket over his shoulders.

One hundred years after the massacre of the Cheyenne by the Seventh Cavalry, the Peace Chiefs made a gesture of conciliation. The scene that followed is hard to describe. People broke down and cried. We cried on one another's shoulders—the Grandsons of the Seventh and the grandsons of Black Kettle.

The captain responded to receiving the blanket by removing from his uniform a Garry Owen pin. That pin symbolized the bugle call for a charge, an attack—something Native Americans have heard so often.

Native Americans have no reason to celebrate events such as the Battle of the Washita or any of the many other incidents that illustrate the deliberate genocide or ethnocide of my people. Similarly, there is little or no cause for Native Americans to celebrate the quincentennial anniversary of the arrival of Christopher Columbus in North America.

But as a young Peace Chief in 1968, I learned the importance of gestures of conciliation from the elder Peace Chiefs. Taking my cue from those Peace Chief elders, I suggested that 1992—and every year after that—be a year of reconciliation!

Lawrence Hart

At the Foot of the Bed

*You're not the same as me, we see things
differently; nevertheless, we share the Earth.*

*The things you do or say might clash with my
own way . . .*

*We come together now, we search for common
ground.*

    James Ahrend, in the song "Dealing with Differences"

During my daily rounds at the hospital, I came across a room where I could immediately tell by looking through the glass doorway that the man inside, though his back was to me, was visibly disturbed. He was anxiously sitting up on the far side of the bed with his feet hanging off while he pulled repeatedly at the unkempt sheets.

Knocking on the door frame, I announced myself: "Hello, I'm Chaplain Jon. Is everything all right in here?"

Pointing to the wall at the foot of the bed, the man replied, "No, there is a crucifix." I sighed as I examined the wall, knowing full well what was there, and I quickly looked at my census list to verify the patient information and faith tradition. I found the room number and the only word I needed to see: *Hindu.*

As a Protestant chaplain serving at a Catholic hospital in the multicultural and interfaith environment of Los Angeles, it was not infrequent for me to find patients perturbed by the presence of a crucifix on their wall. Trying to be diplomatic and defuse the situation, I explained, "If you are offended by the crucifix, I can make arrangements for it to be removed during your stay here." The truth, more accurately, is that some of the more zealous of the Catholic faith had learned of this practice of accommodating people of other faith traditions, and had most of the crucifixes permanently installed on the wall, so the best effort to accommodate patients often was to drape a cloth over the offending relic.

The Hindu patient left me dumbfounded by what he told me next. Turning more toward me and pulling one knee onto the bed, his face wrinkling from being misunderstood, he explained, "I am not offended by the crucifix. I am disturbed that it is at the foot of my bed, which is a place of dishonor in my culture. Every time I lie down, I feel as if I am disrespecting the God of this hospital."

The teacher had just become the student. I was overwhelmed with how much respect this man had for a faith not his own. I couldn't help but think that I had just glimpsed a nugget of human unity whose offspring surely is peace.

Reverend Jon Arnold

8

GIVING BACK

What is giving back?

All our lives we receive love, compassion, lessons, wisdom and knowledge from those around us. Giving back is an occasion when we get to share what we have received with those around us. When we give, we also receive. It is the power of reciprocity. Embrace the gift of giving back.

I am giving back to those around me as well as those who are far away; it is in giving that I am receiving my blessings.

He Achieved the Impossible with a Little Help from His Friends

Nothing is so hard for those who abound in riches as to conceive how others can be in want.

Jonathan Swift

Iqbal Masih spent his childhood shackled to a loom in a dingy carpet factory in Pakistan. At the age of four, when his parents hired him out to repay a sixteen-dollar loan, he worked twelve- to sixteen-hour days, seven days a week, for less than a dollar a month. He never learned to read or write, and was thin and undernourished.

Craig Kielburger spent his childhood in the comfortable suburbs of Toronto, raised by two loving parents who were both teachers. During the day, he attended school. In his free time, he spent his boundless energy in-line skating, swimming and skiing.

Two boys from two entirely different worlds—that is, until the year that they both turned twelve. The impoverished child of the East and the privileged child of the West were symbolically united in a universal effort to liberate enslaved children.

Iqbal was rescued from his factory prison when he was ten. For the next two years, he was treated as an international hero, a living symbol in a brave crusade against bonded servitude in Pakistan's carpet industry. Then, at the age of twelve, Iqbal was murdered, his voice forever silenced.

Halfway across the world, Craig Kielburger read the story about Iqbal's life and death in the Toronto newspaper. At that moment, Craig's carefree days of childhood ended. Fueled by compassion and a sense of justice, Craig vowed to do everything he could to help end the exploitation of child workers. He had the intelligence and foresight to know he couldn't do it alone: he would have to rally others to his cause. People told him that he was too young. They said no one would listen to him. But Craig Kielburger, at the age of twelve, was an effective activist. He knew how to unite others to work toward a common goal.

He read everything he could find about the 200 million children in the world who work in conditions of slavery. But reading wasn't enough. Craig wanted to see for himself the children and the conditions they worked in. At first, his parents refused. After all, Craig wasn't even old enough to travel alone on the subway. But Craig was determined. He sold some of his toys to raise money for the trip. His parents were so moved by Craig's determination that they granted their permission for his seven-week trip to Asia, and with help from other relatives, matched the money he raised.

Armed with a video camera and chaperoned at each stop by local human-rights activists, Craig traveled from Bangladesh to Thailand, and from there, on to India, Nepal and Pakistan. He made his way from windowless sweatshops to airless factories. He met a little girl bagging candy eleven hours a day in a stuffy, overheated room, and a little barefoot boy stitching soccer balls. He talked to each one, child to child, and the children opened up like they never had before. At the end of his journey, Craig made a pilgrimage to the place where Iqbal's own journey had ended: an unmarked grave in a small cemetery.

While Craig was touring Asia, the prime minister of Canada was also there. Craig requested a meeting with the prime minister, but he refused. After all, Craig was just a child, too young to vote. The media, however, were very interested in hearing Craig and two former child laborers tell their stories. The subsequent coverage outraged the public; overnight, the issue of child labor received national attention in Canada. Suddenly, the prime minister wanted to see Craig, too.

Craig knew what he had to do, but he could not accomplish his goal alone. He needed a team. What better partners than his classmates, who, like himself, were "too young to know any better"? Back home, Craig took his shocking photos and horrifying stories into classrooms. Craig said, "Here's the problem. Do you want to help?" His fellow students were more than eager to help. Together, they established a group called Free the Children, which met weekly to share information and discuss strategies. Craig then contacted other organizations for further information, support and contacts. His team was growing.

After hearing Craig speak at the Ontario Federation of Labor's annual convention, two thousand union leaders joined the effort, donating $150,000 to Free the Children. The mayor of Toronto banned fireworks manufactured in child-labor shops. The minister of foreign affairs offered Craig an advisory position in the Canadian government, and the United States Congress invited him to speak. The Canadian government has now become one of the leading nations working toward the elimination of intolerable forms of child labor and the exploitation of children.

"Children have one special quality that gives them a far greater power than adults," Craig said. "They have imagination. They still think they can fly. They even think they can talk to prime ministers as equals."

In two short years, Free the Children became a team of thousands, expanding into an international movement with chapters across Europe and Asia. Free the Children has changed minds. It has changed laws, and it has begun to change the lives of 200 million children.

Kid stuff? You decide.

Cynthia Kersey

You Get What You Give

If you find it in your heart to care for somebody else, you will have succeeded.

Maya Angelou

In 1953, moving into a newly built home in Levittown, Pennsylvania, was the American Dream for a blue-collar worker like my father. These affordable houses included modern automatic clothes washers, radiant heating in the floor, carports and complete landscaping. New schools cropped up, surrounded by parks, pools and baseball fields. It was a dream come true for my family of five, as well as hundreds of other families—providing they were white. Levittown's builder refused to sell to blacks. As an eight-year-old, I was unaware of this racial discrimination. I innocently played with neighborhood kids in the safe streets of Dogwood Hollow, one of the town's subdivisions.

It was four years later when my eyes were opened to the harmful and odious effects of prejudice. That summer, I turned twelve: the age of accountability. I planted a flower garden. I went to a girls' camp with my best friend, and we both changed our names. It was the summer that I was awakened to life's lessons of hate and love, courage and conviction, and the darker side of human nature.

Although Levittown's builder would not sell his homes to black families, there was nothing in the books that prevented a resale to blacks. That is exactly how the Myers family bought their house on Deepgreen Lane, just around the corner from my house. At first, neighbors thought that the black family had come to clean the house for the new residents. But when it became apparent that they were moving in, crowds began to gather around the house and in the street. The crowd turned into a mob that remained outside the house for weeks, terrorizing the Myerses with hurtful remarks, death threats and broken windows. Crosses were burned on roofs and lawns of any sympathizers. The Ku Klux Klan recruited angry homeowners who felt that their property values would decline.

As a naive young girl, I was shocked and horrified by the events taking place in my neighborhood. I couldn't believe that people would hate other people because of their skin color. "Why?" I kept asking everyone. No one could give me an answer that made sense. The unfairness and hatefulness of it all pierced my heart deeply. I had to do something. I had to show this family that they were welcome in *my* neighborhood. I recruited my best girlfriend to help me.

The flower garden I had planted was now in full bloom, so I decided to pick some flowers and take them to the Myerses, my friend in tow. I was oblivious to any dangers or negative consequences of my decision to act. I didn't tell my parents of my plan either. I sensed that they wouldn't approve. Off went my friend and I, through the crowds and up to the front door of the Myerses' home.

Mrs. Daisy Myers answered the door. "Welcome to our neighborhood," I announced as I held out my bouquet of zinnias, snapdragons and marigolds. She smiled and invited us in.

The memory of her smile and her peaceful presence will forever inspire me. Here was a woman whose family was endangered, hated and victimized by members of my community and my ethnic group, yet she graciously invited my friend and me into her home. She trusted us enough to show her little baby girl to us, and she talked to us like equals. It was a time of transformation for me. I walked up to that door thinking that I was doing something good for that family, but it was *my* life that was changed. I saw courage, love, endurance and faith in the kindness that Daisy Myers offered me that day.

In 1999, forty-two years later, the city of Levittown invited Daisy Myers back so that a formal apology could be made to her. At the age of seventy-four, Mrs. Myers drove herself to Levittown from miles away, declining a chauffeur-driven ride in a government car. When I heard of the event, my heart nearly burst with joy. At last, I could be at peace with my hometown. I felt proud that they wanted to rectify the past injustices and create a new memory of acceptance and love. Daisy Myers lit the community Christmas tree in Levittown that year. Her memory still lights my heart.

Terri Akin

Strengthening the Circle of Life

Through our willingness to help others, we can learn to be happy rather than depressed.

Gerald Jampolsky

The bumper sticker on a car at the powwow caught my eye: "My Child Strengthens the Circle of Life." As I looked at my five-year-old granddaughter Chantelle, sitting next to me in the car, I reflected on the statement. Before the day was over, these words would hold much more meaning for me.

"Nana, let's go look at the Native American dolls," said Chantelle, who is part Native American.

I had brought her here hoping to find opportunities for her to connect with that part of her culture. We went to the crafts booth and were mesmerized by the hundreds of dream catchers hanging from the ceiling. Gradually, we found our way to the dolls. She picked one up and hugged it in such a way that I knew she saw herself. When we went to pay for it, I couldn't help but comment to the owner on what a special world he had created with his display of dream catchers.

"Yeah," he said. "Some people like it; others don't. I sold a lot of stuff at the last powwow, but not much at a conference I went to earlier this summer."

"How come?" I inquired.

He looked around the booth to make sure that his partner had things under control, then asked, "Do you have time for a story?"

"Sure," I said, my curiosity piqued.

"The best way I can describe the tone of that conference is to tell you about a young boy who wanted a leather pouch with an animal printed on it. A relative bought it for him. Twenty minutes later he was back with his parents who insisted that he return it. They believed that the pouch was evil because it had an 'animal spirit.' As the boy's eyes met mine, I could see he was embarrassed, sad and disappointed. Thinking about that young boy, though, brought back memories of my childhood."

He continued, "My father had never been part of my life, and when my mother's drinking and prostitution began consuming her days and nights, I was taken out of our home and put into a foster home. It was just as well. I was tired of having to compete for my mother's attention. I hoped a loving family would adopt me.

"As the days, weeks and months dragged on, it was apparent that no one wanted me as their son. I thought it was because I wasn't good enough. So for the next several years, I tried to become good at everything. I excelled in school and participated in every extracurricular activity I could. I went to church every Sunday and was the best-behaved boy in the bunch. Still, no one ever came for me.

"By the time I was eighteen, I was bitter and disillusioned. I took up drinking and vowed that I would never seek out anyone again. I stayed that way until my own son was born. As I looked into his eyes, his tiny soul touched mine. I loved him with all my being. As much as

I tried, I wasn't able to regain my sobriety until he was eleven. When he was twenty-three, I was horrified to learn that he was drinking, yet I understood the forces that can drive a man to drink. One night, he either tripped or passed out on a step leading to the basement. When he landed, he hit his head and went into a coma. A few days later, when I didn't think it could get any worse, they told me he was brain-dead. *How could this be?* I wondered. He was the one person who had filled my heart, and now he was gone. I felt I was breaking into a million pieces.

"I knew my son would want to donate his organs. He was always generous, and his organs could help about a hundred people. However, I didn't want anyone else to pull my son's life-support plug. I knew I had to do it.

"After I mustered up the courage to pull his life-support plug, I went to my car and decided to head for the nearest bar. Sobriety wasn't worth maintaining, not with this kind of pain. As the engine roar died down to a quiet hum, I could hear my car radio. Not wanting to listen, I was about to turn it off when I heard Reverend Robert Schuller saying, 'When your disappointment bears understanding, you shall have peace in your heart.'

"Instead of going to the bar, I decided to drive out to the country. I was determined I was going to sit there until my disappointment bore understanding—not really believing I would ever feel any relief from the pain that engulfed me. No bolt of lightning came out of the sky. No great bird of peace descended on my shoulder, but after several weeks of meditating on Schuller's words, I slowly began to realize that my son had strengthened the circle of life. My understanding came when I realized that each one of the hundred people who had received a part of his body probably had about two hundred people who loved them, and could still love them because my son's organs had kept them alive.

"In that instant, I could feel the love of those twenty thousand people. I knew then that my son's life had been for the greatest purpose of all: love. Not only had he lived for me to love, but also he'd lived for the hundred organ recipients and the twenty thousand people who loved them. They were all impacted by his life."

"I'm number twenty thousand and one," I said somberly, then thanked him for sharing his story.

As Chantelle and I were about to leave, he said, "Here, take this dream catcher. See the hearts around the rim? I give these to anyone passing by who has children. It's a reminder to celebrate the children who come into our lives."

"But, mister, I've got a sister. Can she have one, too?" asked Chantelle.

"Of course," he said, and handed us another one. She and I each gave him a hug in gratitude.

As we walked away, hand in hand, I thought about how natural it was for Chantelle to think of others. I imagined how her gifts to the world would unfold.

As Chantelle ran to give her sister her dream catcher, I made a mental note to check "donor" on my driver's license the next time I renewed it.

Rebecca Janke

Awakening of the Soul

An *eye for an eye would make the whole world blind."*

Mahatma Gandhi

The last time I spoke to my brother Robby was September 7, 2001.

Our daughters both were starting school in Washington, D.C., and he teased me about being able to see them whenever he wanted because he was an executive and I was a teacher. I told him I was planning a trip to D.C. on Veterans Day weekend. We agreed to meet in Washington, then we segued into a lively analysis of who was going to win the World Series. I told him that my team, the Arizona Diamondbacks, would win it all. He chuckled and said I was dreaming.

Four days later, on September 11, my brother was gone. Robby was on American Airlines Flight 77, the hijacked plane that crashed into the Pentagon.

As Veterans Day approached, there was still much trepi - dation about flying, but I knew I still had to go to Washington. Security was on high alert, and the airlines were recommending getting to the airport three hours early. I checked in curbside, ate lunch, was searched by security, and was still at the gate two hours before takeoff. Before finding a comfortable place to wait, I asked an attendant if I needed to get a boarding pass. She looked at my ticket, smiled and told me I already had one. Then she commented that she loved my hat. I was wearing the newly issued Arizona Diamondback World Champions hat. The D-backs had beaten the Yankees in a classic series only a few days before. We talked about the seventh game for a bit, then I settled down to write a letter to my sister-in-law.

I wanted to write to her because putting my feelings about Robby on paper would be like giving her a hug she could have whenever she wanted or needed one. In the upper corner, I wrote the date: 11/9. As I did, a shock ran through me like a bolt of lightning: 11/9 was 9/11 backwards.

At just that moment, the gate attendant came over and asked to see my ticket. She took it, and as I followed her to the counter, I asked what was going on. She told me she was upgrading me to first class and again mentioned that she loved my hat. I was totally surprised. I've been flying all my life and have never been upgraded to first class. I thanked her, and she winked and said, "We really got those Yankees, didn't we?"

The words shook me. I felt as though this was my brother talking to me. These were his words. Baseball was always something we strongly connected on, and here he was acknowledging the Diamondback series victory.

As I walked around the airport, I had a strange but distinct feeling that Robby was somehow right there with me. At one point, I felt directed to enter a sundry store. I never buy anything in airports, but this time I walked directly to the newsstand and picked up the current issue of *Rolling Stone* magazine. Bob Dylan was on the cover—

another strong connection between us. Dylan had always been a major influence in both our lives. We grew up singing and analyzing his lyrics. Robby even coined a term, the "Zimmerman Peak," to describe a superior piece of music. (This, of course, refers to Dylan's real name, Robert Zimmerman.) Through the years, we always spoke of music in terms of how close a song came to reaching the peak.

I opened the magazine and flipped to the Dylan article. At the top of the page, large boldface type announced that "Love and Theft," Dylan's latest album, had been released on 9/11. This sent shivers up my spine: I felt Robby's presence all around me. Through the concourse windows, I could see planes taking off and landing, each one an arrow piercing my heart. I wished I could ask Robby what happened that day on the plane, but the reality of his departure and the possibilities of what actually happened on the plane silenced my thinking.

The next morning in Washington, my daughter and I went to the Pentagon. Sean, an FBI agent, took us to the crash site. I'd met Sean previously at my parents' house on Long Island, where he had taken blood from us for DNA samples. Sean drove us through security, and at a small construction shed, my daughter and I traded our baseball caps for hard hats and walked out to the site of the crash. We sat on the cold ground behind a chain-link fence and stared at the raw earth and boarded-up building walls. We cried, hugged and cried some more. After a while, Sean came over with a policeman and a construction worker. They each hugged us, and we felt the true compassion of the human spirit awakening our souls.

When we got back to the car, Sean asked if there was anything else he could do. I told him I hadn't been sleeping well. The image of my brother on the plane with the hijackers haunted me nightly. Sean took out some color photos of the hijackers. He told us that all the hijackings took place between fifty-eight and sixty-two minutes after take-off. The planes were all above thirty thousand feet. There was a terrorist in the front row of each aircraft, two more in the rear of first class and two at the head of coach. Sean told us that the hijackers herded everyone to the rear of the plane. Many of the passengers were schoolchildren flying with their teachers. They had been winners of a geography contest and were being rewarded with a trip to California.

Robby loved children. He coached his daughter's soccer teams and liked nothing better than having all the kids hang out at his house. "He probably went to the back of the plane and comforted the students," Sean suggested. I could see Robby doing that, joking with the kids and telling them that he'd take them all for Happy Meals when it was over. I believe Robby died a true hero, helping children smile in the face of danger, and at that moment, I wondered if this could be the answer to my thoughts of the day before. It was then that I felt compelled to ask Sean if he knew where Robby had been sitting. He said he had a schematic map of Flight 77. As he pulled out the map, I opened my wallet and looked at my boarding pass from the day before, seat 4B. Sean opened the diagram and there it was: Robert Speisman imprinted over seat 4B. The lightning bolt ran through me again. I had been mysteriously upgraded to the exact seat my brother had sat in.

All coincidence? I don't think so. The lightning bolts, our brotherly connections, the answered questions, the almost surreal feeling of my brother's presence throughout my whole trip were too much to ignore. I believe Robby got my attention to offer comfort and bring peace and closure, and that's exactly what he would have wanted to do.

Not a day goes by that I don't reflect on his fateful journey. Ironically, "love and theft" is what my family and I feel about September 11. For the love, we decided that the best way to honor Robby would be to establish a foundation that would have a positive impact on the lives of children. For the theft, we've come to realize that anger and revenge would do nothing to end our grief, but a loving contribution would be healing. In our hearts, we know that's what Robby would want.

The Robert Speisman Memorial Basketball Foundation was created at the Y in our hometown on Long Island. People donated more than twenty thousand dollars so that underprivileged kids can play on "Speis" teams just like we did. In October 2002, we held a memorial basketball game. Family members and friends flew in from all over the country to play against Robby's Sunday morning basketball buddies. A plaque with Robby's picture was hung in the gym.

Cocopah Middle School in Scottsdale, Arizona, adopted the foundation for their yearlong charity project. They sold lollipops and doughnuts, and at a special assembly, presented a check to my family for twenty-five hundred dollars. Imagine our surprise when Diamondback World Series hero Luis Gonzalez appeared at the assembly and told my parents that he would get tickets for the Speis team to see the Mets play the Diamondbacks in New York. As we posed for pictures with the kids and Luis, I realized that I was holding my Diamondback hat in my hand.

Robby may be gone in body, but he's not gone in spirit. Recently, I drove past a schoolyard and saw kids playing basketball. It got me thinking that maybe some day a young Speis team member will walk into our old gym. He'll look up at that plaque and go out and hit the game-winning shot, inspired by the love my brother left behind.

Steve Speisman

Christa's Field of Dreams

My sister Christa struggled with severe epilepsy throughout her life, which made daily tasks difficult. But she never once complained, and her resilient spirit and faith inspired all who knew her.

Christa had always wanted to visit the cornfield in Dyersville, Iowa, where the famous baseball movie *Field of Dreams* had been filmed. She had planned and prepared, and on July 24, 1992, her bags were packed and Christa was ready to make her dream trip come true. But it never happened. That very morning, she died of a massive coronary at the tender age of twenty-three.

My family was devastated by Christa's death. I chose to honor Christa's memory by climbing Pakistan's K2, the world's second-highest mountain, a dangerous and difficult ascent.

In September 1993, after seventy-eight grueling days on K2, I still had not reached the top. I was physically emaciated and emotionally exhausted. Two local men helped me on the treacherous five-day walk back to the nearest village, Korphe. There, the Islamic villagers shared everything they had with me: They covered me with warm woolen blankets, massaged my legs, and gave me their last eggs and precious food. The Korphe villagers told me that, in their remote Braldu Valley, one in three babies born alive died before age one, and the literacy rate was a dismal 2 percent.

It took a week to regain my strength, and I wanted to repay the villagers for their generosity. Instead of demanding anything, they led me to a local school in a dusty grove above the village. There, I saw eighty-four children sitting in a circle in the dirt. They were huddled together to keep warm. Most students were barefoot, and they wrote on slate boards with sticks dipped in ashen mud. A worn blackboard propped up by stones kept blowing over in the furious, chilly autumn wind. Most amazing of all, there was no teacher. Master Hussein was in the next village teaching that day because the Korphe community could not afford his dollar-a-day salary. He split his time between two villages to make ends meet.

The children's eyes were riveted on me all day. Despite abject poverty, their resilient spirits soared, and I noticed their determination to have an education. Filled with hope, the children asked me to help them build a school. Here, in one of the poorest, most remote frontiers of civilization, I discovered why I had come to Pakistan—not to climb a mountain, but to help the Korphe children's dream for a school come true. I promised to help.

Back in America, I struggled to raise the twelve thousand dollars needed to build a school, meeting challenges at every turn. Many people wondered about my motivation for such a task. But I was determined to follow through with my promise to the children of Korphe. Three years later, in 1996, Korphe School was still not finished. I had paralyzed the project with my micromanagement. I still had so much to learn.

Haji Ali, Korphe's silver-bearded village chief, closely watched the progress of the school. He was a wise man, tempered by seven decades of eking out a life in a harsh environment. Noticing my frustration, he hobbled over to me with his arthritic knees. He led me to a bluff on the side of a hill, which overlooked the vast panorama of Pakistan's Karakoram Mountains. Haji said, "God blessed us with your vision to bring us education. However, you need to do one thing: You need to let us do the work. We have lived in our ancestral land for eight centuries and know what we are doing. Sit down, shut up and stop micromanaging, and I promise you we will succeed."

It was not easy, but I let go. Before my eyes, a miracle took place. Children, grandparents and women all helped build the school by carrying sand from the river, and gathering stones and other materials. Within eight weeks, on the day of the first winter snow in 1996, the school was complete.

Over the years, I visited Haji Ali frequently. We would embrace, and then in a somber shuffle, visit the local graveyard. He would point out the children who had died in my absence. This was his way of acknowledging the changes in his village. One day he told me, "I am old now, and my time to go to heaven is near. Soon, you will be standing here over my grave, and you will be sad. But remember one thing: Listen to the wind." Three months later, Haji died peacefully in his rickety bed.

In October 2001, I visited Korphe and stood sadly by his grave. But I remembered what he said, and I listened to the wind. In that wind, I heard the sweet voices of children in the nearby school. At once I knew that, almost a decade after Christa's death, a promise had been fulfilled: Christa had been honored in a "field of dreams" not in an Iowa cornfield, but halfway around the world in an impoverished mountain village of Pakistan. And I also realized that this revered place had now become my very own "field of dreams."

Greg Mortenson

The Voice of the Future

*The success of our living is measured not by
what we can accumulate for ourselves, but what
we can bestow upon our fellow travelers on life's
tough travel.*

W. Phillip Keller

In late 1997, a sixteen-year-old boy walked into Talking
Drum Studio in Monrovia, Liberia. He had an idea, and he
needed Talking Drum Studio to make it happen. Talking
Drum Studio, a project of Search for Common Ground,
produces—and teaches others to produce—radio programs.
Through news, feature stories, music and soap operas,
Talking Drum Studio aims to encourage dialogue and
defuse violence.

But this boy had more than just a good idea. He had
spirit, perspective and a powerful message. He and a small
group of children had created the Children's Bureau of
Information to give a voice to the children of Liberia, to
help other children—their peers—recover from seven
years of civil war. Before long, the Children's Bureau of
Information and Talking Drum Studio were producing a

weekly show titled *Golden Kids News,* which was aired by
a local radio station. The impact was almost immediate:
Children's voices were being broadcast, and people
stopped to listen.

Golden Kids was such a hit that, before long, there were
more people walking through the doors of Talking Drum
Studio. This time, it was the U.N. High Commission on
Refugees asking whether we would produce another program. The result, *Children's World,* was a program "by and for
children affected by war." This weekly program shared the
experiences of children who were displaced by war and were
trying to rebuild their lives. With adult support, the children
of *Children's World* broadcast poetry, songs, storytelling, news
and music to thousands of listeners every week.

We started a second Talking Drum Studio in Freetown,
Sierra Leone, in April 2000. *Golden Kids News* was the first
program we produced. The impact in Sierra Leone was
even more striking than it had been in Liberia. Soldiers in
the U.N. peacekeeping mission, market people and taxi
drivers all stopped by the studio to comment on the children's programs.

Five years later, thirteen radio stations in Sierra Leone are
carrying *Golden Kids News* and are frequently asked to replay
each program. A nationwide survey conducted in 2004
showed that over 88 percent of the respondents listened to
Golden Kids News and almost all of them (98 percent) reported that the program changed their attitudes toward the
role of children in Sierra Leone. Listeners also thought the
program "made children aware of options besides warfare
and contributed to the healing process after trauma."

In *What's Going On,* a film produced for the United
Nations, Michael Douglas interviewed one of the *Golden
Kids* reporters in Sierra Leone. This young man had been
a former child soldier who joined *Golden Kids News* as a
way to put his horrific past behind him and to help the

other estimated fifteen thousand child combatants. "I interviewed some of my colleagues to explain their stories," he explained to Mr. Douglas, "so the people in the community, they would be able to accept them back."

Search for Common Ground expanded children's radio programming to Angola, Burundi and the Democratic Republic of Congo and is making its methodologies available to organizations around the world.

The remarkable story of *Golden Kids News*, *Children's World* and the Children's Bureau of Information often surprises people. As a producer at Talking Drum Studio said: "Very often, adults believe that kids do not have any thoughts of their own. This is a fallacy. What we have discovered is that children do have their own fears and concerns, and, if given a chance, they express their thoughts very well."

The first time I watched a *Children's World* program being produced in Liberia, I was immediately impressed by the image of a small child with large headphones speaking into an even larger microphone: "My name is Brandy Crawford, and this is *Children's World*, a program produced by children for children affected by war." I suddenly understood on a visceral level the power of the programming. I struggled to hold back tears as the innocence and purity of a child reaching out to other children in the face of horrible atrocities stirred my own heart: to compassion, beauty and hope, the very essence of being human, all of which will need to be cultivated if we are to move beyond war.

As for that sixteen-year-old boy who walked into Talking Drum Studio five years ago, he went on to become a Child Ambassador for UNICEF and is now on a full scholarship at the university. But the most important of his achievements must be that, while still only a child himself, he created a platform for children everywhere to voice their hopes and fears, and to teach us all something about the human spirit.

Philip M. Hellmich

Concepción's Circle

If we lift our eyes, to the moon, the stars, and sun; then might we hear the ancient truth—In spirit we are one.

Frances Key, in the song "The Flag of Living Stars"

After twenty-six hours on Guatemalan buses, I had finally drifted into a fitful sleep. I dreamed of my home in Winnipeg, Canada, and of the teaching job I had left for a year to volunteer in this Central American country as an international accompanier.

Suddenly, the rickety bus lurched to a stop. My fifty-one-year-old body screamed in protest. Then I became aware of the fear that shot tangibly through the bus. Anxious Mayan mothers, dark eyes wide with terror, wrapped their children close to them in colorful, hand-woven scarves. The door was pushed open. Two soldiers entered. They barked out orders in Spanish: "All men, out. Line up beside the bus."

Through dusty windows we watched, scarcely daring to breathe, as each man's papers were checked. This time, thank God, not one man was taken away. The bus rolled on. Two hours later, I arrived in Cantula, the village of returned refugees that had sent an urgent plea for some international accompaniers.

I was in the Ixcan Jungle communities, a full day's bus trip away, when the message came. It was brief and carried a note of alarm. It was decided that I should go to Cantula.

The next morning, after I had had time to settle in, Concepción, one of the returned refugees, came to introduce herself and to invite me for a cup of coffee. Gratefully, I accepted. We walked in silence to her home.

"Siéntese, por favor (Sit down please,)" she urged gently. So I sat, lowering myself onto the rough-hewn bench behind the small, handmade table. Concepción walked the three steps across the dirt floor, fanned the fire gently, then lifted the metal kettle from the fire pit and poured us each a mug of something dark.

"Gracias por ayudarnos (Thank you for helping us)" she breathed as she set the mug before me. The liquid was black, and the flat, metallic taste would linger long in my mouth.

"Don't thank me," I replied. "I haven't really done anything. You are the brave ones." In this windowless dwelling, threads of light sifted through the vertical branches that had been lashed together to create walls. The corrugated metal roof was ominously silent. No rain today; no rain at all this spring.

Concepción's hand, worn and old before its time, traced the knot in the wood of the tabletop. "We were brave that day, a week ago before you came." She was silent. I waited. Did she trust me enough to tell? She breathed deeply and looked up, her eyes searching far into the distance.

"We were alone that day—only the women and the children. Our men had gone to the *milpas* to work this year's bean and corn crops. As you know, the fields are far away, higher up on this mountain. When our Guatemalan government allowed us to return from the refugee camps in Mexico, we asked for international accompaniers. We were afraid to come back to our home where so many of us had been killed. The government agreed, but no accompaniers were available. So alone, we returned to our homes—those of us who had survived. There was nothing left here. After the massacre, the paramilitary had also burned our homes, even cut down our fruit trees and burned our crops. The wounding, the tearing, the destroying was complete, complete. *Ay, Dios mío!* (Oh my God)!

"Yes, and after we had been here eight months, we thought maybe we were safe. The military camp, as you know, is only twenty-five minutes away, but no one had come to trouble us. And on the walls of their military compound, they had painted in large letters: '*Luchar por la Paz* [Work for Peace].' We wanted to believe this. Our worries turned to our food supply. You know that the rains have not come. And our rice?" Concepción glanced at the wrinkled white plastic sack slumping in on itself on the floor. "Of the rice we carried back from Mexico, we have only one week's supply left. And the beans? Now, all we have left are a few cupfuls—so tired and dried out. Well, they do still make a good coffee, don't you think?" We exchanged glances and both smiled sadly.

"But, you want to know why we called you to come here to our community, yes?" Concepción took a deep breath and then leaned toward me, her hands clutching the edge of the table. "Last week, it was a Tuesday, our men had gone early to the fields with their machetes to cut away at the underbrush that had grown unchecked into the fields for eight years. They went with their hoes to hack into the hard dirt around the shriveling plants, to make a soft bed for the rain, if it comes. I was inside, making tortillas. Suddenly, Jose came running in, crying and gasping, 'Mama, Mama, the black men are coming.' My heart lurched into my throat. 'Where is Ana?' Just then, she, too, came running. I grabbed my two little children, and I ran to my neighbors' homes, calling to the women, 'Come quickly. Tell the others.' Their eyes widened with fear, but they listened to me. They came. I could tell they wanted to run. They wanted to hide as we had done uselessly, eight years ago.

"By now the soldiers with blackened faces were in our little settlement, outside the town office. They were as startled as we were to see us coming toward them. We women joined hands, feeling the fear in the damp clasp of skin to skin. The children clung to our skirts, our legs. And then, we surrounded the soldiers. We saw their unease. Their confusion. The soldiers were so young. Some had been drafted into the army from our own Mayan communities.

"The air was heavy with possibility. The guns were loaded. The commands were waiting to be barked out. Then the leader looked around and said defiantly, 'You hate us, but we work for peace.'

"'Peace?' I heard the word explode from my mouth. 'What do your blackened faces and your guns have to do with peace—the peace you write about on your compound walls?'

"I spoke—from what well the words came forth, I cannot say. I spoke of family. I spoke of seeds pushed gently into Mother Earth. I spoke of waiting and of hope. And one of the soldiers, tall and very young, began to cry. Slowly, all the soldiers lowered their weapons to the ground. Then, silently, they left."

I wiped tears from my eyes.

"Years ago," Concepción continued, "they would have come, and we all would have been hiding, helpless."

"So I am here to honor you and your path toward wholeness," I said.

"And to be a link to the rest of the world. We also need the strength of the international community in our circle. Our hands are still sweaty and our knees tremble." Again Concepción looked far off into the distance. "Who knows? In my heart, I see a day when our circle will include Mayan women, children, men, people from across the world and also . . . ," she paused briefly, "and also those wounded, wounded ones who carry the weapons."

Madeleine Enns

Seeds of Justice, Seeds of Hope

First keep the peace within yourself, then you can also bring peace to others.

Thomas à Kempis

In the midst of the toxic atmosphere of Watts, seeds are sprouting, organic gardens are thriving, young people are discovering a vocation, and healthy, whole foods are becoming part of everyday life.

If you could imagine a place that has the highest crime rates, the largest drug saturation, the greatest welfare-recipient population, and the fastest growing HIV-positive infection rates in one of the richest cities, in the richest state, in the richest country in the entire world, then you could begin to imagine Watts, California—a district in South-Central Los Angeles.

My name is Anna Marie Carter, but I am also known as "The Seed Lady" of Watts. I am a certified Master Gardener through the University of California. I practice direct action by building free, organic gardens for people who suffer from HIV/AIDS, cancer, diabetes, high blood pressure, obesity and other illnesses. My advocacy takes me to drug- and alcohol-rehabilitation centers, mental-health facilities, community centers, schools, housing projects and shelters that house women who are returning to our community from prison. I teach people how to grow their own food, organically. But that is not all I teach them.

The environment in Watts is toxic. We are told not to drink the water. The air is polluted, and there is not much rain. Multigenerational gangs, drug abuse, carnal value systems resulting from being institutionalized by the welfare system for generations and low morality all add up to no self-esteem, depression, overcrowding, crime and escapism through unprotected sex and drugs. Where it seems there is no hope, there also is no reason to be happy or to act decently—or to dream.

External forces dictate here. I have yet to meet a drug addict who harvests his own drugs. There are no coca plants or poppies growing here. All this madness is imported by the tons to this community—daily! The health of the community is further jeopardized by the lack of real food. The food available in South-Central Los Angeles is genetically engineered, pesticide laden, hybridized and irradiated. The majority of people here eat food that is bagged, bottled, canned, boxed or frozen. A majority of this food comes from South America and Mexico through free-trade agreements. We do not even get food grown in California. The pesticide DDT is still widely used in Latin America. There is no access to whole foods here. The highly processed food and low-quality meats affect the health, both physical and mental, of everyone here.

I had an organic vegetables, seeds and plants store many years ago on Crenshaw Boulevard. The first day I went to open the front door, I looked behind me, and there stood three little boys, lined up in a row, like they were in the army. I opened the door, and they came in after saying "Good morning," and proceeded to take all my plants outside and set up the organic vegetable and flower stands for the day. They were sent to me by a higher source. I taught them many things. Out back, we planted tomato plants that grew over seven feet tall. The boys sold the tomatoes and used the money for school clothes and supplies. One even paid his mother's utility bills. They are grown now, but when I see them, they kiss and hug and thank me.

After I graduated as a Master Gardener, I began my internship at the former Watts Family Garden. We lost the battle to save the garden from sale, so I took my newly formed garden club into the City of Los Angeles's recreation center inside the Jordan Downs Housing Projects. Here, we taught a class called the Value of a Seed, taking the children to the gardens and planting the ingredients that go into pesto, salsa, coleslaw and other products. We taught the children how to design recipes and logos for their food products.

With the help of donations to the Watts Garden Club, we bought our own center in the heart of Watts in 2002. At the club, we have our own Community Supported Agriculture (CSA) project, which provides fresh farm produce to the invisible populations here, and we operate our own produce stand and farmers' market. We train youth in agricultural entrepreneurship (which includes classes in manners, grooming, hospitality and vendor relations). We teach the Value of a Seed on organic gardening and creating value-added products. Participants in the Made in Watts class make their own bath products for sale to our community. The Organic Greenhouse class teaches people to grow lettuce, herbs and flowers indoors. The center will soon have a greenhouse in the courtyard. The Kitchen course covers vegan and vegetarian cooking. We also hold anti-drug/anti-gang rallies, HIV-support groups and holistic-health workshops. We involve the community in garden construction, and we network with other low-income communities of color. We have more than two hundred students at our center, and we go out to where the people are to plant gardens and teach classes.

One of the students in the Watts Garden Club is a young man we will call David. He has never met his father, who is serving a life sentence in prison. His mother is on drugs, and his stepfather is a drug dealer. David is hyperactive and cannot stop moving his hands. He is asthmatic, uses an inhaler and takes Ritalin. At eleven years old, he is a prime target to join a gang. He is talkative and likes to work with his hands. I taught him how to build containers and plant herbs, flowers and vegetables. He learned how to ask retailers if he can beautify their landscape with his creations. He has a portfolio of his work and is always very successful. Now, the biggest hurdle to clear is his inability to save.

We also offer think-tank sessions at the Garden Club. Here, we plant the seeds of change, knowledge and remembrance by facing our history and tasting the bitterness of slavery, oppression, injustice and self-hatred. We take these emotions, bond with each other like never before, and then, fast-forwarding to later on in the twenty-first century, we take a full assessment of where we stand today, here in Watts, California. In a circle, with the help of a facilitator, we have two-hour jam sessions that make the sweetest music—the sound of thinking people who are awakened fully to the calling of addressing our communities' problems and creating viable solutions. We are networking and forming alliances to initiate direct action to expedite change.

If you look at history, you can see it takes only one person to change an environment—one person who takes a stand, an advocacy, an action. It takes only one person to change the entire world. Once upon a time, we were taught here in Watts, "Power to the People." I have lived through that to tell you what I know for sure, and that is people *are* the power. And it only takes one: you!

Anna Marie Carter

Copper or Plastic?

Thoughtless words can wound as deeply as any
sword, but wisely spoken words can heal.
Proverbs 12:18

Our growing rural congregation in Central Pennsylvania was in the process of building a Sunday school addition. Who would have thought that a church situated among sparsely populated farmland would outgrow their facilities? Excitement and enthusiasm for the project ran high.

Money wasn't plentiful, but determination was! As a cost-saving factor, the men of the church were volunteering all the labor for the undertaking. In our little corner of the Susquehanna Valley, many of the families had proudly stick built their own homes and were truly experienced in construction. Several of these people made up the building committee.

One evening at a planning meeting for the building, the members were discussing the type of pipe to use for the plumbing. Earl, a gentleman from the 'old school' insisted on copper, while Dave, a younger man who worked for a local trailer manufacturing company, claimed plastic was the only logical choice. In a matter of minutes what started out as a difference of opinion turned into a heated argument with flaring tempers, raised voices, and unkind innuendoes.

My husband, Dick, pastor of the church, had commented to me many times that maintaining good relationships throughout the building project far outweighed the project itself. From past experience we knew that building construction added strain and stress to a church, not just financially, but physically and spiritually also. Dick felt responsible for assuring good communication and interaction.

Though several people tried to interject a calming word or two, it soon became evident that no peaceful resolution to the conflict would be forthcoming during the meeting. Dick stood and, in a precisely controlled voice, informed the committee that they would be adjourning immediately. He requested that each member go home and pray about this situation, not just for wisdom about the choice of materials, but also for a spirit of cooperation. Not wanting to let the problem fester, he advised the group that they would re-convene at the same time the next evening.

When I heard Dick coming in the back door that night I glanced at the clock and was surprised at the time.

"My, you're home early! How did the meeting go?"

One look at his face and I knew the answer to that question.

Sighing as he flopped down on the couch, he proceeded to tell me all about the seemingly innocent discussion that escalated into a full-blown argument. Dick despises conflict and agonized all evening about what had happened in those few short minutes, replaying the scene over and over in his mind.

We also discussed possible outcomes. Would both men quit the project? Would the members of the committee discuss this with others and spread the contention? And —most distressing of all—would our church lose two fine families over this? Dick planned his strategy for tomorrow night's meeting. We discussed what he would say and how he could handle several scenarios that might occur. Then we prayed together and went to bed, trusting that the outcome of the meeting did not rest with Dick.

The next evening the group warily gathered in a Sunday school classroom, uncomfortable with each other after the way things had ended the night before. Dick opened the meeting with prayer and as soon as the "Amen" was said, Earl asked to speak. "I just want to start off by apologizing for my behavior last night. No matter how I felt about the issue, I shouldn't have handled the situation the way I did. I'm sorry, Dave, for what I said and how I said it."

Then turning to the committee Earl said, "I also have a suggestion to make that might resolve the conflict we have here." Dick signaled that they were all listening and would welcome any solution Earl might suggest.

"I have a lot of experience with siding and roofing. Dave here does a lot of indoor construction. How about if I oversee the outside of the building and Dave oversees the inside? And we just trust each other's decisions on the project. What do you think?"

Everyone turned their head in Dave's direction. With a mildly surprised but admiring look in his eyes and a slight smile, Dave nodded his agreement. A collective sigh of relief went up from the group as they embraced the wisdom of Earl's idea. All the agonizing and dramatizing of the night before had been needless. We had forgotten for a moment the good will and integrity of the men involved.

The meeting ended with smiles, handshakes and good-natured slaps on the back.

Just as quickly as the argument had flared up, the point of contention and source of conflict was resolved with the cooling balm of a few humble, well-chosen words.

Pamela D. Williams

It Begins Within

The day started in typical form as snowflakes fell outside the window. It was Sunday morning, our normal day to clean the house. I took the kitchen while the kids went into their bedroom and closed the door. Soon the house became silent. I became suspicious and went and checked on Anthony and Ryan. As I opened the door, I was met by two smiles and a room covered in toys scattered evenly across the floor. We were expecting guests soon, and the house looked a lot like their room—a big mess. Even though Anthony was only four, my patience was beginning to wear thin. I told him that if he did not get the room cleaned, I was just going to take all his "good stuff" away.

As he looked me in the eye, he said, "You can't."

"And why not?" I asked.

My four-year-old restored order to the house as he proclaimed, "Because all the good stuff is in my heart."

Bryan Hayes

Who Is Jack Canfield?

Jack Canfield is one of America's leading experts in the development of human potential and personal effectiveness. He is both a dynamic, entertaining speaker and a highly sought-after trainer. Jack has a wonderful ability to inform and inspire audiences toward increased levels of self-esteem and peak performance. Jack most recently released a book for success titled *The Success Principles: How to Get from Where You Are to Where You Want to Be.*

He is the author and narrator of several bestselling audio- and videocassette programs, including *Self-Esteem and Peak Performance, How to Build High Self-Esteem, Self-Esteem in the Classroom* and *Chicken Soup for the Soul—Live.* He is regularly seen on television shows such as *Good Morning America,* 20/20 and *NBC Nightly News.* Jack has co-authored numerous books, including the *Chicken Soup for the Soul* series, *Dare to Win* and *The Aladdin Factor* (all with Mark Victor Hansen), *100 Ways to Build Self-Concept in the Classroom* (with Harold C. Wells), *Heart at Work* (with Jacqueline Miller) and *The Power of Focus* (with Les Hewitt and Mark Victor Hansen).

Jack is a regularly featured speaker for professional associations, school districts, government agencies, churches, hospitals, sales organizations and corporations. His clients have included the American Dental Association, the American Management Association, AT&T, Campbell's Soup, Clairol, Domino's Pizza, GE, Hartford Insurance, ITT, Johnson & Johnson, the Million Dollar Roundtable, NCR, New England Telephone, Re/Max, Scott Paper, TRW and Virgin Records. Jack has taught on the faculty of Income Builders International, a school for entrepreneurs.

Jack conducts an annual seven-day training called Breakthrough to Success. It attracts entrepreneurs, educators, counselors, parenting trainers, corporate trainers, professional speakers, ministers and others interested in improving their lives and lives of others.

For free gifts from Jack and information on all his material and availability go to:

www.jackcanfield.com
Self-Esteem Seminars
P.O. Box 30880
Santa Barbara, CA 93130
phone: 805-563-2935 • fax: 805-563-2945

Who Is Mark Victor Hansen?

In the area of human potential, no one is more respected than Mark Victor Hansen. For more than thirty years, Mark has focused solely on helping people from all walks of life reshape their personal vision of what's possible. His powerful messages of possibility, opportunity and action have created powerful change in thousands of organizations and millions of individuals worldwide.

He is a sought-after keynote speaker, bestselling author and marketing maven. Mark's credentials include a lifetime of entrepreneurial success and an extensive academic background. He is a prolific writer with many bestselling books, such as *The One Minute Millionaire*, *The Power of Focus*, *The Aladdin Factor* and *Dare to Win*, in addition to the *Chicken Soup for the Soul* series. Mark has made a profound influence through his library of audios, videos and articles in the areas of big thinking, sales achievement, wealth building, publishing success, and personal and professional development.

Mark is the founder of the MEGA Seminar Series. MEGA Book Marketing University and Building Your MEGA Speaking Empire are annual conferences where Mark coaches and teaches new and aspiring authors, speakers and experts on building lucrative publishing and speaking careers. Other MEGA events include MEGA Marketing Magic and My MEGA Life.

He has appeared on television (*Oprah*, CNN and *The Today Show*), in print (*Time*, *U.S. News & World Report*, *USA Today*, *New York Times* and *Entrepreneur*) and on countless radio interviews, assuring our planet's people that, "You can easily create the life you deserve."

As a philanthropist and humanitarian, Mark works tirelessly for organizations such as Habitat for Humanity, American Red Cross, March of Dimes, Childhelp USA and many others. He is the recipient of numerous awards that honor his entrepreneurial spirit, philanthropic heart and business acumen. He is a lifetime member of the Horatio Alger Association of Distinguished Americans, an organization that honored Mark with the prestigious Horatio Alger Award for his extraordinary life achievements.

Mark Victor Hansen is an enthusiastic crusader of what's possible and is driven to make the world a better place.

Mark Victor Hansen & Associates, Inc.
P.O. Box 7665
Newport Beach, CA 92658
phone: 949-764-2640
fax: 949-722-6912
Visit Mark online at: *www.markvictorhansen.com*

Who Is Candice C. Carter?

Candice C. Carter, Ph.D. is a student of peace who has spent her lifetime thinking about how unnecessary violence is for conflict resolution. Experiences with, and observations of, violence sensitized her awareness of them and motivated her pursuit of peace through education.

Candice has been a career teacher, then professor of education, in USA as well as a consultant for and researcher of peace through education in other countries. Her writings focused on learning peace in schools and beyond can be read in the *Journal of Peace Education, Theory and Research in Social Education, the Journal of Social Alternatives, Multicultural Perspectives,* and *Academic Exchange Quarterly* as well as in book chapters and online in web-based literature that focus on prosocial education. As a resource for peace through education, literature, the arts, and other means, Candice provides The Peace Maker SiTe at *www.peacemaker.st.*

To advance peace education, Candice is currently working in the American Educational Research Association and the Peace Education Commission of the International Peace Research Association to develop guidelines and standards for peace through education. She is also the founder and sponsor of a human rights group where she currently lives. Candice enjoys relaxation in, and protection of, nature. She a leader of educational nature outings that are sponsored by the Sierra Club. Candice delights in teaching others about the natural treasures in our world, of which we are all stewards.

Presently Candice lives on the edge of a preserve by the Atlantic Ocean and considers all of the creatures in her ìyardî as a part of her global family. She finds peace through deep listening to nature at home and active listening to humans who are experiencing conflicts in all regions of the world where she learns, teaches, and conducts research. Candice can be reached at:

phone 904 620-1881
fax: 904-620-1025
e-mail: *ccarter@peacemaker.st*

Visit The Peace Maker Site to find many resources that helped the authors in this book nonviolently resolve conflicts and contribute in other ways to the better world that we are building: *www.peacemaker.st*

Who Is Susanna Palomares?

Susanna Palomares has been involved in the development, publishing and marketing of education curricula and programs for over twenty-five years. She is the president of Innerchoice Publishing, and continues producing K–12 educational materials for teachers and counselors. She has authored or co-authored over twenty-five books and activity guides addressing a wide range of topics in the social-emotional and life-skills domains. Her most recent releases are *Lessons in Tolerance and Diversity, How to Handle a Bully* and *Teaching Kids Right from Wrong.*

Her materials have found their way around the world, having been translated into many languages. One of her programs has served as the basis for teaching peace and cooperation to people who are caught in the Israeli-Palestinian conflict. This program brings together Christians, Jews and Muslims from all cultures to develop a forum of understanding and respect.

Susanna's background is in education, and she has a master's degree in Curriculum and Instruction. She began her career as a classroom teacher working in migrant education at the elementary level. As a publisher, she continued her teaching by working with students and adults within the scope of the programs she has developed and published.

Susanna has a vision for education based on the fact that students who develop strong intrapersonal and social skills move into adulthood better prepared for success in all parts of their lives. She has worked with groups of concerned educators and parents all over the nation and is an advocate for school counselors and the role they play in helping young people have success in their first careers as K–12 students.

Today, in addition to her other pursuits, Susanna has a passion for service that is expressed as an active volunteer with Junior Achievement and in her work in a refugee program sponsored by the school district of Palm Beach County.

Susanna lives with her husband, David, and their Golden Doodle dog Chimay in their homes in Florida and New York. Susanna can be reached at *Susanna@susannapalomares.com.*

Who Is Linda K. Williams?

Linda K. Williams was born in Toledo, Ohio, and has lived in San Diego since fifth grade. She has a BA in Linguistics and an MA in Education/Reading.

She has been married to her high-school sweetheart since 1973, has taught Kindergarten-sixth grades in English and Spanish since 1973, and has found great satisfaction in teaching Reading Recovery (*www.rrcna.org*) to the neediest first-grade readers in inner-city schools since 1994, helping them to joyfully declare, "I can do it!"

Linda's peace-making roots began in the Church of the Brethren (*www.brethren.org*), of which she is an active, longtime member; she is Decade to Overcome Violence coordinator for her congregation. Linda began her passionate peacemaking efforts after an elderly family member was murdered in 1981; since then she has co-authored *Caring and Capable Kids* (includes "If You're Angry and You Know It," *www.ProEdInc.com*), designed to help kids become compassionate and responsible, and has written and recorded over one hundred songs for children and adults on the themes of self-esteem, conflict resolution, drug abuse prevention, inner peace, dealing with feelings, and other pro-social and spiritual themes (*peacemaker.st*). Also please visit "Let's Overcome Violence with Education, Empathy, and Empowerment" (*www.cob-net.org/docs/williams.htm*).

After the Columbine School shootings in 1999, Linda felt compelled to bring the message of nonviolence to as wide an audience as possible, and was convinced that a *Chicken Soup for the Soul* book would be the best possible venue. This has been a book long in the making! She was thrilled when a volunteer story reader/rater thanked *her*, saying, "Reading these stories has helped me see that there are so many ways of dealing with conflicts without resorting to violence!" What a heart-warming, hope-filled moment! May all our readers be so blessed!

Linda lives in San Diego with her patient, supportive, understanding husband Rob, their "most wonderful daughter in the world," Cherilyn, and their rambunctious pound-puppy mutt, Toby. Linda cherishes time with family and friends and loves to "play with her plants," play the guitar, and harmonize. She finds pulling weeds—and prayer, and yoga—to be great for inner peace! Linda can be reached at *LKW_BetterWorld@yahoo.com*.

Who Is Bradley L. Winch?

Bradley Winch, Ph.D., J.D., is a noted international scholar, published scientist, businessman, lawyer, lecturer, educator, author and award-winning publisher. He has been affiliated with Wayne State University and the University of Karlsruhe (Germany), and he was an exchange scientist in the Soviet Union in 1963–64. His business history includes stints with Parke, Davis, General Mills and Mattel. He was also a practicing attorney.

Bradley has, since 1971, been active in publishing activity-driven books to help students grades K-12 develop social, emotional, ethical and peaceful conflict resolution skills. Titles from his educational company, Jalmar Press, have been translated into more than thirty-five languages and are distributed around the world. In 2003, Bradley formed Personhood Press: Books For ALL That You Are! to publish books on anger management, peaceful conflict resolution, psychology, self-help, spirituality and relationships.

Bradley is dedicated to empowering children (and adults) worldwide to develop strong conflict resolution skills so that they may begin to value, respect and honor life within themselves and around them. His goal is to create a peaceful, loving, esteeming world filled with people who live from the "inside/out," understanding that in all situations the choice is theirs.

Bradley is chairman of the board of the B. L. Winch Group, Inc. and CEO of Intercontinental Diversified, Inc., which does international licensing. He is on the advisory board of Friends of Fawnskin, a group of interested citizens in the Big Bear Lake area striving to protect endangered species and the environment.

He spends most of his time in Fawnskin, California, on the beautiful North Shore of Big Bear Lake, seven-thousand feet in the San Bernardino Mountains, with his wife, Cathy, and their dog, Shyloh. To contact him, write, call or e-mail:

The B. L. Winch Group, Inc.
P.O. Box 370
Fawnskin, CA 92333-0370
phone: 909-866-9479
fax: 909-866-2767
blwjalmar@att.net
www.personhoodpress.com

Contributors

Terri Akin holds an M.A. in Human Behavior and an M.S. in Education. After a twenty-eight-year career as an elementary school teacher, she is now completing her doctorate in Energy Medicine. A teacher trainer and educator, Terri has authored and coauthored many educational books. She enjoys dancing, hiking and traveling.

David H. Albert is an author, magazine columnist and speaker. He is the editor of two books on storytelling, *The Healing Heart-Families* and *The Healing Heart-Communities*, and several books on home schooling, and he writes two regular columns: "MY Word! in *Home Education Magazine,* and "What Really Matters" in *The Link.* He can be reached through his Web site at *www.skylarksings.com.*

Karen Alexander is a reading specialist and published poet. She enjoys writing children's poetry books, conducting poetry workshops and performing her poems for children and mid-life girls! Visit Karen's Web site at ABC Poet-Tree or email her at *karenalexander@abcpoet-tree.com.*

Nuraddin A. Ali is a native of Somalia. Nuraddin holds a B.S. in Agricultural Extension and Education from the Somali National University.

Dr. Oscar Arias, Costa Rican president 1986–1990, was awarded the 1987 Nobel Peace Prize for efforts to negotiate an end to the Central American wars. The monetary award went to establish the Arias Foundation for Peace and Human Progress, which continues Arias's pursuit of demilitarization, democracy and human security. Visit the Web site *www.arias.or.cr.*

Jon Arnold is an ordained minister with the Church of God (Anderson, Indiana). He received his M.Div. from Fuller Theological Seminary and is a board-certified chaplain with the Association of Professional Chaplains. Jon promotes a spirit of peace by encouraging a multiplicity of truths. Please e-mail him at *genxchap@aol.com.*

Leslie Baer's career has spanned journalism, public relations, marketing and community development. For work on behalf of the poor, the environment and building cultural understanding, she has been honored by Congress, the California Senate and numerous community service organizations. She holds a B.A. in Communications, a master's in Organizational Management, and is the founder of a Guatemalan aid organization, *www.xelaaid.org.*

Palmer Becker served as a relief worker and educator in Taiwan from 1958 to 1963 and as a pastor and leader in the Mennonite Church before becoming director of pastoral ministries at Hesston College in 1998. He has nurtured social intimacy through books and workshops on small groups. Palmer enjoys traveling, public speaking and writing. You can e-mail him at *PalmerB@Hesston.edu.*

Jodi H. Beyeler is a 2000 graduate of Goshen College in Indiana, where she is currently employed as the news bureau director/writer. Jodi enjoys books, amusement parks and road trips. You can e-mail her at *jodihb@goshen.edu.*

Adrianne Bowes is an RN in Northern California and a Licensed Practitioner with the Center for Spiritual Living in Santa Rosa, California. A lover of nature, Adrianna is actively pursuing a publication venue for her personal essays. You can e-mail her at *adribowes@yahoo.com.*

Janna Bowman worked in Bogotá, Colombia, with the Colombian Mennonite peace organization Justapaz from 2001 through 2004. She currently works with Witness for Peace in Washington, D.C., as the national grassroots organizer on Colombia. You can e-mail her at *jannalbowman@yahoo.com.*

Anna Marie Carter is a certified Master Gardener through the University of California. Ms. Carter is founder and CEO of the Watts Garden Club. She specializes in creating economic development in low-income communities and is a motivational speaker.

Jimmy Carter, thirty-ninth president of the United States of America, Nobel Peace Prize laureate, author of nineteen books, volunteer for Habitat for Humanity (*www.habitat.org*), and founder of The Carter Center (*www.cartercenter.org*) with his wife, Rosalynn. The Center has improved the quality of life for people in more than sixty-five countries by international peacemaking, promoting democracy, fighting disease, and championing mental health issues.

Joan Chittister, O.S.B., is a noted national and international lecturer, columnist and widely published author of over thirty books. She is a social psychologist and communications theorist with a doctorate from Penn State University. She is also the founder and executive director of Benetvision, a resource and research center for contemporary spirituality. Visit her at the Web site *www.benetvision.org.*

Lynea Corson-Hadley received a Ph.D. in Psycho-Educational Process (Temple University) and is a Clinical Member of ITAA. She coauthored *I Know It and I Show It* (award-winning character-building test preprogram K–6) and *Secret of Super Selling*—endorsed by Og Mandino, Zig Ziglar and Dr. Norman Vincent Peale. You can e-mail her at *lynea@mac.com.*

Florence Crago received her Ph.D. in Education from Claremont Graduate School in 1975. Her career roles have included: college professor, social worker, medical secretary, business administrator, gift shop manager, and co-pastor with her late husband Glen. Retirement for Florence means more time to write. You can e-mail her at *cragocorner@cox.net.*

Maureen Murphy DeLucia has taught kindergarten for thirty-two years. She was the recipient of a 1996 Teacher of the Year award. Maureen lives with her husband, Tony, and two sons in Wallingford, Connecticut. She is the author of *Keeping Your Word*, a book on parenting, published in 2005 by iUniverse. You can e-mail her at *adelucia67@aol.com*.

David S. Diamond received his bachelor's degree in Elementary Education from The Ohio State University and a master's of education from SUNY Plattsburg. He teaches third grade in the Adirondacks. He runs the Adirondack Writer's Guild, a gifted and talented program for grades 4–6, and writes children's books for and with students. You can e-mail him at *dsdiamond@hotmail.com*.

Gerry Dunne is a speaker, teacher, counselor and author on anger and conflict management, parenting today's kids, communication in the organization, harassment prevention, and career continuation. She earned her Ph.D. in Psychology at the Saybrook Institute in San Francisco, an M.S. degree at the University of Southern California, and a B.A. degree at Chapman University, where she was selected Alumna of the Year, 2002.

Helen Engelhardt is a writer, poet and storyteller. Her memoir, *The Longest Night: A Personal History of Pan Am Flight 103*, will be published later this year. She is actively involved with groups supporting and sustaining peacemakers in the Middle East. You can e-mail her at *Helen.Engelhardt@verizon.net*.

Madeleine Enns, a retired teacher, lives in Winnipeg, Canada. She has lived and worked in Guatemala, Taiwan and China. She continues to be involved in peace and justice issues. Her stories have been published in several magazines, including *Rhubarb* and *Sophia*.

Jan Thompson Eve is a leadership coach, working with corporations to develop their high potentials and executives. She grew up in Texas, but has lived in San Diego, California, for the last twenty years.

Bob Filner has served the people of Southern California in Congress since 1992 and is deeply committed to the battle for justice and equity. While a professor at San Diego State University, he was elected to the San Diego Board of Education and the San Diego City Council.

Susan Finney was a classroom teacher for over twenty-five years, a consultant presenting seminars for teachers for over ten years and a Scholastic author. She currently resides in the Northwest where she is enjoying retirement, her grandchildren and many new interests.

Kathy Gerst has Bachelor of Science degrees in Math, Biology and Chemistry. She currently is working in a large pharmaceutical company as a chemist. She and her husband have adopted all of the foster children she wrote about. As a mother of seven, she keeps busy participating in activities with her children.

Terri Goggin-Roberts is an R.N., writer and mother of two incredible children. She created the "Strong & Wise" Workshop and upcoming book. Teri lives with her charming husband in Pennsylvania. "Left Foot Forward" is dedicated to her grandparents, who were a constant source of love. You can e-mail her at *Indigomuse63@aol.com.*

Richard Gutherie dedicated his career at Ford to the transformation of an autocratic work culture. This story is a prelude from his book, *Working with Spirit: To Replace Control with Trust at Ford,* an award-winning journey about empowerment, diversity and the bottom-line impact. You can e-mail him at *rgutherie@comcast.net* or visit his Web site at *www.LeadershipForDiversity.com.*

Share **Nadja Halilbegovich**'s passion for a peaceful tomorrow by helping to rebuild her homeland. Contact Our Children, Musala Street 51, 71000 Sarajevo, Bosnia Herzegovina. Telephone 011-387-71-442-464 or fax 011-387-71-531-833.

Thich Nhat Hanh is a Vietnamese Buddhist monk, poet, scholar and human rights activist. In 1967, he was nominated by Martin Luther King Jr. for the Nobel Peace Prize. He is author of more than fifty books. He lives at Plum Village, a meditation center in France, and travels worldwide, leading retreats on the "the art of mindful living."

Ian Harris and **Sara Spence** have been married twenty-four years. They have raised two children and two dogs nonviolently. Ian is the founder of a peace studies program at the University of Wisconsin–Milwaukee. Sara has a background in early childhood education.

Lawrence H. Hart is a Cheyenne member of the Cheyenne and Arapaho Tribes of Oklahoma. He is one of the traditional peace chiefs and is one of four principal chiefs in the Council of Forty Four. He is the executive director of the Cheyenne Cultural Center.

Jo Clare Hartsig graduated from Colgate University with a B.A. in Peace Studies and from Yale Divinity School with an M.Div. for Ministry with an emphasis on Social Change. She was ordained in 1983 in the United Church of Christ. Jo Clare lives with her family in Minnetonka, Minnesota, where she works on disability advocacy in congregational settings.

Bryan Hayes is a soulful poet and writer. He is a former president of Toastmasters Club 9086, the designer of the "7 Keys to Lasting Happiness," a Life Coach, and the proud single dad of Anthony and Ryan. You can write to him at 1400 NW 15th Avenue #5, Boca Raton, FL 33486, or call (561) 866-0976.

Regina Hellinger lives in Orlando, Florida, with her husband and two sons, Andrew and Ethan. She has been in education for over a decade as a classroom teacher and consultant in character education. You can e-mail her at *RHellinger@cfl.rr.com.*

Philip M. Hellmich grew up in Greensburg, Indiana, with his ten siblings. He joined the Peace Corps in 1985 after graduating from DePaul University. He works for Search for Common Ground (*www.sfcg.org*), an international organization working to transform how the world deals with conflict. He loves gardening and kriya yoga. You can e-mail him at *phellmich@sfcg.org.*

Roberta and **Warren Heydenberk** are education professors who have conducted extensive conflict resolution research in schools. Their publications include a textbook, a children's book and numerous research articles. PK, the boy who inspired their story, was a third-grade student who they had the honor of working with in an urban school.

Thomas Ann Hines holds a B.S. in Criminal Justice and refers to her favorite pastime as "going to prison." She has been invited to speak in facilities throughout the United States, and has been featured on *Oprah, 48 Hours,* numerous TV and radio stations, as well as in newspapers and magazines. She receives numerous letters from both victims and offenders, and sends a personal reply to each one. You can contact her at Box 864499, Plano, TX 75086–4499, or e-mail her at *tahines@aol.com.*

Lee Hargus Hunter is a freelance writer now living in Florida. Her works have appeared in both Christian and secular publications throughout the United States and Canada. She also writes Sunday school curriculum and teaches creative writing to home school enrichment groups. She is also a motivational speaker. You can e-mail her at *HJL114@aol.com.*

Rebecca Janke received her Master of Education degree at Xavier University in 1981. She is the cofounder and executive director of Growing Communities for Peace. She is the coauthor of *The Compassionate Rebel* and codeveloper of *www.humanrightsandpeacestore.org,* which provides resources for building a culture of peace.

Wollom A. Jensen is a retired captain, Chaplain Corps, USN. He earned his Doctor of Arts from George Mason University and is an ordained pastor of the ELCA. Wollom is currently the Executive V.P. of Gettysburg Lutheran Seminary. He and his wife Rita make their home in Alexandria, Virginia.

Laurie Beth Jones, an internationally acclaimed author, has published nine books, including *Jesus CEO, The Path* and *Jesus Life Coach.* She founded The Path Community Services, which teaches life skills to youths in juvenile justice facilities, YMCA Youth Programs and some school districts. You can visit her Web site: *www.Lauriebethjones.com.*

Joel Kauffmann has produced the cartoon strip *Pontius' Puddle* for twenty years. It appears in two hundred publications in a dozen countries. Joel also writes for the screen and television. Disney has produced two of his recent screenplays. You can e-mail him at *joelkauffmann@aol.com.*

Cynthia Kersey is a nationally known speaker, columnist and author of the bestseller *Unstoppable,* and an upcoming sequel, *Unstoppable Women.* Cynthia captivates audiences by delivering presentations on how to be unstoppable in their business and life pursuits. To learn more about joining the FREE "Unstoppable Community" or bringing Cynthia to your next meeting, visit the Web site *www.unstoppable.net.*

KEV™ (Kevin Rones) is a San Diego–based acoustic performer whose mission is to inspire. Please visit *www.kevmusic.com.*

Azim Khamisa is founder/CEO of the Tariq Khamisa Foundation (*www.tkf.org*). He is an emissary of peace, an international inspirational speaker and the award-winning author of *From Murder to Forgiveness,* as well as an audio program called *Forgiveness: The Crown Jewel of Personal Freedom.* He is a recipient of over fifty national and international awards, and has been featured in countless media publications. You can e-mail him at *azim@azimkhamisa.com.*

Sister Chân Không was born in a village on the Mekong River Delta in 1938. She has devoted her life to the development and practice of nonviolence grounded in the Buddhist precepts of nonkilling and compassionate action. She is part of the community of Zen master Thich Nhat Hanh and lives in Plum Village, France.

Joanne Klassen of Heartspace Associates in Winnipeg, Canada, facilitates personal transformation and writing workshops. She is the author of *Learning to Live, Learning to Love, Tools of Transformation,* and *Trouble in Grandpa's Golf Bag.* Contact Joanne at 204-452-1941 or *jklassen@write-away.net.*

Erik Kolbell is an author, ordained minister and licensed psychotherapist living with his wife and daughter in New York City. His most recent book, *Were You There?* was published by Westminster Press. Erik was the inspiration for the character Rev. Eric Camden on the television show *Seventh Heaven.*

Kristin Krycia received her M.Ed. from University of San Diego. She lives and works as a school counselor in Virginia. She's married and has three children. Much of her life and work revolves around children with special needs. You can e-mail her at *Kristinkrycia@cavtel.net.* For more information on the program visit the Web site *www.operationrespect.org.*

George Lakey, sixty-seven, is a Quaker activist great-grandfather who has taught in universities and led fifteen hundred workshops on five continents. He has led social change campaigns from neighborhood to international levels, and directs Training for Change (*www.TrainingforChange.org*).

Linda Lantieri is coauthor of *Waging Peace in Our Schools* and director of Project Renewal, a project of the Tides Center. She has been in the field of education for thirty-five years as a classroom teacher, administrator and founding director of the internationally recognized Resolving Conflict Creatively Program. She lives in New York City. Visit the Web site *http://projectrenewal-tidescenter.org.*

Warren Lehrer, an award-winning writer, designer and photographer, and **Judith Sloan,** a critically acclaimed actress, oral historian and audio artist, are cofounders of EarSay, a nonprofit arts organization documenting and portraying lives of the uncelebrated. Their book, *Crossing the BLVD,* won the 2004 Brendan Gill Prize, among others. Visit the Web sites *www.earsay.org* and *www.crossingtheblvd.org.*

Sylvia Boaz Leighton credits her German/Puerto Rican heritage for her love of baking and dancing. Her family's mission is Micah 6:8 and to share God's love with everyone. She plans to write a book about her "Cookie Fairy" adventures.

You can e-mail her at *sylvia@library.ucsd.edu.*

Julie Madsen, RN, Ph.D., began her career as a nurse, working in psychiatry and public health in Cleveland, Ohio. After earning a doctorate in Counseling Psychology from The University of Akron, she spent seven years in private practice. In 1995, disillusioned by the increasing focus on violence, she and her husband Bruce traded high-paying jobs for a life on the road as gypsy journalists. Their book *Inner Views: Stories on the Strength of America* offers ninety-five stories of hope from all around the United States. The Madsens reside in San Francisco, California. You can e-mail her at *juliemadsen2003@yahoo.com.*

Krista Martinelli is an avid playwright and founder of the Boca Playwrights Group. She was previously a theater reviewer and English instructor. Krista wrote a short story for the book *An Ear to the Ground* and wrote a book on leadership for Office Depot. She lives with her supportive husband Joe in Lake Worth, Florida. You can e-mail her at *kmartinelli@earthlink.net.*

John McCutcheon is an internationally known performer, songwriter, recording artist and peace activist. His songs have been loved and recorded worldwide. He has written short stories, poetry and children's books and is a regularly featured performer at the U.S. National Storytelling Festival.

For further information on **Steven McDonald,** Johann Christoph Arnold and their peace work in New York schools, visit the Web site *www.breakingthecycle.us.*

James McGinnis is the founder of the Institute for Peace & Justice and international co-coordinator with his wife, Kathleen, of the Parenting for Peace & Justice Network. He is an author, speaker, parent, grandparent, peace educator, activist and clown. Please visit *www.ipj-ppj.org.*

Simone McLaughlin was born and raised in New York City and was encouraged to write by both her middle- and high-school English teachers. She graduated from New York City Lab School in 2003 and presently attends UMass Amherst majoring in pre-veterinarian studies. Her family and friends have always supported her. You can e-mail her at *simmac20@gmail.com.*

LeDayne McLeese Polaski is the Summer Conference Coordinator of the Baptist Peace Fellowship of North America. Her part-time job with the Peace Fellowship (along with incredible support from her husband Tom) allows her to stay home with their daughter, Kate.

Dee Montalbano is a teacher, a teacher of teachers, a communication consultant and a writer. She is mom to two grown daughters, grandma to three great kids and guardian to one Labrador Retriever. When she's not hiking the Colorado trails, she drums, studies Italian, and enjoys music and film.

Greg Mortenson is founder of the nonprofit Central Asia Institute (CAI), which sets up schools especially for girls in remote regions of Pakistan and Afghanistan. To date, Mortenson has established fifty-two schools that educate over twenty thousand children. Mortenson, a military veteran survived a

1996 kidnapping and received a Red Cross Humanitarian Award. His biography, *Three Cups of Tea*, published by Viking/Penguin, will be released in 2006.

Jeff Moyer is an internationally known author, songwriter and advocate for the dignity and inclusion of all people. Moyer's published materials are at work in schools, homes and communities, healing exclusion, ridicule and violence against those devalued because of their differences. His work can be reviewed at the Web site *www.jeffmoyer.com*.

Ilene Munetz Pachman, author of the children's book *Like a Knot in My Shoelace/A Yahrzeit Remembrance* (United Synagogue), was the "Motherhood" columnist for the (Philadelphia) *Jewish Times*. She has written for the *Washington Post* and the *Philadelphia Inquirer,* and was the primary advocate of the Raoul Wallenberg 1997 U.S. stamp.

Andy Murray is the director of the Baker Institute at Juniata College in Pennsylvania. He serves on a joint commission of the United Nations and the International Association of University Presidents for Arms Control Education. He was a consultant to the special U.N. project on Peace Building in West Africa.

Michael Nagler founded and teaches nonviolence and meditation in the Peace and Conflict Studies Program at University of California–Berkeley. He does public speaking and conducts workshops for the Blue Mountain Center of Meditation in Northern California and the award-winning Search for a Nonviolent Future.

Rik Palieri is a long-established professional singer, musician, TV show producer and world traveler. Rik recently published his first book, *The Road Is My Mistress: Tales of a Roustabout Songster.* For more information about Rik, his music and tales from the road, you can e-mail him at *rik@banjo.net.* Visit his Web site *www.banjo.net.*

Carol Lynn Pearson is the author of numerous books and plays, most notably *Goodbye, I Love You, The Lesson, A Stranger for Christmas, Consider the Butterfly,* and a one-woman play, *Mother Wove the Morning.* She lives and works in Walnut Creek, California.

As a teacher, **Barbara Pedersen** knew the importance of providing meaningful curriculum and experiences to allow students to reach beyond their potential. She created a curriculum model called Connecting Learning Assures Successful Students. Barbara strives to help educators discover themselves as professionals through C.L.A.S.S. You can e-mail her at *bjpeders@comcast.net.*

Ellie Porte lives knee-deep in snow in upstate New York, where she and her husband are raising two boys. She writes, does pottery and hones her negotiation skills. She has a Ph.D. in psychology and is interested in international adoption issues. You can re-mail her at *Ellieparker@hotmail.com.*

Pierre Pradervand has had a varied and rich career as researcher, program leader for the American Friends Service Committee, journalist, international consultant and now trainer and writer in his homeland, Switzerland, where he runs workshops on simpler, more holistic living at seven thousand feet in the Swiss alps. You can e-mail him at *prader@iprolink@ch*.

For any information regarding Bittersweet Ministries, please contact **Gilbert Romero** at (323) 721-5544.

Angie Rubel teaches middle school in Alpharetta, Georgia. She enjoys gardening, as well as spending time with her husband, Doug.

Wayne Sakamoto is a safe school coordinator for the San Diego County Office of Education. He is a recipient of the 2005 California Wellness Foundations California Peace Prize. He is currently focusing attention on bully strategies for schools. You can e-mail him at *wsakamot@sdcoe.net*.

Marilyn Savetsky received her bachelor's and master's degrees from Hunter College. A New York City native, she is retired from the school system there, happily painting, swimming and traveling with her husband. She has had her paintings exhibited in New York City and in upstate New York.

Joyce Seabolt has been a nurse for over forty years and a freelance writer for four. She has never forgotten the lesson of keeping a peaceful spirit. Joyce and her husband, Hal, live in Norrisville, Maryland.

Joanne Shenandoah is a Wolf Clan member of the Iroquois Confederacy, Oneida Nation, and a two-time Grammy-nominated singer and composer. Her many recordings, including "Peacemaker's Journey," are available on Silver Wave Records (*www.silverwave.com*). Her husband Doug George, of the Akwesasne Mohawk Territory, is a freelance columnist and a nationally recognized authority on Iroquois politics and culture.

Glenn Smiley was a Methodist minister from Texas who worked for the Fellowship of Reconciliation for twenty-five years. He served a prison term as a conscientious objector in World War II. He is best remembered for his work with Martin Luther King Jr., beginning with the Montgomery bus boycott.

Stacy Smith is a freelance writer who thrives on writing about cultural and spiritual experiences while traveling. Between her journeys and quests for inspiration, she pays the bills by writing copy for businesses of all sizes. You can contact her through her Web site *www.wordsmith-writing.com*.

Barbara Smythe, recently retired from city and school administration, is enjoying a shift in focus. Instead of writing grants and proposals, she is doing creative writing, leading to some exciting opportunities. She has published several short stories and poems, and done editing and ghostwriting for many successful authors. You can e-mail her at *blsmythe@earthlink.net*.

Christian Snyder holds a bachelor of science degree summa cum laude in Social Sciences from Canisius College. Christian started his cartooning career in 1994. Christian's cartoons have appeared in *Chicken Soup for the Prisoner's Soul, Chicken Soup for the Volunteer's Soul* as well as numerous books, magazines and trade journals.

Cathy Som lives on a remote private lake on the Kitsap Peninsula in northwest Washington State. She worked many years in the forests and feels a true bond with nature. "It is God's creation, and we should respect it as that, not exploit and destroy it. Nature can live without us, but we cannot live without it." You can e-mail her at *mahoniabear@msn.com*.

Steve Speisman is a high-school teacher and adjunct professor in Scottsdale, Arizona. He is a published author and accomplished guitarist/songwriter. Steve has been appointed to the Arizona Governor's Task Force to develop a September 11 Memorial so that the tragic events of that day will never be forgotten. You can e-mail him at *AZSpeis@aol.com*.

Belle Star is a graduate and currently a staff member of the Nine Gates Mystery School. She has also studied extensively with Dr. Brugh Joy. When not doing aura readings at major holistic health conferences, Belle lives with fiction author J. D. Townsend and works as a life coach in Boulder, Colorado.

Michael Stern is a songwriter and inspirational speaker from Seattle, Washington, where he also works as a clinical researcher. His music and presentations focus on nurturing peace, compassion, hope, healing and wonder at the beauty of creation and human diversity. Visit the Web site *www.mikesongs.net* for more about Michael's music and creative programs.

David Stratman edits *New Democracy World.org*, a Web site committed to democratic revolution. He is a former Washington director of the National PTA and a former Education Policy Fellow. He received his Ph.D. from the University of North Carolina, studying as a National Defense Fellow. You can e-mail him at *newdem@aol.com*.

Len Traubman, a retired pediatric dentist, cofounded the twelve-year-old Jewish-Palestinian Living Room Dialogue on the San Francisco Peninsula. After 152 meetings, it is the oldest of its kind. Through face-to-face and Internet communication, he continues to help "enemies" meet and become partners in the public peace process. You can e-mail him at *LTraubman@igc.org*.

Karen Waldman, Ph.D., loves working as a psychologist. She also enjoys writing, dancing, music, acting, playing in nature, traveling with her husband Ken and spending time with their wonderful families, friends, children and grandchildren (Lisa, Tom, Lana, Greta, Alyson, Brian, Eric, Maryann, David and Laura). You can e-mail her at *krobens@aol.com*.

Pamela Williams received her Bachelor of Arts in English from Shippensburg University in 1975. Pam writes from her life experiences and has been published in various Christian magazines and cat publications. She enjoys working closely with her husband in pastoral ministry and travel, and visiting with her children and grandchildren.

Margaret Wolff is a writer and trainer who leads women's spirituality retreats throughout the United States. Her book *In Sweet Company: Conversations with Extraordinary Women About Leading a Spiritual Life,* from which this excerpt is taken, is enjoyed by readers worldwide. You can contact Margaret through the Web site *www.insweetcompany.com* or e-mail her at *margaret@insweetcompany.com.*

Pattty Anne Zeitlin teaches Nonviolent Communication (based on Dr. Marshall Rosenberg's work *www.cnvc.org*) in Seattle, Washington. Please visit these Web sites for more information *www.psncc.org,* and *www.cnvc.org.* She is an author, singer-songwriter with many recordings for children and a former nanny. For twenty-five years, she taught young children and trained teachers. She has an M.A. in human development and adult education. You can e-mail her at *pattipaz@psncc.org.*

Howard Zinn is a historian, playwright and activist. He has taught at Spelman College and Boston University. He is the author of many books, including *A People's History of the United States* and his memoir, *You Can't Be Neutral on a Moving Train.* For speaking engagements or more info, visit the Web site *www.HowardZinn.org.*

Permissions

A Risky Ride for Freedom. Reprinted by permission of Bob Filner. ©2004 Bob Filner.

Truth at a Tender Age. Reprinted by permission of Gerry Dunne, Ph.D. ©2003 Gerry Dunne, Ph.D.

The Last Day of My Life. Reprinted by permission of Helen Engelhardt. ©2003 Helen Engelhardt.

A Bully's Transformation in Room 7. Reprinted by permission of Kristin Krycia. ©2005 Kristin Krycia.

Peace on Earth, Goodwill to Men. Reprinted by permission of Barbara Mosier Smythe. ©2001 Barbara Mosier Smythe.

Shopping for a New Coat. Reprinted by permission of Krista Koontz Martinelli ©2003 Krista Koontz Martinelli.

Labib's Café. Reprinted by permission of Warren Lehrer and Judith Sloan. Excerpted from *Crossing the BLVD: Strangers, Neighbors, Aliens in a New America.* Published by W.W. Norton, ©2003.

Hulk Heaven. Reprinted by permission of Dolores M. Montalbano. ©2004 Dolores M. Montalbano.

Roses for Dinner. Reprinted by permission of Cathryn M. Som. ©2001 Cathryn M. Som.

The Christmas Truce. Reprinted by permission of David Stratman. Excerpted from *We Can the Change the World, The Real Meaning of Everyday Life.*

Christmas in the Trenches. Reprinted by permission of John McCutcheon. ©1984 John McCutcheon.

Left Foot Forward. Reprinted by permission of Theresa M. Goggin-Roberts. ©2001 Theresa M. Goggin-Roberts.

A Spa for the Heart. Reprinted by permission of Janet Bailey Thompson Eve. ©2001 Janet Bailey Thompson Eve.

Beginning Anew. Reprinted by permission of Parallax Press. ©1998 Parallax Press.

The Mystery of the Thatch. Excerpted from *Coals of Fire* by Elizabeth Hershberger Bauma. ©1954, renewed 1982, 1994 by Hearald Press, Scottsdale, PA 15683.

Common Ground. Reprinted by permission of Jodi Sue Hochstedler Beyeler. ©2003 Jodi Sue Hochstedler Beyeler.

Saving Oleg. Reprinted by permission of Lionel Traubman. ©2004 Lionel Traubman.

Drafted by Mother Teresa! Reprinted by permission of Leslie Carol Baer. ©2004 Leslie Carol Baer.

At the Foot of the Bed. Reprinted by permission of Jon Douglas Arnold II. ©2004 Jon Douglas Arnold II.

He Achieved the Impossible with a Little Help from His Friends. Reprinted by permission of Sourcebooks and Cynthia Kersey. ©1998 Cynthia Kersey. Excerpted and adapted from *Unstoppable.*

You Get What You Give. Reprinted by permission of Terri Akin. ©2002 Terri Akin.

Strengthening the Circle of Life. Reprinted by permission of Rebecca Janke. ©2002 Rebecca Janke.

Copper or Plastic? Reprinted by permission of Pamela Dawn Williams. © 2004 Pamela Dawn Williams.

Awakening of the Soul. Reprinted by permission of Steven Barry Speisman. ©2004 Steven Barry Speisman.

Christa's Field of Dreams. Reprinted by permission of Greg Mortenson. ©2005 Greg Mortenson.

The Voice of the Future. Reprinted by permission of Philip M. Hellmich. ©2005 Philip M. Hellmich.

Concepción's Circle. Reprinted by permission of Madeleine Ruth Enns. ©2003 Madeleine Ruth Enns.

Seeds of Justice, Seeds of Hope. Reprinted by permission of Anna Marie Carter. ©2003 Anna Marie Carter.

It Begins Within. Reprinted by permission of Bryan Hayes. ©2003 Bryan Hayes.

Improving Your Life Every Day

Real people sharing real stories—for nineteen years. Now, Chicken Soup for the Soul has gone beyond the bookstore to become a world leader in life improvement. Through books, movies, DVDs, online resources and other partnerships, we bring hope, courage, inspiration and love to hundreds of millions of people around the world. Chicken Soup for the Soul's writers and readers belong to a one-of-a-kind global community, sharing advice, support, guidance, comfort, and knowledge.

Chicken Soup for the Soul stories have been translated into more than 40 languages and can be found in more than one hundred countries. Every day, millions of people experience a Chicken Soup for the Soul story in a book, magazine, newspaper or online. As we share our life experiences through these stories, we offer hope, comfort and inspiration to one another. The stories travel from person to person, and from country to country, helping to improve lives everywhere.

Chicken Soup for the Soul

Share with Us

We all have had Chicken Soup for the Soul moments in our lives. If you would like to share your story or poem with millions of people around the world, go to chickensoup.com and click on "Submit Your Story." You may be able to help another reader, and become a published author at the same time. Some of our past contributors have launched writing and speaking careers from the publication of their stories in our books!

Our submission volume has been increasing steadily — the quality and quantity of your submissions has been fabulous. We only accept story submissions via our website. They are no longer accepted via mail or fax.

To contact us regarding other matters, please send us an e-mail through webmaster@chickensoupforthesoul.com, or fax or write us at:

Chicken Soup for the Soul
P.O. Box 700
Cos Cob, CT 06807-0700
Fax: 203-861-7194

One more note from your friends at Chicken Soup for the Soul: Occasionally, we receive an unsolicited book manuscript from one of our readers, and we would like to respectfully inform you that we do not accept unsolicited manuscripts and we must discard the ones that appear.

Chicken Soup for the Soul

www.chickensoup.com